The Rose

Project Editor
Leslie Firth

Editorial Director
Chris Milsome

Managing Editor
Susan Ward

Production Manager
Chris Fayers

Design
Ruth Prentice

Picture Research
Anne Marie Ehrlich

Illustration
Marion Appleton
Harriet Bailey-Watson
Gordon Cramp
David Mallot
John Rignall/Linden Artists
Anne Winterbotham

Library of Congress Cataloging in Publication Data

The Rose

Includes index.
1. Roses. 2. Rose culture. I. Mechlin, Stuart.
SB411.R656 635.9'33'372 79-10375
ISBN 0-8317-7498-3

Manufactured in Italy
First American Edition.

The Rose

Consultants
Stuart Mechlin, Janet Browne

MAYFLOWER BOOKS
NEW YORK

Photographs

Pictures are listed by page number; additional numbers read in order from top to bottom and left to right taken together i.e. top left first, bottom right last.

Bodleian Library 25/1, 30/1, 30/2
Pat Brindley 62/2, 80/3, 81/1, 91/1, 94/2
British Library 13/3, 17/1, 18/1, 56/1
British Museum 19/2 (photo Ray Gardner), 35/2
Julia Clements 69/1, 70/1, 71/1 (photo Jon Whitbourne), 71/2 (photo Jon Whitbourne), 71/3
Anne-Marie Ehrlich 24/1
Mike Fear 25/2
C. Gregory & Son Ltd. back cover, 64/1, 64/2, 64/3, 65/1, 65/2, 74/3, 90/1, 91/4, 94/3
Sonia Halliday Photographs 3/1, 11/1, 34/1
Robert Harding Associates 46/1, 51/2, 53/1, 75/1, 75/2, 91/5
Peter Harkness 87/2
Iris Hardwick Library 59/2, 61/3, 62/1
Angelo Harnak Photograph Library 27/2, 35/3
John Johnson Collection/Bodleian Library 38/1
Kunsthistorisches Museum, Vienna 13/2, 22/1 (photo Meyer), 23/2 (photo Meyer)
H. Le Rougetel/Biofotos 49/2, 50/1, 51/3, 61/1
The Mansell Collection 12/1
John Mattock Ltd. 3/3, 67/1, 73/1, 74/1, 74/2, 80/1, 80/2, 80/4, 80/5, 87/1, 87/4, 87/5, 91/2, 94/1
Courtesy of Mayorcas Ltd./Photo Mike Fear 37/1
Stuart Mechlin 63/1
Musée de la Malmaison (photo Studio Laverton) 3/2, 43/1
National Galleries of Scotland (photo Tom Scott) 23/3
National Gallery, London 21/1
National Trust 35/5 (photo John Bethell), 37/2 (photo John Bethell), 37/3 (photo Country Life), 60/1 (photo John Bethell)
Michael Newton 3/4, 40/1, 41/1, 97/1
Réunion des Musées Nationaux, Paris 19/1
Royal Horticultural Society/Photo Eileen Tweedy front cover, 21/3, 28/1, 30/3, 31/1, 33/1, 33/2, 33/3, 53/2, 54/1, 54/2, 57/1, 57/2, 57/3, 57/4
Royal National Rose Society 6/1, 62/3
Ronald Sheridan 14/1, 23/1 (Musée de Carnavalet)
Harry Smith Horticultural Collection 46/2 46/3, 48/1, 49/1, 51/1, 52/1, 58/1, 58/2, 59/1, 59/3, 61/2, 61/4, 66/1, 86/1, 87/3, 91/3
Smithsonian Institution 44/1
Sotheby 14/2, 16/1
Studio Hermann Wehmeyer 13/1
Maureen Thompson/Photo Eileen Tweedy 27/3, 27/4
Victoria and Albert Museum 17/2, 21/2, 21/4, 27/1 (photo Sally Chappell), 29/1 (photo Eileen Tweedy), 29/2 (photo Eileen Tweedy), 30/2 (photo Eileen Tweedy), 35/1 (photo Eileen Tweedy), 35/4 (photo Sally Chappell), 36/1
Walker Art Gallery, Liverpool 20/1 (photo John Mills (Photography) Ltd.)
Walters Art Gallery, Baltimore 26/1

With special thanks to the staff of the Royal Horticultural Society Library

Front cover: *Rosa centifolia foliacea* by Pierre-Joseph Redouté (Royal Horticultural Society).
Back cover: 'Piccadilly' (C. Gregory and Son).

The Consultants

Stuart Mechlin Curator of the International Rose Test Garden at Portland, Oregon, USA. Judge for the All-America Rose Selections and Consulting Rosarian to the American Rose Society. Author and contributor to magazines including *The American Rose* and *Horticulture*.

Janet Browne Horticulturist and gardening consultant. Journalist and author of books on gardening, and a horticultural correspondent for *The Times*.

The Authors

Julia Clements VMH International judge, teacher and writer on flower arrangement, author of 18 books and a regular contributor to *Garden News*, *Flora* and other women's papers.

Tony Gregory Rose grower and breeder and past Chairman of the Rose Growers' Association.

Domini Gregory Founder of a cottage industry producing traditional English country wines, the speciality being rose petal wine.

Jack Harkness Rose breeder, author, Secretary of the British Association of Rose Breeders and Editor of the Royal National Rose Society's Annual and other publications.

John Mattock Rose breeder, Vice-president of the British Association of Rose Breeders, Chairman of the Gardens Committee of the Royal National Rose Society, and a council member of the Royal Horticultural Society.

Noël Riley Art journalist and contributor to *Country Life*, *Collector's Guide* and *Art and Antiques Weekly*.

Peter Russell Garden designer and consultant, and garden consultant and correspondent for *House and Garden*.

Contents

Foreword	8
Introduction	9
The Rose in Art and Legend	10
The Rose in Legend and Custom	12
The Classical World	14
The Rose in the Orient	16
A Medieval Ideal	18
The Renaissance and After	20
An Age of Naturalism	22
A Nineteenth Century Passion	24
The Decorative Rose	26
An Inspiration for Engravers	28
The Botanical Illustrators	30
Jewellery, Porcelain and Glass	34
The Rose in Textiles	36
The Useful Rose	38
The Lore of Pot-pourri	40
The Rose in Bloom	42
The Ancestry of the Rose	44
The Wild Rose	46
The First Hybrids	48
Old Cultivated Roses in Europe	50
Old Cultivated Roses: the Chinese Influence	52
Old Cultivated Roses: the Persian Influence	54
A Brief History of Rose Gardens	56
The Rose in the Formal Garden	58
The Informal Rose Garden	60
Great Rose Gardens of Today	62
How Specialist Breeding Evolved	64
The Rose Breeders: Examples of Success	66
Cutting Roses for Arrangement	68
Arranging Roses: Basic Techniques	70
The Modern Rose	72
Hybrid Tea Bush Roses: Introduction	74
Hybrid Tea Bush Roses: A-Z	76
Floribunda Bush Roses: Introduction	80
Floribunda Bush Roses: A-Z	82
Modern Shrub Roses: Introduction	86
Modern Shrub Roses: A-Z	88
Climbers and Ramblers: Introduction	90
Climbers and Ramblers: A-Z	92
Miniature Roses: Introduction and A-Z	94
The Rose in Your Garden	96
Life Cycle of the Garden Rose	98
Planting and Cultivation	100
How and When to Plant	102
Feeding, Mulching and Watering	106
Pruning and Trimming	108
Pergolas, Walls and Pillars	112
Roses for Hedges	116
Propagation: Budding and Grafting	118
Propagation: Other Methods	120
Controlling Pests and Diseases	122
Roses in the Greenhouse	124
Growing Roses for Exhibition	126
Planning a Rose Garden	130
Town Gardens and Patios	132
Rejuvenating Roses	133
Seasonal Survey of Care	134
The Fellowship of the Rose	135
Plant Patents	136
Glossary	137
Index	141

Foreword

In *The Rose* contributors and editors have worked together to produce what I believe to be a unique volume. Some of the world's most authoritative writers have combined their specialist knowledge to provide the reader with a mine of information on the rose: its history from earliest times to the present day, its development from a wild ancestry to the infinite variety of form and colour of our modern blooms, its appeal to artists and writers, its cultivation and care in our gardens, and its use in decorative arrangements in the home.

A tremendous amount of painstaking research has gone into the compilation of this book. While there exist several hundred books on roses and rose-growing, and no one volume could claim to contain all there is to know about roses, this work must come very near to meeting such a claim. Furthermore, the text is profusely illustrated with skillfully selected photographs, reproductions and line drawings, which add enormously to its interest and value.

This is no formally written text-book, nor should it be regarded as simply a reference work. It is written in an eminently readable style and I am confident that all those fortunate enough to acquire this splendid production will read it with great pleasure and profit.

Everyone responsible for the compilation and publication of this remarkable work is warmly congratulated, and I confidently recommend it to a wide circle of readers.

Eric Elwes
President
Royal National Rose Society

Introduction

The Rose was conceived to appeal to a large public – to amateur and professional rose growers, to general gardeners and to those with a more casual interest in the history and development of the world's favourite flower. The simple double-page spread presentation is designed for easy reading and reference, while the wealth of illustrations, over fifty per cent in colour, supplies the richness and clarity of information and detail which words, however carefully chosen, cannot always convey.

The well-known authors were selected for their specialist expertise. The result is a generous collaboration of time and talent, reflecting the deep knowledge, dedicated research and personal enthusiasm of each contributor.

The book is divided into four sections: The Rose in Art and Legend, The Rose in Bloom, The Modern Rose, and The Rose in Your Garden. The first of these sections provides an historic insight into the traditions of rose lore. It explores the formal inspiration of the rose in decorative art and investigates its more utilitarian contributions to herbal remedies, sweet-smelling concoctions and delicate wines and jellies.

The Rose in Bloom takes the reader back to the earliest rose, a fossil some 60 million years old. It follows the historical evolution of the rose genus and species, and explains the specialist breeding which has produced the disease-resistant, many-coloured variations which abound today. The section also covers famous rose gardens and takes the flower from the outdoors into the home, via the techniques of floral arrangement.

The Modern Rose consists of carefully compiled, international lists of prime examples from the five main types of rose. Over 175 varieties are detailed; the name of each rose is accompanied by a brief but distinguishing description, together with the particulars of its breeder, date of introduction, origin, antecedents, availability and awards.

The Rose in Your Garden explains the best methods for growing and caring for the different groups of roses, and their assorted uses in both large and small gardens. Training and preparing flowers for exhibition is also covered simply and thoroughly. The final pages provide a summary of world Rose Societies, an explanation of plant patents and classification, a useful glossary and comprehensive index.

As consultants from either side of the Atlantic, we are proud to be associated with everyone who has worked on *The Rose*. I hope that our readers experience as much satisfaction in reading and *using* it as we did in producing it.

Janet Browne

S. Mechlin

Janet Browne
Stuart Mechlin

The Rose in Art and Legend

The Rose in Legend and Custom

The rose, probably the most celebrated and persistently used adornment of human civilization, existed long before the advent of man. Fossils of rose plants millions of years old have been found in America, Europe and Asia. Evidence suggests that all roses were originally native to the northern hemisphere; they were taken south of the equator by man.

The Greek myths

Nearly every culture seems to have had its own folklore about the rose, and almost all regarded it as the queen of flowers. According to one Roman poet, 'the rose was either born from a smile of Cupid or else it fell from the hair of Aurora as she combed it'. The Greeks provide some of the most picturesque myths, many of them associated with Aphrodite, or Venus, as the Romans called the goddess of love. In one story Venus was hurrying through a thicket when she stepped on a thorn. From her blood sprang the first red roses. A variation suggests it was the blood of her lover, Adonis,

which was responsible; the jealous Mars incited a boar to kill the youth and roses grew to mark the spot. Jealousy also accounted for the actions of Cybele, who created the rose to make a rival for Venus' beauty. But the gentlest version says merely that roses grew from the foam which covered the lovely goddess as she rose from the sea.

Modesty colours the myth – and rose – of Bacchus, who was chasing a beautiful nymph through the woods when she was trapped by the spikes of a thorny shrub. In gratitude, Bacchus touched the shrub with his stick and ordered it to be covered with flowers to match the nymph's blushes; pink roses were the magic result.

The expression 'sub rosa', implying confidentiality, has its origins in Greek legend. According to one story Cupid gave the first rose to Harpocrates, the god of silence, on the condition that he should not reveal the amorous activities of his mother, Venus. Another explanation places it in a more historical context. After their defeat on land by Xerxes in 479 BC, the Greeks retired to a rose bower to discuss a surprise attack on Xerxes at sea. Their secret talks were thus 'under the rose'. The rose's connection with secrecy, whatever its origin, led to the convention of roses being carved on the ceilings of council chambers.

Below
The Birth of Venus by the Renaissance painter Botticelli (*c*.1445–1510). The goddess rises from the sea in a spray of roses.

Other Greek myths involved the transformation of people into roses. For example Rhodanthe, a beautiful queen of Corinth, sought refuge from over-importunate suitors in the temple of Diana. On seeing her beauty the people began to worship her instead of Diana. In revenge, Diana's brother, Apollo, turned Rhodanthe into a rose bush and her suitors into a worm, a fly and a butterfly. Similarly Zephyr (the west wind) changed himself into a rose to make himself more attractive to Flora, whose only passion was flowers. She kissed him and their union was consummated.

The Arabs had their theories, one of which was that the rose grew out of the sweat of the prophet Mohammed. More picturesque is the story of the flowers' complaint to Allah that the queen of flowers, the lotus, slept at night. So Allah created the white rose. The story did not end there. The nightingale fell in love with the white rose and during a passionate embrace was pricked by its thorns; the drops of blood which fell from the nightingale stained the white rose red.

Medieval legends

According to medieval belief, the first roses appeared in answer to a maiden's prayers. A girl from Bethlehem, unjustly condemned to be burnt at the stake, prayed for help. God answered by turning the already smouldering embers into red roses and the unburnt sticks of wood into white ones. Another legend holds that a white rose bloomed in the Garden of Eden – it blushed when Eve kissed it and turned into a red one.

Medieval Europe was rich in rose legends, nearly all of them associated with miracles or the lives of saints. The most famous is probably the story of the Hildesheim Abbey rose. According to one version, it was planted by the Emperor Charlemagne, but romantics prefer another legend. The Emperor Ludwig had lost his way in the forest while out hunting. Realizing that he would have to spend the night alone in the open, he hung his crucifix and chain on a thorn bush and prayed for protection. The next morning his companions found him asleep and safe beside a fully grown rose tree. The Emperor had a chapel built in thanksgiving and this was eventually the site of the cathedral. The rose still exists and is now 10 metres (30 feet) high.

The saints

There are many saints associated with roses. St Dorothy, for example, was martyred for her Christian beliefs. As she was led to her death she declared that she was on her way to her wedding and that her fiancé was Jesus Christ. Theophilus, a scribe who was standing by, jeered at her and suggested she should send some 'roses or apples' from her bridegroom's paradise. Shortly after her execution a young boy appeared, on a cold February day, with a basket containing three apples and three roses in full bloom. He gave them to Theophilus, who was converted to Christianity and eventually became a martyr himself.

The Virgin Mary must lay claim to more associations with the rose than any other figure. She is said to have appeared at Fatima and at Lourdes from a circle of roses. The origin of the rosary is traditionally associated with her gift of a chaplet of beads, perfumed with roses, to St Dominic.

Absorbed into the liturgy as a title of Mary, Mystical Rose, the flower·became the symbol of a paragon, or one without equal, and of Christian purity. Red roses symbolize the Virgin's sorrow, white roses her joy and gold roses her glory. In other Christian symbolism the rose is also associated with the blood of martyrs, the wounds of Christ and the crown of thorns.

Top
The rose bush at Hildesheim Abbey. Medieval legends associate it with Charlemagne and the Emperor Ludwig.

Centre
Flora in the Garden by Pieter van Avout, 17th century. The flowers and trees were painted by Jan Breughel the Younger.

Left
The Rosary of passion, an illustration from a 15th century Dutch prayerbook.

The Classical World

Right
Part of a fresco at the Palace of Knossos which includes the earliest known painting of a rose.

Below
Roses of Heliogabalus, a Roman banquet portrayed by the Victorian painter, Sir Lawrence Alma Tadema.

The painted frescoes of the Palace of Knossos in Crete are thought to contain the earliest recognizable representations of roses. If they are genuine and not, as some people have suggested, part of a much later restoration scheme they would date from 2000–1700 BC when the Palace was built. Minoan goldsmiths of this time are believed to have used the rose as a motif in their jewellery, though to date only scant evidence has been found to support such claims.

Not long after this, in about 1500 BC, a rose appears in an Egyptian tomb painting. There are early allusions in classical literature to the rose. According to Homer, Hector's shield was decorated with roses and when he died Venus anointed his body with rose ointment. A little later the Greek poet, Sappho, described the rose as the 'queen of flowers'.

The cult of the rose

The Egyptians and the Greeks both adopted the rose as a cult flower. In Egypt it was sacred to the goddess Isis and rosy garlands were offered at her altars. The enchantress Mythris was buried in a rose-filled tomb. Large quantities of roses were grown in the Nile valley. They were used for domestic and religious purposes and exported to the rest of the ancient world.

According to Herodotus, it may have been King Midas of Phrygia who first introduced the rose to Greece in about 700 BC. He apparently brought one or more varieties of rose with him from Asia Minor and started extensive rose gardens in Macedonia. Pindar, in about 500 BC, wrote of the Athenians wearing wreaths and crowns of roses. They were used for decorating the houses of the living and for scattering on the tombs of the dead.

The Greeks grew roses in their gardens and sometimes in special 'gardens of Adonis' where rose bushes were grown in silver pots. Epicurus is said to have had a rose garden so that he could have fresh roses at any time. Roses grew in abundance on the island of Rhodes and the flower is thought to have been stamped on her coinage. Theophrastus, who died in 287 BC, wrote about the people of Philippi collecting wild roses from the Pangaeus Mountains and planting them in their gardens. But it was the island of Kithira, also renowned for the cult of Venus, that was regarded as the home of the rose in ancient Greece.

Roman opulence

The Greeks enjoyed and cultivated roses in good measure but the Romans were obsessed with them. They wore them in garlands, as crowns and in sweet-smelling sachets. They slept, sat, and even walked on them. Roses were given as prizes for victories and festooned or scattered on tombs. They were used in jellies, honey, medicines, bath essence and wine.

Roses were planted all over the country. There were large market gardens at Tibur (Tivoli) and Praeneste (Palestrina). The chief rose-growing centre, Paestum, became famous throughout the ancient world as a fashionable resort in the rose season. Roses were cultivated in private gardens and there was scarcely a farmer who did not use a part of his land for rose growing. Horace complained that grain fields and orchards were being planted with roses instead of food crops, so lucrative was rose culture.

The Romans succeeded in growing winter-flowering roses in heated greenhouses, but the rich still imported their out-of-season supplies from Egypt. The Egyptians exported roses made of chips of wood, paper or cloth dipped in rose oil to give them fragrance. On one famous occasion Queen Cleopatra gave a dinner for her lover Mark Antony and commanded that the floor of the banqueting room be covered in roses up to the guests' knees; they sat on rose-filled mattresses and wore wreaths of roses on their heads.

The Emperor Nero was probably the most extravagant of all rose-lovers. He held banquets in which the guests lay on rose-filled cushions on rose-strewn floors. Rose petals cascaded on them (some unfortunates were suffocated by their weight) and rosewater ran in the fountains. Nero once spent the equivalent of about £45,000 on roses to cover the beach at the resort of Baiae. Even the public baths were filled with rosewater on festive occasions. After Nero the Roman emperors continued to hold rose banquets, though in a slightly less opulent manner. Some historians claim that this indulgence in the appetite for roses contributed to the economic disintegration of Rome and, as the Empire declined, so the rose cult sank, disreputably, with it.

The Rose in the Orient

Above
The nightingale and the rose, an illustration on a Persian book cover of the mid 19th century.

Right
A 16th century plate from Isnik, Turkey, decorated with roses and hyacinths.

Far right
A Persian miniature illustrating the legendary Duel of the Roses. One of the physicians is seen collapsing after sniffing the fatal rose.

The Chinese probably cultivated roses well before the Minoan artists were painting them on the walls of Cretan palaces or fashioning them in gold. It is thought that there were rose gardens in China as early as 2700 BC, and roses certainly flourished in the Imperial gardens of Peking during the fourth and fifth centuries BC. At this time, according to Confucius, the Imperial library contained as many as 600 books on roses.

Important people of the time perfumed themselves with attar of roses, while lesser mortals carried dried rose petals as a protection against evil spirits. It was from Chinese originals, grown there for centuries but only imported to Europe during the late eighteenth and the nineteenth centuries, that many of our modern roses were bred. Yet the Chinese, though they held the rose in great esteem, accorded it less importance than the lotus, the poppy, the chrysanthemum or the prunus blossom, and recognizable roses appear comparatively rarely in Chinese art. This seems to be true also of the Japanese. Although it is known that the Japanese cultivated the rose almost throughout their history, the flower is hardly found in Japanese art.

The Middle East
Some of the earliest references to the rose are found in the Middle East rather than the Far East. Some stories are so ancient that it is

impossible to be certain which are legend and which are fact. The Sumerian King Sargon is said to have returned from a campaign bringing 'vines, figs and roses to his country' in about 2200 BC. This anecdote probably provides the earliest known reference to roses in history.

It is likely that the Hanging Gardens of Babylon contained roses. These terraced gardens, which became one of the Seven Wonders of the World, were begun about 1200 BC by King Nebuchadnezzar, for his wife Amytis. She loved roses above all other flowers, so they would not have been left out of a garden built to please her.

In Persia, roses were evidently grown from an early period and King Kyros II of Persia took the rose as his official symbol of power in the sixth century BC. The main rose-growing areas were always in the north of the country. According to an Englishman writing in more recent times, 'in no country in the world does the rose grow in such perfection as in Persia; in no country is it so cultivated and prized by the natives. Their gardens and courts are crowded by its plants, their rooms ornamented with roses . . . and every bath strewed with the full-blown flowers . . .'

The image of the rose appears from time to time in Persian literature. The thirteenth century poet Sadi, originally a slave, is supposed to have appealed to his master with a rose: 'Do good to thy servant whilst thou hast the power, for the season of power is often as transient as the duration of this beautiful flower.' The man's compassion was successfully aroused and Sadi was released from bondage. He later named one of his books the *Gulistan*, or rose garden. Much earlier, the poet Omar Khayyam (who wrote in the eleventh century) had mentioned roses again and again in his works, and it is known that a rose grew on his grave in Nishapur.

One of the most famous Persian rose legends is the story of the Duel of the Roses, recorded by the twelfth century poet Nizami. Two rival physicians fought a duel with poisons: one forced the other to swallow a deadly pill, but the victim saved himself with an antidote. The other insisted that his opponent should sniff a rose over which he had cast a spell, whereupon the physician collapsed

and died. This scene is depicted in Persian miniature paintings of the sixteenth century.

Ceramics

The rose motif was used lavishly in Persian and Turkish ceramics of the sixteenth, seventeenth and eighteenth centuries. Anatolian pottery of the sixteenth century was decorated with plant motifs in shades of blue, turquoise and green on white backgrounds. Roses as well as other flowers can be recognized on various wares including dishes, lamps, jugs, vases and tiles. Although it originated in Turkey, this type of pottery is often known as Damascus ware, probably because tiles of its kind are to be found on some of the mosques of that city.

The Isnik wares of north-west Turkey are the most famous of all Turkish ceramics. They were produced in abundance from the mid-sixteenth to the end of the seventeenth century and they are sometimes referred to as Rhodian wares. This is rather misleading as they were not originally produced on the island of Rhodes. Isnik pottery was decorated with a range of naturalistically drawn flowers, in which the rose was a favourite. During the eighteenth century a type of semi-faience known as Shiraz ware was produced in Persia. Characterized by naturalistic flower decoration in strong colours that included pink, its motifs included the rose.

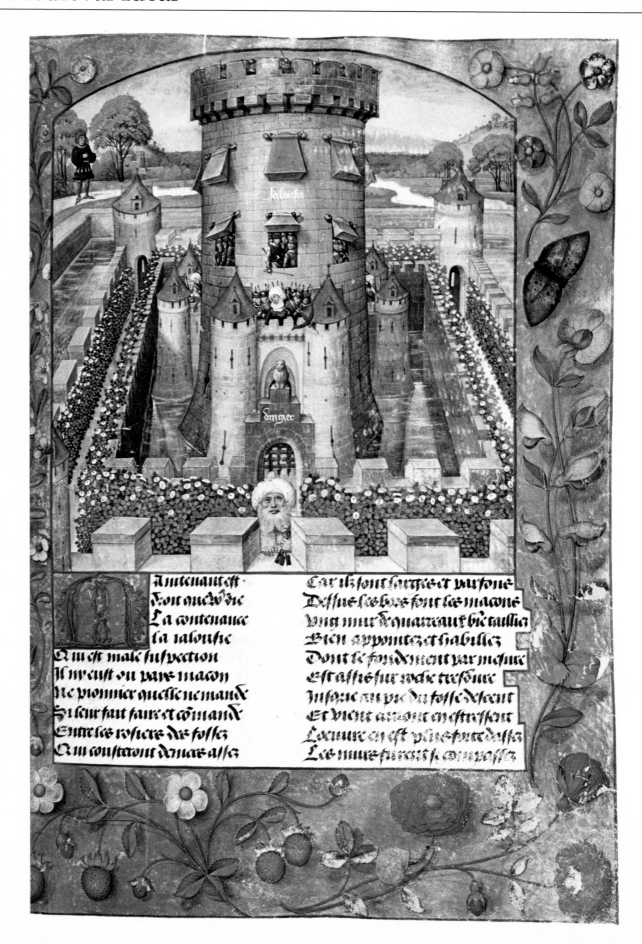

Roman excesses brought the rose into disrepute with the early Christians – it seemed more symbolic of debauchery and extravagance than the pure and virtuous love embodied by the goddess Venus. After a lapse of four or five centuries, however, the rose began to regain its position as the queen of flowers and became linked with the Christian equivalent of the goddess of beauty, the Virgin Mary.

The rose was used in various ways. The first rosaries were probably made of dried rose petals or rose-shaped beads. Roses were placed once again on tombs and graves. Their perfume freshened homes and they were used for love charms. In times of plague, roses were considered an essential purifying agent and on church feast days rosewater filled the holy water stoups.

As if confirming the rose's reinstatement as the symbol of purity and goodness, Pope Leo IX instituted the Order of the Golden Rose in 1049. Originally this was a reward for virtuous women; the Order was later extended to include cities, churches, organizations or people who had rendered particular service to the Papacy. King Henry VIII was awarded it twice, ironically enough. The fourth Sunday in Lent, the day on which the Pope traditionally blesses the Golden Rose, is sometimes called Rose Sunday.

It was in medieval times that the rose was first widely grown in northern Europe. The Crusaders brought back several new varieties from the Holy Land, among them probably the Damask rose. This was the rose used mainly in rose perfumes, and from early times the trade was supplied by the extensive rose-growing areas of Bulgaria. Damask roses, which are among the most pungent of all varieties, were also cultivated further north and west in Europe.

The rose in medicine

Rosa gallica may also have come to Europe with the Crusaders. A variety of this is known as the Rose of Provins or the Apothecary's rose because of its predominating use in medicine. The chief centre of cultivation was the Champagne area of north-east France from where it was exported to the rest of Europe and as far east as India. By the sixteenth century Provins was the centre of the medicine trade: the town had a whole street of apothecaries' establishments - among their specialities was a rose conserve.

Monasteries were the chief rose-growing centres at this time. Monks were the universal providers of medical care and, like the apothecaries of Provins, they used roses and rose hips for making a veritable battery of potions and remedies. Their gardens were havens of peace and fragrance and roses were also grown for their own beauty. The Benedictines were at the forefront of rose propagation in this golden age of monastery gardening.

The heraldic rose

The rose has been used extensively in heraldry, notably by members of the British royal family. Edmund, Earl of Lancaster (Edmund Crouchback), was one of the first to do so. He married Blanche of Artois in the thirteenth century and lived for a time at Provins, so his use of the rose was particularly appropriate. The medieval kings Edward I, Henry IV and Edward IV used the rose in their heraldic devices, and the Tudors then made it especially their own. Nearly all British monarchs and many members of their families have used it in one or other of its basic four shapes: the single dog rose; the double Tudor rose; the 'rose-en-soleil' (a white rose surrounded by the rays of the sun) and the slipped rose – a Tudor rose with a stalk and leaves. The rose in heraldry is also specifically the mark of cadency of a seventh son. In English coinage, the rose noble, current during the fifteenth and sixteenth centuries, was a gold coin stamped with a rose.

The rose remained the symbol of earthly love as it had been in classical times. The famous medieval French allegory of love, the *Roman de la Rose*, is typical of this association. Written mostly during the thirteenth century, it was one of the most lastingly popular literary works of the entire medieval period. Chaucer is supposed to have been responsible for a large part of the English version, published in the fifteenth century. The rose in the poem symbolizes virginal purity, innocence and unattainable beauty. This can be seen in an episode in the French romance *The Siege of the Castle of Love*, often portrayed in carving on ivory mirror cases and caskets of the later medieval period. Glamorously caparisoned knights in armour storm a castle full of fair damsels whose only weapons are the roses they shower down on the invaders. No doubt the subject was depicted on other objects but most have perished in the course of time.

Opposite page
An illustration from the *Roman de la Rose*, a famous medieval allegory of love. Bel Accueil is imprisoned in the castle by Jalousie. Her lover can be seen outside.

Far left
The Golden Rose of Basle which is thought to have been awarded by Pope Clement V to a bishop of Basle in the 14th century.

Left
A rose noble, a gold coin minted during the reign of King Edward IV.

The Renaissance and After

The rose continued to flourish as the queen of flowers and the symbol of all earthly and heavenly love in the sixteenth and seventeenth centuries. Countless painters of the Renaissance depicted the Virgin in a garden or a bower, surrounded by roses, or angels wearing rosy wreaths in their hair. Others used the rose to symbolize romantic, secular love. Botticelli's *The Birth of Venus* and Nicholas Hilliard's *Portrait of a Young Man* (possibly Sir Philip Sidney) are spectacular examples.

Roses were carved over confessionals (to indicate secrecy) or into the wooden panelling of rooms; stone or plaster roses appeared on the ceilings of banqueting or council chambers; jewelled or embroidered ones danced on the dresses of rich ladies. Rosewater was used for washing the hands at noble tables; it was carried in magnificent silver ewers and poured into bowls of matching sumptuousness. By this time the rose was indeed everywhere.

The Tudor rose

In England the rose's enormous advance in fashion may partly be accounted for by the fact that it had become the emblem of the sovereign and the country. Henry VII united the red rose of the Lancastrians with the white rose of the Yorkists in the memorably stylized Tudor rose. This mythical flower subsequently appeared in every possible medium and situation. It was eagerly taken up by the London Pewterers' Company as a symbol of excellence. During the sixteenth century, pewter of the highest quality made by the Company's members was stamped with a rose and crown. In the seventeenth century the same touch mark was used on exported pewter and later on any fine pewter. Evidently 'the Rose and Crown', a favourite among British public house names, also originated during this period. 'The sign of the rose' was not uncommon for other premises besides taverns.

Gardens of the Renaissance

Horticultural interest in the rose itself was growing. The Renaissance spirit of curiosity gave an impetus to scientific and geographic enquiry and botany in particular became a subject of intense interest. Explorers returned from their great voyages with exotic new plants. The tulip and the sunflower, for example, made their first appearance in Europe in the mid-sixteenth century, and new varieties of many existing plants, among them the rose, came from far and distant parts about this time.

On the whole this was an era of peace and prosperity, especially in Elizabethan England, and this led to more time and thought being given to home comforts. Gardening had once been the preserve of those living in monasteries and castles. Now most of the large houses, and many of the smaller ones, had their own flower gardens. For the first time horticulture was becoming a more popular pastime.

Roses were favoured 'to be placed with the most glorious flowers of the world' in the garden. The European fashion for collecting roses began, and many a romantic connoisseur planted his 'rosarium' with the new as well as the well-loved old varieties. The rose still had a huge range of culinary and medicinal uses and even the humblest gardener was bound to cultivate a few to furnish the domestic needs of his household.

Some of the first botanically accurate records of roses, generally watercolour drawings, appeared during the Renaissance. These in turn were copied to make woodcuts for the herbals which began to appear from this time onwards. And so, in the sixteenth century, we have some of the earliest pictures of identifiable rose varieties.

Above
Nicholas Hilliard's portrait of Queen Elizabeth I. Her gown is embroidered with roses in blackwork, a form of fine embroidery using black silk.

Left
The Concert, an early 16th century painting by Lorenzo Costa. A stylized rose motif is cut into the soundboard of the lute.

Above
The outer covers of the Armada jewel, showing a rose and Noah's ark in enamelled gold. It is thought that Queen Elizabeth I presented it to Sir Thomas Heneage. English, *c*.1588.

Far left
A romantic view of the rose in Hilliard's *Portrait of a Young Man*.

Left
A botanical illustration of a rose, *c*.1590, by Theodor Jacob of Berg Zabern who was known as Tabernaemontanus.

An Age of Naturalism

Above
Intense detail is characteristic of Jan Breughel the Elder's flower pieces. Here, roses are seen together with tulips, lilies and other flowers.

The seventeenth century was an age of famous gardeners. The most celebrated horticulturist of all was probably John Tradescant who became botanist to Queen Henrietta Maria, wife of Charles I, and later director of the royal gardens. Another of Charles I's gardeners, Parkinson, recommended planting rose hedges round flower gardens in his *Garden of Pleasant Flowers* published in 1629. Wealthy people spent fortunes on their gardens, which became as important as their homes for showing off worldly splendour.

This interest in horticulture found expression in flower paintings not as accurate records of plants but as flamboyantly decorative pieces in themselves. The Dutch led this tradition of painting, just as they were pioneers in the development of new plant strains at this time.

The Dutch flower painters
The flower painting tradition is thought to have begun in the late sixteenth century when a Dutch woman employed Jan Breughel the Elder to paint the flowers she could not afford to buy. Astonishing as it may seem, in those days artists' services cost less than rare plants. In fact Breughel was not the first Dutch artist to make flower studies (roses were his forte) but he appears to have started a fashion for naturalistic floral painting.

Among those whom Breughel influenced were Ambrosius Bosschaert the Elder, Daniel Seghers and Balthazar van der Ast, all working in the early seventeenth century. They were followed by Davidsz de Heem, van Aelst, Verelst, Rachel Ruysch and Jacob Walscapelle. These and many others brought the tradition to a climax of popularity in Europe at the end of the century. The final brilliant strokes were added in the early eighteenth century by virtuosos such as Jan van Huysum, van Os and Gerard van Spaëndonck. Their style evoked almost *trompe l'oeil* effects, with dewdrops about to fall off the flowers and insects crawling realistically on their canvases.

Never before had flowers been painted so naturalistically – one can almost smell the roses and hear the bees buzzing in them. This approach had enormous impact on other fields. Furniture, especially in the Low Countries, was inlaid with marquetry flowers in swags and bunches, and ceramics were decorated with posies and sprays which invariably included roses. Embroidery of the early eighteenth century was worked with vases and baskets of full-blown pink and white roses and other blossoms.

The roses of Versailles
Perhaps the most famous and most enthusiastic of rose-lovers were Madame de Pompadour and her successor as Louis XV's mistress, Madame du Barry. They gave their names to particular shades of rose pink porcelain; in portraits they appear with roses in their hands or hair. Madame du Barry's rose-decorated bedroom at Versailles is a legend in the history of interior decoration. Her bed was surmounted with a rosy canopy and from its four corners hung festoons of rose-embroidered silk. The curtains and upholstery were also of silk decorated with roses, and she herself frequently wore the most sumptuous rose-embroidered dresses.

In 1759, the Lancashire Fusiliers went to the Battle of Minden wearing roses. They were victorious and ever since then the 'Minden rose' has given them the nickname of the 'Minden Boys'. To this day officers of this regiment have to eat a rose at the annual Minden dinner.

Roses maintained their artistic and romantic appeal in the eighteenth century. They were celebrated in poetry and in paint and were cultivated enthusiastically in the gardens of Europe.

Left
A 17th century naturalistic study of flowers and insects by Ambrosius Bosschaert.

Right
The symbolic *L'Amour Triomphant* by Fragonard.

Below
Fragonard's portrait of Madame de Pompadour, one of the most famous rose-lovers in history.

A Nineteenth Century Passion

Until the eighteenth century, only a few varieties of rose were known in Europe. Although they were often highly scented, they were on the whole less spectacular than those of today. The Dutch were among the first to develop new strains, particularly of red roses, but by the end of the eighteenth century there were still only two or three hundred varieties; these could all be contained in a single rosarium. During the nineteenth century there was an enormous increase in rose varieties, the result of intense activity on the part of rose breeders.

The roses of Josephine

Probably the greatest – and certainly the most influential – of all rose-lovers was Josephine de Beauharnais, who became Napoleon's wife. At the Palace of Malmaison Josephine amassed the greatest rose collection anywhere. She began by acquiring many of the recently developed Dutch varieties and later, helped by some of the most famous gardeners of the time, she had roses brought to her from all over the world. Even at the height of the war with England, Josephine's rose agents were allowed to pass unmolested between England and France.

Josephine's collection stimulated great interest in rose growing. One of her most valuable legacies was her patronage of the artist Pierre-Joseph Redouté. Redouté had been taught by the Dutch painter Gerard van Spaëndonck (himself a pupil of Jan van Huysum) and was already a botanical illustrator of great repute when Josephine commissioned him to record the flowers of her garden. The best known part of this work was *Les Roses*, published in three volumes after Josephine's death in 1817.

The 'Dean of Roses'

Another important figure in rose-growing history was the Englishman Samuel Reynolds Hole, Dean of Rochester from 1877 to 1904. In 1856, while he was still a young curate at Caunton near Nottingham, his general interest in horticulture was apparently transformed, quite suddenly, into an obsession for roses. The queen of flowers never had a keener champion. He began to form a rosarium and within ten years had accumulated about 5,000 varieties – the largest collection then known. He was the initiator

Above
An illustration from *The Floral Telegraph, or Affection's Signals,* by Captain Marryat R.N. According to the language of flowers, the message reads 'I shall be at No. 33 after the Opera'.

The Language of roses

Red rose: I love you
China rose: Beauty always new
Damask rose: Brilliant complexion
Garland of roses: Reward of virtue
Japan rose: Beauty is your only attraction
Burgundy rose: Unconscious beauty
Cabbage rose: Ambassador of love
Carolina rose: Love is dangerous
Deep red rose: Bashful shame
Dog rose: Pleasure and pain
Hundred-leaved rose: Pride; dignity of mind
Musk rose: Capricious beauty
Single rose: Simplicity
Thornless rose: Early attachment
White rose: I am worthy of you
Yellow rose: Declining love; jealousy
A full-blown rose placed over two buds: Secrecy
White and red rose together: Unity
Red rosebud: Pure and lovely
White rosebud: Girlhood
Moss rosebud: Confession of love
Rose leaf: You may hope

of the National Rose Show in Britain (first held in 1858) and later, in 1876, was instrumental in forming the National Rose Society. This 'Dean of Roses' as he has been called, was a man of unquenchable enthusiasm and humour whose love of roses must have been highly infectious. Lest one should imagine that he was any less successful as a cleric it must be mentioned that, according to a contemporary journalist, there were 'few more popular men among the dignitaries of the Church of England'.

The general interest in roses, whether growing or in decoration, increased throughout the nineteenth century. All over Europe the rose continued to be used as a motif in architectural ornament, on ceramics and in textiles. The pink cabbage rose was still very popular, particularly among enthusiasts of Berlin woolwork, although later in the century the adherents of the Arts and Crafts movement in Britain began to favour the simple dog rose. The majority of late nineteenth century rose motifs appeared in fairly humble situations. Etched on the glass of bars and public houses, cast into coal-hole covers, woven into lace curtains and printed on tiles, there was no escaping them.

The language of flowers

As a symbol of romantic love, the rose must have reached its zenith in the late nineteenth century with the advent of the printed Valentine. These passionate declarations of love and devotion flew to and fro, most of them embellished with verses of dubious literary merit and almost all decorated with roses. There was great variety in the roses and other flowers that appeared in these Valentines. This was not the result of chance or whim, but was dictated by a sentimental code known as the language of flowers. Different flowers had different meanings, and the rose in its various forms had several.

Right
A late 19th century label from a bottle of rosewater.

Below
A photogravure of the *Council Chamber* by Edward Burne-Jones, part of his Briar Rose series of paintings illustrating the story of Sleeping Beauty.

The Decorative Rose

Before the medieval period the rose was rarely portrayed in a realistic manner. However, its stylized form, the rosette, appears as a decorative motif from very early times. It seems reasonable to assume that the rosette was used primarily in those cultures and areas of the northern hemisphere where the rose was actually grown. Thus the ornamental rosette is found on Mesopotamian friezes and seals as early as 3000 BC. It is also seen in Assyrian reliefs, on Phoenician stelae, Mycaenean gold jewellery and Hellenistic marble columns.

During Roman times, when the rose probably reached the summit of romantic popularity, the rosette was used in designs for mosaic pavements, gold jewellery, shields and metalwork, and in stone and ivory carving. After a period of disgrace in the post-Roman world, the rosette began to appear again. It features in Christian ivories of the fifth and sixth centuries, in seventh century Byzantine metalwork, eleventh and twelfth century architectural stonework, thirteenth century Limoges enamels and early medieval ceramic tiles.

Even after naturalistic illustration and decorative use of the rose became widespread, the rosette maintained its popularity. In Persian and Turkish art, for example, the naturalistic rose is rare, in keeping with the Islamic traditions of those countries, but stylized roses appear frequently, notably in architecture, carpets and embroideries.

Architecture

An interesting example of the stylized rose translated into architecture is the rose window. It is likely that the Crusaders brought the idea to Europe during the twelfth century, when the great age of cathedral building was just beginning. What more suitable motif than the rose, symbol of the 'spotless rose', the Virgin Mary, could be introduced into the architectural scheme? Dazzlingly beautiful, especially in the setting sun, and often monumental in size, rose windows were incorporated into French cathedrals from the twelfth century onwards. Among the finest examples are those at Rheims, Amiens, Chartres, Laon and Angers. A little later, the rose window was to be adopted by the English cathedral builders, with particularly splendid effect at York, Westminster and Lincoln.

Musical instruments

During the Renaissance, the rose was used as a stylized motif in the sound-board holes of musical instruments. In reality some of these sound-hole decorations were not rosettes at all, but patterns of interlacing ribbons, stars or snowflake designs. But whatever its shape, the sound-hole decoration has now come to be known as the 'rose'. In Italian keyboard instruments – harpsichords, spinets and so on – the rose was generally a Gothic tracery of intricately cut parchment and veneer, not unlike a medieval rose window. In Flanders it was most commonly of gilded metal. From the sixteenth to the eighteenth century, roses, whether formal or naturalistic, also decorated other parts of musical instruments. They were carved in wood and inlaid in ivory but most often painted, especially on keyboard instruments.

In metalwork and gunsmithing the rose was given similar decorative treatment. It appears in rosette form, or among swirling plant stems, on clock cases and gun barrels, chased on silver or fused in enamel. The rose has been depicted on many coins and regimental badges of the British Isles. It is sometimes shown as a Tudor rose, as in the Henry VII sovereign, and sometimes as a slipped rose, denoting the badge of England.

Above
The north rose window at the 15th century cathedral of Angers in France.

Furniture

The rose was used extensively in late seventeenth and eighteenth century furniture. This fashion began with the influence of the Dutch flower painters on furniture and other applied arts. Naturalistically conceived flower compositions in contrasting woods were inlaid in furniture, particularly in Holland. Later, in the mid-eighteenth century, the 'patera' or carved wood rosette began to appear on the corners of mahogany cupboards, as terminals for the arms of chairs or in rows edging tables and sideboards. This ornamental motif continued to be used on all kinds of furniture for nearly a century. Roses and rosettes were inlaid in marble tables, carved in stone as architectural ornament and moulded or painted in ceramics. Towards the end of the eighteenth century there was a revival of naturalistic floral inlay in furniture all over northern Europe. Roses are often to be found. During the same period a great deal of furniture was also painted with roses and other flowers.

Paper mosaicks

From the seventeenth century onwards ladies of leisure occupied themselves with some form of artistic handicraft. Some of them painted and almost all embroidered. Others, often highly gifted, pursued more esoteric pastimes by making objects out of such materials as beads, shells, and curled paper. Flowers, especially roses, feature as a principal motif in a great number of these decorative fancies.

Among the most unusual – and the most celebrated – feminine creations were the cut paper flowers made by the famous Mrs Delany towards the end of the eighteenth century. She called them 'paper mosaicks'. Each bloom was composed of pieces cut from coloured papers and pasted onto black card. She made nearly a thousand altogether, including several sorts of rose, and although she was very old when she began the 'Flora Delanica', each specimen is botanically accurate.

The rose in silverwork

One of the most elegant users of the rose for ornament was the silversmith Omar Ramsden. His *repoussé* roses – Tudor, slipped, naturalistic briar or stylized rosette – are among the triumphs of early twentieth century silverwork. He was greatly influenced by the Arts and Crafts movement of the 1870s and 80s and by Art Nouveau a decade or so later. In both these movements the rose had played an important part – in textiles, wallpaper, ceramics, book design, furniture and metalwork.

Left
'Halifax rose', a paper mosaick by Mary Delany (1779). Each part of the bloom was cut from different coloured papers and pasted on to black card.

Above
A silver sweetmeat dish by Omar Ramsden, London, 1925.

Left
'Sleeping Beauty' wallpaper, 1875, designed by Walter Crane.

Above
A canal boat table top from the late 19th or early 20th century. It is decorated in typical style, with a border of roses and other flowers.

An Inspiration for Engravers

By translating painted or drawn illustrations of roses into reproducible form, engravers and printmakers enabled them to be widely distributed. As a result many pictures of roses became extremely popular. Some botanical artists owed a great part of their success to the skill of the engravers who reproduced their work.

Herbals and florilegia

The herbal was the first medium for the dissemination of the printed rose. Until the seventeenth century herbals and florilegia had been illustrated by fairly crude woodblock engravings. From the early seventeenth century onwards however, etching and engraving on metal began to be used for botanical illustration. These techniques were more complicated and costly but more suited to fine detail and gradations of shading.

Rich horticulturists spared no expense in commissioning the most able artists they could find to record the rarities in their gardens. Many of their illustrations were then printed in books. Some were hand-coloured while others relied on subtle tones of line or stipple for their effect. Basil Besler's *Hortus Eystettensis*, published in 1613, was one of the most impressive of these printed florilegia (as collections of flower illustrations are known). At least six engravers were employed to produce the 374 plates from Besler's drawings. No less than 21 different varieties of rose are illustrated. Another decorative example is the *Hortus Floridus*, published in 1614. Its author, the Dutchman Crispin de Passe, was both artist and engraver and the majority of its two hundred-odd plates were done by him.

Nurserymen published lavish catalogues that were illustrated by well-known flower artists. Some of the best are Dutch, but an Englishman, Robert Furber, produced a splendid example in 1730 which contained 14 varieties of rose.

The French flower print

The flower print made to delight, rather than instruct or record, was a particularly French phenomenon. It was made possible as an art form by the advances in printing techniques. One of its chief exponents was Jean-Baptiste Monnoyer, whose voluptuous baskets and ribbon-tied bouquets almost invariably included roses.

The flower print tradition in France was followed and nurtured by a succession of official royal artists. Nicholas Robert, one of the earliest, was himself a competent engraver who made important contributions to the *Receuil des Plantes*, an official national record, considered by many to be the finest collection of seventeenth century flower engravings. Robert's eighteenth century followers, Aubriet, Madeline de Basseporte, van Spaëndonck and others, continued this tradition of decorative flower prints. These had a great influence on wallpaper and textile printing. One of van Spaëndonck's many gifted pupils, Jean-Louis Prévost, published a book of flower prints in 1805 which was meant specially for designers and manufacturers.

England led in botanical science in the eighteenth century and artists from all over Europe were enticed to make drawings for the plates for English botanical works. Jacob van Huysum (younger brother of Jan) provided the artwork for John Martyn's *Historia Plantarum Rariorum*, produced between 1728 and 1736. Another example was Georg Dionysius Ehret (1708–70) who contributed illustrations of roses and other plants to several of the major works of the period.

Mary Lawrance, whose book *A Collection of Roses from Nature* (1799) was the first to be devoted exclusively to any single flower,

Above
An engraving of the 'Rose de Provins' by J. Godefroy, from a painting by Gerard van Spaëndonck.

did both the drawing and the engraving of her designs. Similarly, H. C. Andrews described his *Roses* (1805–28) as 'a monograph of the genus Rosa, containing coloured figures of all the known species and beautiful varieties, drawn, engraved, described and coloured from the living plants . . .'

New printing techniques

Great strides in engraving and colour printing techniques made possible the astonishing perfection of such works as Redouté's *Les Roses*. Stipple engraving – the technique used for reproducing his watercolours on vellum – was originally a French invention but it had been developed most successfully in England where Bartolozzi had cleverly combined its possibilities with a new method of colour printing. Redouté adopted a similar form of colour printing from a single stipple-engraved plate and the result had, in his own words 'the softness and brilliance of a watercolour'.

An important English work was Thornton's *Temple of Flora*. This was a series of 30 large colour plates produced by Dr Robert John Thornton from 1798 onwards. He used a mixture of aquatint and mezzotint. His original intention was to publish 70 plates, but his funds failed to cope with the great cost of the work. While Thornton himself designed the roses, the best artists and most skilled engravers of the day were employed for the execution of his delicate blooms.

By the 1820s lithography was being used for printing botanical illustrations. From then onwards there was a steady trickle of sentimental flower books, mostly designed for romantic young ladies. Grandville's *Les Fleurs Animées*, published in France in 1846, was among the most interesting. The most common theme was the 'language of flowers' and, despite their nostalgic charm, little originality was shown in the designs.

In more recent years the engraved rose has flowered abundantly on the postage stamps of the world. Among the countries to have produced rose series are Bulgaria, Taiwan, Hungary, Pakistan, Russia, Switzerland and Britain.

Above
The title page of a set of plates illustrating flowers in vases by J. B. Monnoyer, published *c*.1665.

Left
A plate from *Hortus Floridus* by the Dutchman Crispin de Passe, 1641.

The Botanical Illustrators

Roses depicted for botanical rather than purely artistic purposes fall into two basic categories – those drawn to illustrate herbals and those meant to be pictorial records of plants. This does not mean, however, that many of the roses illustrated in, say, medieval manuscripts or Dutch flower paintings were not botanically accurate. It is simply that the purpose of painting them was primarily artistic rather than scientific.

The first herbal of any significance was that of the Greek, Dioscorides, in the first century AD. It was illustrated in 512 by 'A Byzantine', probably a monk from Vienna, who produced what are almost certainly the oldest botanical drawings in existence. Like the information in the herbal itself, these drawings were plundered repeatedly by subsequent compilers. As late as 1526 a woodcut of a rather undistinguished rose, similar to one of Dioscorides' roses, appears in the *Grete Herball*.

Illuminated manuscripts

It seems that between Dioscorides and the late medieval period few recognizable roses were drawn. Among the first naturalistic renderings were those painted for the borders of illuminated manuscripts. This tradition was started by the Flemish miniaturists whose masterpiece was the *Très Riches Heures du Duc de Berry* of the early fifteenth century. The genre reached a stunning climax with the manuscripts of the Ghent-Bruges school. Their illuminations for the early sixteenth century Books of Hours contain roses and other flowers, and insects such as butterflies, all executed with a three-dimensional realism.

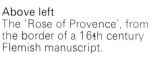

Above left
The 'Rose of Provence', from the border of a 16th century Flemish manuscript.

Above
Roses and forget-me-nots, an illustration from a 16th century Book of Hours.

Left
'Rose de Canelle', from the herbal of the Flemish botanist de l'Obel.

Frontispiece

Above
The frontispiece to *A Collection of Roses from Nature* by Mary Lawrance, published in 1799. This was the first book devoted exclusively to the rose.

Left
A water-colour of the 'Royal Virgin Rose' by Georg Dionysius Ehret.

31

The Botanical Illustrators

Painters in the Low Countries and in Italy soon took on the illuminators' habit of including flowers in their work. The most distinguished of these carefully observed blooms came from artists such as Memling, van Eyck and van der Goes in the Low Countries and Pisanello, da Fabriano and the della Robbias in Italy.

The development of printing techniques from the late fifteenth century onwards had a tremendous impact on herbals. Illustrated books of herbs and flowers for medicinal and domestic use were published all over Europe during the next century. Among the most notable herbals were those of the Flemish botanists Dodoens, de l'Ecluse and de l'Obel (who illustrated ten different kinds of rose) and the Germans Fuchs and Brunfels. Their work was copied, often inaccurately, by many less original compilers, especially in late sixteenth and early seventeenth century England. The most roguish borrower of them all must have been John Gerard whose *Herball* of 1597 gained enormous and quite unmerited popularity.

Before this, however, a steadily growing interest in horticulture had stimulated the art of flower illustration. The demand for florilegia was met admirably by such artists as Georg Hoefnagel who was patronized by Albrecht V, Elector of Bavaria and the Emperor Rudolf II of Austria, and Giacomo Ligozzi, court painter to the Grand Duke of Tuscany in Florence. They recorded all kinds of plants, among them roses, in the great botanical gardens of sixteenth century Europe.

The most important botanical artist of this period for roses was the French Huguenot, Jacques Le Moyne de Morgues, who fled to England from the Massacre of St Bartholomew in 1572. His *Clef des Champs* (1586) was illustrated from delicate water-colours of fruit, flowers, and some birds and animals.

French and Dutch illustrators

Although England was at the forefront of developments in botanical science at this time, the French and the Dutch led in the field of illustration. Among botanical works of great importance were Pierre Vallet's *Le Jardin du Roy tres Chrestien Henry IV* (1608) and the *Florilegium Novum* (1611) by Johann Theodor de Bry. Basil Besler's *Hortus Eystettensis* (1613) was an immense and highly decorative record of the garden of the Bishop of Eystet in Bavaria.

The French artist, Nicholas Robert (1614–85), was employed by Gaston d'Orléans to record the plants in his famous botanical garden at Blois and later to do flower paintings on vellum for Louis XIV. Robert was one of the first contributors to a magnificent series of flower paintings on vellum commissioned by successive kings of France. By the nineteenth century the collection amounted to more than a hundred volumes. Later royal flower painters on vellum included Claude Aubriet and Gerard van Spaëndonck. Their work is now housed in Paris at the Jardin des Plantes.

One of Robert's most charming works, and the one which first brought him fame, was the *Guirlande de Julie*, an album of flowers painted upon vellum, given by the Baron de Sainte-Maure to his fiancée Julie d'Angennes, daughter of the Parisian hostess Madame de Rambouillet. The rose, of course, was included in this romantic compendium of all the most beautiful garden flowers.

The naturalistic roses by the Dutch flower painters of the seventeenth century are at once identifiable, unlike those in many of the earlier herbals. The Dutch school had a great influence on plant illustration, particularly in eighteenth century France where the decorative approach prevailed over the scientific.

Amateur and professional artists

During the eighteenth century, amateurs, especially in England, were busy making delicate water-colour studies of the plants in their gardens. Some were taught by eminent professional artists such as Georg Dionysius Ehret (1708–70) whose own work was a brilliant combination of artistic imagination and scientific exactitude. Others turned for instruction to the proliferating manuals designed for aspiring flower painters. Robert Sayer's *The Florist* (1760) was one of the earliest of these; it was re-vamped by Carrington Bowles at the close of the eighteenth century when it became the more famous Bowles's *Florist*. Others included Henderson's *The Seasons, or Flower Garden . . . with a Treatise or General Instruction for Drawing and Painting Flowers* (1806), George Brookshaw's *A New Treatise on Flower Painting or Every Lady her own Drawing Master* (1818), and Ackermann's *Elements of Flower and Fruit Painting* (1814).

Scientific botanical works illustrated by well-known artists were popular in Europe during the eighteenth century. But it was not until 1799 that the first book devoted exclusively to roses appeared. This was by Mary Lawrance, a teacher of botanical drawing. It is not a distinguished work, from either the scientific or artistic standpoint, but it is nevertheless charming and it led to several other books on roses. Among these were Roessig's *Die Rosen*, published in Leipzig between 1802 and 1820, Henry Andrews's *Roses* (1805–28) and John Lindley's *Rosarum Monographia* produced in 1820. None of them compares with Redouté's sumptuous three-volume *Les Roses* published from 1817 to 1824.

The life of Redouté

Pierre-Joseph Redouté came from a family of artists and was already earning his living, however precariously, at the age of thirteen. The work of van Huysum and the other Dutch flower painters made an early and powerful impression on him. Although he worked for a while as a set painter in the theatre, flowers soon became his primary interest. Redouté eventually met the botanist L'Heritier de Brutelle who commissioned him to contribute drawings to be engraved for his books. This led to the honorary post of 'Draughtsman to the Cabinet of Marie-Antoinette' which in turn brought his work to the notice of Gerard van Spaëndonck, the most fashionable flower artist and teacher in France at that time. Van Spaëndonck was Redouté's greatest influence and their best work is remarkably similar. Redouté adopted van Spaëndonck's technique of watercolour on vellum and obtained equally subtle results.

With van Spaëndonck's encouragement and the patronage of eminent people, Redouté's talent and energy brought him great recognition. After Josephine's death he remained one of the most acclaimed artists of his day, patronized by royalty as a flower painter and as a teacher. He amassed enormous wealth, but was an inveterate spendthrift. When he died of a stroke in 1840 he was, unbelievably, in dire financial straits.

Nearly a hundred years were to pass before the appearance of an illustrated work on the rose of a stature comparable to Redouté's *Les Roses*. This was Ellen Willmott's *Genus Rosa*, published between 1910 and 1914 with illustrations by Alfred Parsons. Parsons was already a well-known landscape painter when he was commissioned to undertake the watercolour drawings for Ellen Willmott's monumental opus, and he succeeded in combining botanical accuracy with sparkling artistry.

Top
Rosa centifolia foliacea by
Pierre-Joseph Redouté.

Above
Rosa lutea from the Reeves
collection of Chinese water-
colours, 1812–31.

Left
Rosa (indica) chinensis, a
water-colour by Alfred
Parsons for Ellen Willmot's
Genus Rosa published
between 1910 and 1914.

Jewellery, Porcelain and Glass

The rose, the symbol of beauty, is quite appropriately celebrated in jewellery, the most luxurious of crafts. The rose itself could be thought of as a jewel. A mid-sixteenth century portrait of Diane de Poitiers, mistress of Henry II of France, shows her choosing jewellery from an overflowing casket. Strewn round it are red and white roses, as though she intended to pick one or two to wear among her pearls and rubies.

Jewellery

As we have seen, the Greek and Roman jewellers fashioned *repoussé* roses in gold and the Byzantine goldsmiths included formal rosettes in their work. In the late medieval period realistically executed roses in enamel began to appear. The magnificent fourteenth century gold cup of the Kings of France and England, now in the British Museum, is decorated with applied enamel roses. A little later Benvenuto Cellini, the Italian Renaissance goldsmith, was creating roses in enamel, gold and pearls.

The rose-cut diamond made its appearance in Holland in the mid-seventeenth century. Before this, diamonds had either been shaped into a pyramid or given a flat, mirror-cut surface. The rose-cut diamond could have up to 24 facets, giving it greater brilliance.

Enamelling lends itself better than most other jeweller's techniques to the fashioning of naturalistic roses, but many settings of rubies and diamonds were undoubtedly intended to be roses. The Italians, during the eighteenth century, were notably successful in making some of their stone-set clusters look more like roses than any other flower and later still, during the nineteenth century, they were to triumph again with *pietra-dura* jewellery of the utmost realism. In these miniature pictorial plaques (known as Florentine mosaics) birds, butterflies and flowers carved out of lapis lazuli, onyx, jasper, coral, agate, malachite and other coloured hard-stones were laid into marble. These created a brilliant if garish effect. Other jewel-like roses were carved in ivory, inlaid in tortoiseshell or even plaited and pincered out of human hair.

Among more recent exponents of the rose in jewellery are the Russian Carl Fabergé and his American contemporary Louis Comfort Tiffany, who both worked at the turn of the century.

Porcelain

No flower was used for decoration more often or with prettier effect than the rose in porcelain. From the mid-eighteenth century onwards, when pottery and porcelain factories were being established all over Europe, the rose, enamelled or realistically modelled, became extremely popular. The Meissen factory, where European hard-paste was first made, was among the first of the producers of porcelain roses. Blossoms in pink, white and yellow were strewn at the feet of many of the figure subjects of such famous modellers as J. J. Kändler.

Many factories continued to make earthenware and other pottery glazed in various ways. Almost without exception they produced china decorated with roses. Sometimes, in pink festoons, they formed the border decoration on dishes and tea wares. Often, as in the Meissen figure groups, they were incidental embellishments; single moulded or modelled roses formed knobs and finials on handles and covers, or appeared on clocks and centrepieces for tables. Roses came in bunches and garlands, in single sprigs and in delicate sprays. Most often, they were part of enamelled posies of mixed flowers.

The factories had different characteristic bouquets, identifiable by the roses alone. At Strasbourg, for example, a full-blown rose

Above
Fabergé's rose trellis egg, made in 1907 for Tsar Nicholas II. It is fashioned in gold and enamel and latticed with rose-cut diamonds. Height 8cm (3in).

often appears at the centre of a softly painted cluster of flowers – the shapes are built up by shading rather than outline. From Mennecy a more rounded, half-opened bloom is painted in a soft pink in an irregularly shaped bouquet. From the Comte d'Artois factory at Limoges comes a similarly rounded rose but with a more strongly shaded centre. This is sometimes scattered in single blooms and sometimes part of a cluster of mixed flowers.

No factory, in France or anywhere else, equalled the royal porcelain factory (first at Vincennes and later Sèvres) in the production of rose-decorated ceramics. Situated near Madame de Pompadour's Chateau de Bellerne on the way from Paris to Versailles, it received immense patronage from the King's favourite mistress. She used to receive him surrounded by banks of porcelain flowers made at Vincennes and later became especially fond of the shade of bright pink known as rose Pompadour. This colour was later copied at some of the English factories. Madame de Pompadour died in 1764. Her successor in Louis XV's affections, Madame du Barry, was another enthusiast for the rose porcelain of Sèvres. Her particular shade of pink, rose du Barry, was used mainly on nineteenth-century English porcelain.

Among the most luxurious of all the Sèvres productions were the flower-enamelled plaques used to embellish furniture of the late eighteenth century. Roses predominate in these overflowing baskets and bunches of delicately painted blooms which were set into some of the finest furniture of the French *ébénistes*.

From 1760 onwards, roses appeared in different guises from nearly every factory in England. Some of the most charming – generally in bouquets characteristic of their respective factories – come from Leeds, New Hall, Swansea and Derby. Coalport and Coalbrookdale also produced elaborate rose-encrusted pieces. Most curious were the spectacular cabbage roses of the Wemyss factory in Scotland in the late nineteenth century, when the rose was being used to decorate cheaper cottage wares as well as the expensive products of the most important factories.

Glass

The rose does not perhaps have a very obvious association with glass, but it has made a few noteworthy appearances. The most celebrated is on Jacobite glasses, made to toast 'the Cause' of the descendants of James II of England. Among other emblems such as the thistle, the star, portraits of Bonnie Prince Charlie and various mottoes, the heraldic rose with varying numbers of petals and either one or two buds, occurs with frequency. Different aspects of 'the Cause' were depicted in various ways. The rose probably represents the crown of England and the buds the Old and Young Pretenders, but opinions are somewhat divided on these details.

Roses also appear on the opaque white glass made in Bristol in the third quarter of the eighteenth century. Vases, bottles, tea caddies, candlesticks and other items were decorated with roses and other flowers very much in the manner of pottery and porcelain. Examples of this opaque glass are now extremely rare and are valuable collectors' pieces.

Much later, in the late 1840s, the rose made an illustrious appearance in the paperweights of the Clichy factory. The Clichy rose, as it is called, appears like a signature on a large number of Clichy weights. Most commonly it is pink and green, sometimes white and more rarely blue, yellow or red. The Baccarat factory also used the rose, either by itself or in a bouquet with other flowers, in its flower paperweights. Early examples from both factories are prized by collectors.

Top
Rose-strewn porcelain. From left to right: a mid 18th century Strasbourg dish and cover, a Mennecy teapot and a Sèvres jug.

Centre
A Baccarat paperweight of the mid 19th century, showing a pink rose with other flowers.

Above
An opaque glass baby-feeder made in Spain during the 18th century.

Right
An example of Jacobite glass depicting the heraldic rose.

The Rose in Textiles

Right
Seventeenth century rose
point lace from Venice. The
delicately worked flowers
joined by intricate stems and
loops are a feature of this
kind of needlepoint lace.

Soft, sensuous and versatile in terms of design, the rose has been a favourite of embroiderers and weavers since the sixteenth century. Exploration and discovery at that time stimulated developments in botany, and gardening became a popular pursuit. The predominating peace and prosperity led to a greater degree of civilization and an interest in home comforts generally. Until this time the best embroidery had been worked for the grander establishments and for the Church; now it was taken up by ladies at home who embroidered furnishings and decorated their own dresses. Quite naturally they drew inspiration for their designs from the flowers in their gardens.

Designs from herbals

By the end of the sixteenth century there were plenty of patterns for them to copy if they were unable to create their own. Many of the herbals and other books of plant and animal illustration were published as much for embroiderers and other craftsmen as for herbalists and those interested in the study of botany. One such book, the *Clef des Champs* (1586) was intended for those engaged in painting, sculpture, goldwork, embroidery and tapestry. Its author, Jacques Le Moyne de Morgues, dedicated it to Lady Mary Sidney, mother of Sir Philip Sidney.

Royal embroiderers

Royal ladies were among the most notable embroiderers of the day. Some of the happier hours of the ill-fated Mary Queen of Scots must have been spent with the needle. The embroidery she did during the 15 years she was in the custody of Bess of Hardwick, herself a famous needlewoman, has become almost legendary.

In France, Marie de Medici, wife of Henry IV, was a passionate embroiderer of flowers. In 1608 the artist Pierre Vallet dedicated his book, *Le Jardin du Roy tres Chrestien Henry IV* to her. On the title page he described himself as 'brodeur ordinaire'. His compilation, which included two kinds of rose, was intended to provide the Queen with designs for her embroideries. The fashion for embroidering flowers soon spread through the French court.

As one of the the most appealing of floral motifs, the rose took various forms. There were sprigs, trailing briars and, most popular of all in England, stylized Tudor roses. Many of them were made as slips – plant motifs embroidered on canvas which were cut out and appliquéd. Roses were also used in blackwork, the fine embroidery in black silk on linen, popular in the Elizabethan period for items of clothing such as hoods and coifs, collars, sleeves and stomachers. Cushions, book covers, purses and clothes were decorated with exquisitely stitched flowers often embellished with seed pearls, sequins and metal threads.

Lace was among the most luxurious of materials and many people spent fortunes on it. In one year alone, it is recorded, Queen Anne spent £1,000 on bobbin lace. A large number of laces carried rose motifs. One of these, called rose point, was a fine Venetian needlepoint lace, a variety of what is known as *punto in aria*. It consisted of small rose florettes joined by wavy stems and decorative loops and was made principally between 1650 and 1720.

Dress fabrics

The herbal-based, rather stylized roses in embroidery were superseded by more naturalistic treatment in the late seventeenth century. The influence of the Dutch flower painters had filtered down to the embroiderers. This led to naturalism in textile design and other kinds of decoration. Some of the most sumptuous of dress fabrics were now being produced by the silk weavers of Lyons whose rich, often rose-strewn brocades were being worn by the elite in France and those who could afford them elsewhere.

Dress fashions in the eighteenth century generally became less stiff, and while women's dresses remained wide-skirted and tight-bodiced, they were sensuous and flouncy. Their materials, often light in both colour and texture, lent themselves to decoration with flowers. The pink cabbage rose, echoing the period's predilection for frilliness, appears constantly: embroidered, woven or real, worn in the hair or on the corsage.

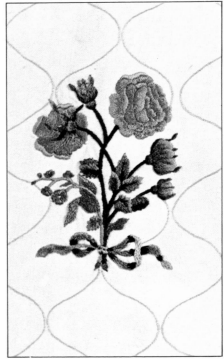

Above
An embroidered rose on a mid 18th century chair cover.

Above left
Cabbage roses on a Berlin woolwork carpet.

Left
Detail of embroidery from Hardwick Hall, thought to be by Mary Queen of Scots.

Furnishing textiles

In furnishing textiles too, the rose acquired a billowing naturalness in contrast to the graphic neatness of Elizabethan slips. Professional embroiderers and ladies at home ambitiously worked sets of chair coverings, screen panels, table tops, bedcovers and even carpets with colourful bouquets of flowers. Their designs were influenced by Dutch flower paintings, and they nearly always included pink or white roses.

In the late eighteenth century this interest in embroidery for furnishings gave way to less arduous embroidered decorations – small panels for firescreens or tea caddies, pictures or costume accessories, worked in coloured silks on silk or satin backgrounds. Flowers, particularly roses, were among the most usual subjects, fashioned into garlands and bouquets.

By the early nineteenth century the women of New England were producing a wide range of homespun items, including some soft, white woollen blankets known as rose blankets. These were woven on the loom and then embroidered in the corners with a stylized wheel or rosette design in coloured yarns.

The rose was prominent in Berlin woolwork, the facile but apparently addictive form of canvas embroidery pursued by European ladies in the mid-nineteenth century. Voluptuous cabbage roses were everywhere – on footstools and fenders, bell-pulls and braces, slippers, waistcoats and every conceivable keepsake or decorative inutility.

Berlin wool roses were so common that it would be easy to overlook the delicate briars characteristic of Arts and Crafts embroidery. William Morris and Edward Burne-Jones led the field and others, including a stalwart phalanx of female embroiderers, followed. Their designs are still enjoyed today.

The Useful Rose

Above
This 19th century perfume label features the deeply fragrant rose of Provence (*Rosa centifolia*).

Since time immemorial the rose, more than any other flower, has been used for making medicines and perfumes, soaps and cosmetics. Dioscorides, who compiled his famous *Herbal* in the first century AD, drew substantially from earlier works such as that produced towards the end of the second century BC by Crataeras, physician to King Mithridates of Pontus. Almost certainly the Chinese, Persians and other ancient peoples were using roses for medicinal purposes long before that.

Dioscorides' *Herbal* was regarded as the definitive textbook on the medicinal properties of plants for the next 15 centuries. It formed the basis for several of the herbals published as late as the sixteenth and seventeenth centuries. An English translation was made in the mid-seventeenth century by the botanist John Goodyer.

Hips, roots and flowers

In affirming that the fruit of 'The Doggs bush' (*Rosa sempervirens*) 'being dryed stops the belly', Dioscorides provides an early instance of rose hips being used in medicine. Rose hips have been used for all sorts of ailments throughout history. It was not until our own century that the high vitamin C content of rose hips was recognized, so confirming their value in medicine during the last 2,000 years. The name 'Dog rose' is thought to have come about,

incidentally, from the belief that its root was a cure for hydrophobia, or rabies.

Dioscorides writes at some length on the properties of *Rosa lutea*, whose flower 'doth coole and binde . . . the iuice must be prest out of them whilst they are yet but young cutting off first that which is called the Naile, which is the white that is in the leafe, but the rest must be beaten and pownded in ye shade in a mortar till it grow thick, & soe be set up for eye salves . . . The straining of the drye Roses sod in wine is good for the head-ach, for the eyes, the eares, ye gummes, for ye paine of ye seat, of the Intestinum rectum, of the Vulua, being anointed on with a feather or washt ouer with it . . . They are burnt also for medicines to make the eyelids looke faire . . . The heads being dranck doe stop a loose belly and the spitting of bloud.'

Dioscorides gives recipes for pomanders of roses, recommending dried balls of rose mixture 'to be put about women's necks instead of necklaces, dulling the unsauourie smell of the sweat. They use the same also being beaten small in medicines made to repress the sweat, & in ointments to anoint withall after bathing.'

A universal cure

The most famous medical writer of the Roman period was Pliny, who listed more than 30 medicines made from roses. He repeated much of the information given by Dioscorides and reaffirmed the rose's efficacy in treating stomach and bladder disorders, eye diseases and nervous problems. Headache and toothache were said to be cured by rose preparations and subsequent writers repeated this theory. The Romans, followed by generations of heavy drinkers, optimistically believed that rose petals dropped into wine would delay drunkenness. Roman ladies trusted that rose petals on their faces at night would smooth out wrinkles and, added to bath water, would preserve their youth and beauty.

In the Middle Ages, the rose was considered 'surpassing all other herbs in virtue and scent'. It was widely cultivated in monastery gardens and made into salves and lotions, honey, vinegar, jams, wine and all kinds of medicinal remedies. Rose petals were thought to have a purifying effect. They were strewn on floors during the medieval and Tudor periods, especially in times of plague. Certainly they must have helped to freshen the often putrid air. The nursery rhyme, 'Ring-a-ring o'roses' is sometimes associated with the Great Plague: a rosy rash was a symptom, posies of herbs were carried as a protection, and sneezing signalled the onset of the fatal illness. However, according to Iona and Peter Opie, compilers of the *Oxford Dictionary of Nursery Rhymes*, this connection is not proven.

The rose in perfume

It is commonly held that the eleventh century Arabian doctor, Avicenna, was the first to extract an essence from roses. Princess Nur Jahan, wife of the Indian Moghul Jahangir, is said to have discovered rose oil in the early seventeenth century. On her wedding day she was boating on a lake full of rosewater when she noticed that the sun had caused an oily scum to form on the surface. When this was skimmed off she found it to be heavily perfumed. However, it seems likely that the Chinese made rose oil and rose essence long before this time.

Since the medieval period, when the rose products of the apothecaries of Provins first became famous, France has been at the forefront of the perfume and cosmetics trade. Although we use few medical preparations containing roses today, the flower is still an important ingredient in the manufacture of beauty products.

Rose petal wine

There is a long-standing tradition among English country people for making a delightful and refreshing wine from both wild and cultivated rose petals. Modern recipes have been considerably updated but have not lost any of their original character. The techniques used by winemakers today eliminate the risk of contamination and failure to ferment so often experienced by our forebears in this field. Rose petal wine can easily be made by every rose-lover who has a taste for unusual wine and wishes to enhance his cellar with this speciality. It is best served as a sweet dessert wine, or when dry, as a light table wine.

Ingredients
The following are the ingredients for 4.5 litres (1 gallon) of wine. Adjustments may be made according to the size of jar used.
450gm (1lb) fresh, red, scented rose petals
1.1 kg (2½lbs) white sugar (this amount will make a medium wine)
Juice of 1 lemon (or 1 heaped tablespoon of citric acid)
1 teaspoon good wine yeast
1 nutrient tablet
4.5 litres (1 gallon) water

Method
First put a large funnel in the neck of a glass jar. Pour the sugar through the funnel into the jar, together with the lemon juice or citric acid. Boil the water in a large saucepan and add the rose petals, cooking them for about 15 minutes until all the colour and perfume have been extracted. When the liquid has cooled to about 21°C (70°F) in the saucepan, strain it through a sieve into the jar, stirring to dissolve the sugar and acid. When this has melted, add the yeast and nutrient tablet. Do not stir the yeast into the liquid, but leave it to ferment in its own time from the top – usually 24 hours. Fit on an airlock tightly and fill the jar half full of cool boiled water. Leave the liquid to ferment in a warm place. If the yeast is kept at extreme temperatures it will die.

When the fermentation has slowed down after about two months, siphon the wine off the lees (sediment) into a clean jar. Refit the airlock and place the jar in a cool dark place to finalize the fermentation. When all signs of activity have ceased, i.e. no more bubbles rise to the top of the jar, it is time for bottling.

Be sure that no more fermentation takes place, otherwise the bottles may blow their corks or even explode. Do this by adding one stabilizing tablet (potassium sorbate) and one Campden tablet (sodium metabisulphite) to every 4.5 litres (1 gallon) and leaving the wine a day or two before finally putting it into bottles.

As with all home-made wines, this may be drunk when you feel it is ready, but the quality will be improved if you can leave it for about six months.

Rose hip syrup

Rosa canina, or the common Dog rose, grows in wild profusion throughout Britain. Although syrups and jellies were made from its hips as long ago as the Middle Ages, it was only in the 1930s that its real food value was discovered.

During the Second World War, a national campaign was launched to collect hundreds of tons of rose hips to make into syrup. This was the result of experiments which showed that the common rose hip contained more vitamin C than any other fruit or vegetable – as much as 20 times that in the same weight of oranges.

Ingredients
1kg (2lb) rose hips
3 litres (6 pints) water
500g (1lb) sugar

Method
Wash the wild rose hips well, top and tail them and mince them coarsely. Add them to 2 litres (4 pints) of boiling water, bringing them back to the boil, and then remove the pan from the heat. Allow the mixture to stand for about 15 minutes then strain through a jelly bag, extracting as much of the juice as possible.

Repeat this process with the pulp in a further 1·1 litres (2 pints) of water, leaving the mixture to stand for a further 10 minutes, and then strain it as before in a clean jelly bag.

Boil the juice from these two extracts until it is reduced to about 1 litre (2 pints). Add the sugar and stir until it is dissolved, bringing it to the boil and keeping the syrup at boiling point for 5 minutes. Pour the syrup into warm, clean bottles and seal them at once with sterilized corks or other stoppers. As the syrup does not keep for very long once opened, use only small bottles.

Sterilize the filled bottles by placing them on a pad of newspaper, or other padding, in the bottom of a large saucepan. Fill the pan with water to the liquid level of the bottles. Bring the temperature of the water up rapidly to 88°C (190°F) and maintain for 20 minutes, taking care not to exceed the time limit as this may impair the flavour of the syrup.

Rose petal preserve

Preserves are generally used as a topping for ice creams, blancmanges, cream parfaits and trifles. It is advisable to use the old-fashioned species roses, or even wild roses, as these are more delicate in flavour and texture than the modern varieties of hybrid tea or floribunda roses. In any recipes using roses, take care not to use plants which have recently been sprayed with chemicals.

Ingredients
55gm (2oz) red or pink rose petals
225gm (½lb) fine white sugar
55ml (2 fl oz) water
1 tablespoon lemon juice
1 tablespoon orange juice
Cochineal (red colouring)
    optional

Method
Remove the yellow base of the petals. Wash the petals well and dry them. Boil the sugar, water and fruit juices gently until a syrup is formed. Add the rose petals, finely chopped, and simmer on the lowest possible heat, stirring all the time. Cook for about 30 minutes until the mixture is thick. Pour into a small pot and cover well.

The rose petal bath

Anyone who grows roses in sufficient quantities may enjoy a rose petal bath. Fill a large bucket with fragrant, freshly-picked red rose petals. Place the petals in the bath and pour very hot water over them. Leave the water until the desired temperature is reached then soak for as long as you wish.

Your skin will be pleasantly perfumed and refreshed because of the astringent qualities of the rose petals.

The Lore of Pot-pourri

It may be a disappointment for many to learn that the word pot-pourri means 'rotten pot'. Derived from the French verb *pourrir*, which means to ripen, to perish, to rot, the term was used in English as early as 1611 for culinary purposes when describing a hotch potch or a mixture of various meats. This may not mean that rotten meat was eaten, but it could have meant second-choice meat or inferior cuts which were preserved by boiling. However at that time the word was used for many kinds of mixtures, including dried flower petals and spices, and as such the term was handed down through families and to travellers. Pot-pourri is a common term in music and literature, meaning a medley of musical airs or writings. But its strongest association is with the scented rose petals and spices which one mixes and stores in jars or bowls in the home.

The ancient Greeks, when entertaining, sometimes gave guests little cloth bags filled with sweet-smelling petals and leaves, rather like the pot-pourri sachets of garden flowers that are sold today. In 1749 Lady Luxborough, in a letter to Shenstone on 28 November, wrote 'it might be called a pot pourri which is a potful of all kinds of flowers of several perfumes . . .' This indicates that the word was used in England at that time to refer to a mixture of flowers. It appeared also in 1863 when Lytton, writing in *Caxtoniana*, referred to 'a blue china jar filled with Pot Pourri'.

Medicinal pot-pourri

More sinister references associate pot-pourri with its value in combating infection at the time of the Great Plague in London (1664–5) when rose petals, dried rosemary, juniper, bay leaves and frankincense were burned in a chafing dish and carried from room to room. Increasing trade and commerce at the end of the fifteenth century, though it brought benefits, also brought the problem of disease. At the time of the Great Plague a proclamation was fixed to the doors of churches listing certain preventive measures. Diets and exercises were recommended and at the same time it was strongly advised that all dwellings were to be filled with the scent of roses, violets, bay leaves, fennel, mint and aromatic herbs. So it seems that these mixtures were being used long before Lady Luxborough called hers a pot-pourri.

In fact these mixtures were constantly being experimented with in the still rooms of the upper classes, especially in the Elizabethan era. It is known that Queen Elizabeth I had a still room at her country residence, where ladies of the Court amused themselves concocting different mixtures for perfumes, powders, pomanders and sweet bags.

Elanour Sinclair Rohde, the great herbalist, wrote in one of her early books that the womenfolk of England turned to their gardens in Elizabeth's time for their mixtures, rather than to the products of the east which were being introduced to Europe. So popular did the use of scented bags and other devices become that later even the smallest of country houses had a still room, perhaps as one would have a conservatory today. Socrates, however, said that perfumes and pomanders were unnecessary for women 'for they themselves smell sweet'.

Make your own pot-pourri

People generally create their own pot-pourri recipes to suit their tastes. Add what you like until, like the expert 'noses' who test and concoct the perfumes in the south of France, you discover the most attractive blend. Too much spice is objectionable to some, while too much orange and lemon rind could be too sharp for others. In all cases, however, scented rose petals should form the basis of pot-pourris. The most scented roses such as *Rosa centifolia* and the Damask roses are the best. Pick the roses just before they are in full bloom and after they are dry from the morning dew (if damp, they will encourage mildew). After stripping the petals place them on muslin or thin paper in the airing cupboard, or a cool/warm oven, turning them now and again. The quicker they dry (this does not mean a hot oven) the quicker the scent is sealed in.

Recipe for pot-pourri

Ingredients
Dried rose petals to form the bulk
Dried lavender flowers
Any other strong-smelling flower such as heliotrope, clove, carnations, honeysuckle
Scented leaves (no stems), dried and crushed, such as mint, sage, fennel, lemon verbena and scented geranium
Grated nutmeg
Crushed cloves
Small amount of allspice (optional)
Grated, dried orange and lemon peel

Method
Mix the ingredients together and let them rest, stirring occasionally later. When the scents fade, a pot-pourri reviver can be bought and used, or a few drops of oil of roses or lavender can be added. When your supply of pot-pourri has been used up, start again, varying the ingredients to suit your taste.

The Rose
in Bloom

Ancestry of the Rose

Evolution remains something of a mystery, not only in respect of roses but also for the human race itself. The factors influencing the creation of life appear to have been chemistry, heat, movement and light. Chemistry is what happens when different elements combine in various proportions and under various conditions. Heat and movement are two conditions well known from general experience to make things happen. Light is the activator of movement in plants, providing their initial energy. Almost certainly there were other factors involved in the creation of life, among which may have been radioactivity and waves or signals of energy.

It is generally assumed that when the earth cooled down after its creation, the seas contained simple life forms which evolved gradually over millions of years into the phenomena of life that exist today. However, life may have begun at an earlier stage of the earth's history and the cells involved in this process may not have been as simple as is supposed. Nor is it necessarily true that the evolutionary process was gradual. Long periods of little change may have been interrupted by short periods of violent change. It is clear that whole lines of evolution perished for ever from the face of the earth, as fossils bear witness. It would seem premature to assume that the process of evolution is yet complete.

Evolution of the rose

The earliest evidence of roses is in fossils. Geologists ascribe these fossils to the Tertiary Period, which has several divisions ranging from the Pliocene (two to seven million years ago) to the Palaeocene (44 to 63 million years ago). Fossils of roses are mostly dated in the Miocene division (seven to 26 million years ago), with a few thought possibly older.

The fossil remains are quite clearly pieces of rose growth, usually leaves. They have been discovered in three continents: Europe (in Austria, Bulgaria, France and Germany), America (in Alaska, California, Colorado and Oregon), and Asia (in China and Japan). No doubt there are more to be found. The rose is native only to the northern hemisphere. It has never been found as an original wild plant in the southern hemisphere, despite its wide distribution around the temperate zones of the north.

The wide distribution of fossil remains suggests that the rose was created from slightly different forms of primitive cell structures. Fossils have not yet been found in central Asia, the fourth area of present-day natural distribution. However, it is unlikely that central Asia got all its roses by encroachments from east and west, because roses are found there which are unknown in the wild elsewhere. If it can be speculated that roses grew in different forms from the beginning, this may account for wide divergences within the genus. Smaller differences may be accounted for by natural variation.

Major differences between wild roses

The major differences among the wild roses of the world follow. The genus *Rosa* can be grouped according to them into various sub-sections.

Simple leaves: The leaf is one entire piece and not sub-divided into leaflets in the normal way. Only one rose answers this description, namely *R. persica* from Iran; sub-genus Simplicifoliae.

Prickly hips: The hips of most roses are either smooth or hairy. A few, including *R. persica*, have prickles on their hips – real prickles, not just bristly hairs. These are the sub-genus Hesperrhodos, from the United States, consisting of two species, and the sub-genus Platyrhodon from China, consisting of one species. The rest of the

genus has smooth, hairy or bristly hips and belongs to the sub-genus Eurosa.

Free stipules: Stipules are the small leafy growths on each side of the base of the leafstalk. Normally they are joined to the leafstalk firmly but in a few roses they are joined only at the base. These are of the sub-genus Eurosa, sections Banksianae, Laevigatae and Bracteatae. There are five species, four from China, one from India.

Protruding styles: The styles, the little stems of the female organs, are at the centre of the flower. In most roses they grow long enough to place their tips about level with the base of the flower. But in two sections they stick further out. These are of the sub-genus Eurosa, sections Indicae and Synstylae. In the latter not only do they jut out but they are also fused together. There are 26 species of which 22 come from eastern Asia, two from Europe, one from Turkey and one from the United States.

Solitary flowers: Most roses bear their flowers in clusters, with little flower stalks arising in the same head. But a few usually produce their flowers in a head of only one. They are of the sub-genus Eurosa, sections Gallicanae and Pimpinellifoliae. There are 13 species, from central Asia to Korea, two spreading also to Europe.

Curved thorns: The remaining roses possess in each case the antithesis of the previous five headings. Those with curved thorns are of the sub-genus Eurosa, section Caninae. These are the 30 species of Dog rose. They are nearly all European, with some spreading to Asia.

Straight thorns: Those which remain have straight thorns and are of the sub-genus Eurosa. Section Carolinae has seven species, all American. Section Cinnamomeae has 56 species, mostly either Chinese or American.

Whatever the secrets of the ancestry of the rose, these are the varied types of wild rose which man found waiting when he entered the world some millions of years later.

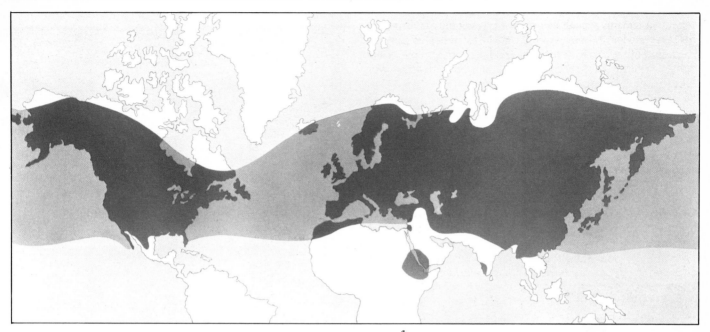

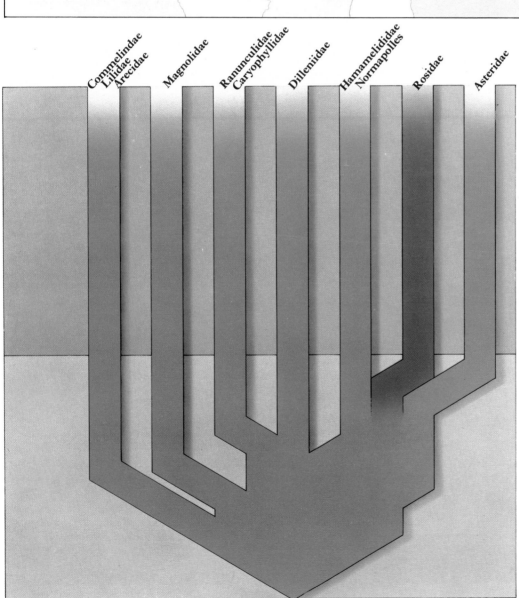

Commelindae
Lilidae
Arecidae
Magnolidae
Ranunculidae
Caryophyllidae
Dilleniidae
Hamamelididae
Normapolles
Rosidae
Asteridae

Above
The rose is native to the temperate zones of the northern hemisphere. It has never been found as a native wild plant in equatorial regions or the southern hemisphere.

Left
Most of today's garden roses are the product of modern rose breeding techniques. However fossil evidence suggests that wild roses came into existence long before the appearance of man. Fossils of the rose are ascribed to the Tertiary Period, with most dating from the Miocene Epoch, about 7 to 26 million years ago.

Opposite page
A fossil of a wild rose leaf with five leaflets. Rose fossils have been found in Europe, North America and Asia.

The Wild Rose

Above
The pale pink flowers of *R. canina* are followed by hips rich in vitamin C.
Left
R. californica plena, from the United States, bears arching sprays of deep pink blooms.
Below
The deep red, single blooms of *R. moyesii* from western China.

The rose is not a simple plant, as one might expect, but on the contrary is one of the most baffling for botanists to understand. It is not even certain how many different species of wild rose there are. One botanist recorded 4,266 species of which, an unkind critic said, he could find several on a single plant.

A rose species may roughly be defined as a distinct kind of wild rose plant which reproduces itself exactly from its own seed. This description has to be qualified to allow for the exceptions that appear both in cultivation and in nature. Taking this definition however, it would appear that there are 141 species. This number might be reduced to about 80 if a proper study were made.

The diversity of the rose
The diversity of the genus may be understood by a brief survey of the sub-divisions outlined in the previous chapter.

Sub-genus Simplicifoliae: This is exceptional because it has simple leaves and no stipules. Botanically it is not a rose but a hulthemia, however it is very closely related. Its one species is a semi-desert plant, distinguished by yellow flowers with a prominent red eye. It is *Hulthemia* (or *Rosa*) *persica*.

Sub-genus Hesperrhodos: The two species are rare, their habitat restricted to fairly small areas of southern California and New Mexico. *R. stellata* has leaves and thorns like those of gooseberries and its twigs are covered with hairs, almost looking like white lichen. It is known as the 'Gooseberry Rose' and has brilliant pink flowers.

Sub-genus Platyrhodon: R. roxburghii, from China, is the 'Chestnut Rose', so called because its hips have prickles like those of the sweet chestnut. It has large pink flowers.

Sub-genus Eurosa is divided into the following ten sections:

Banksianae: Very vigorous, almost thornless, climbers. *R. banksiae lutea* is the famous 'Banksian Yellow'.

Laevigatae: Only one species, from China, a white climber with highly polished leaves. It is naturalized in America and known there as the 'Cherokee Rose'.

Bracteatae: Only one species, from China. It is a white climber with foliage strongly resistant to blackspot.

Indicae: Only two species, namely the 'China Rose' (*R. chinensis*) and *R. gigantea*, the latter from south-west China and Burma.

Synstylae: These are nearly all Chinese, but a notable exception is *R. arvensis*, the 'Field Rose', which is the only wild climbing rose native to Britain. Three of the Chinese species are vigorous, growing through trees in their homeland and flowering in huge sheets of bloom. They are *R. filipes*, *R. helenae* and *R. longicuspis*. All three are white and very fragrant. Much of the scent comes from the stamens, not the petals. A close relative is the famous 'Musk Rose', *R. moschata*, which was taken to Europe in the fifteenth or sixteenth century and for many years was the only climbing rose widely grown. It is rare today.

A quite different member of the Synstylae is *R. multiflora*, a bush with small white flowers in great abundance.

R. sempervirens holds its leaves through most of the winter and is therefore known as the 'Evergreen Rose'. It is a white climber from southern Europe. *R. setigera*, the 'Prairie Rose', is American, a white climber that layers itself in the wild as a blackberry does. *R. sinowilsonii*, from China, has extraordinary huge leaves. *R. wichuraiana* trails along the ground.

Gallicanae: Only one species, from west Asia and Europe. It is a pink shrub – the ancestor of most of the old European roses.

Pimpinellifoliae: These contain most of the yellow to be found in wild roses. *R. foetida* is 'Austrian Yellow', from the area Iran to

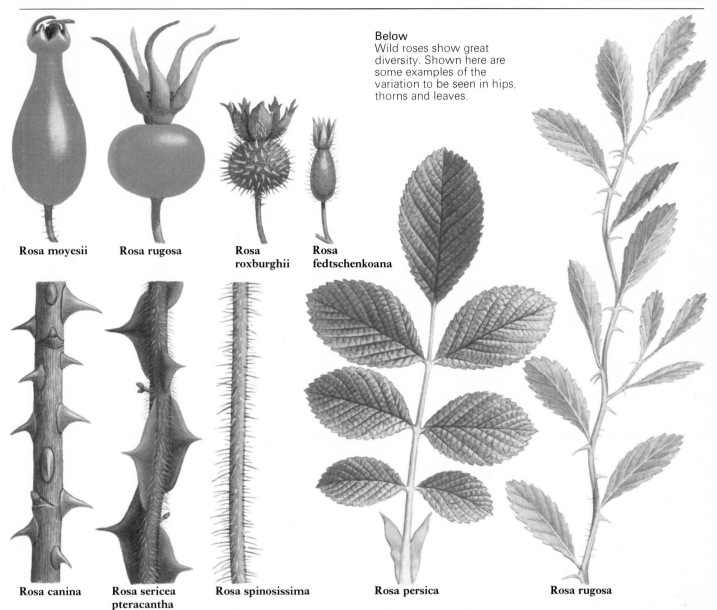

Below
Wild roses show great diversity. Shown here are some examples of the variation to be seen in hips, thorns and leaves.

Rosa moyesii　　**Rosa rugosa**　　**Rosa roxburghii**　　**Rosa fedtschenkoana**

Rosa canina　　**Rosa sericea pteracantha**　　**Rosa spinosissima**　　**Rosa persica**　　**Rosa rugosa**

Turkey. *R. hugonis*, *R. ecae* and *R. xanthina* are also wild yellow roses. In this section are also *R. sericea pteracantha*, with its extraordinary winged thorns, and the 'Scotch Rose', *R. spinosissima*, noted for hardiness and its black hips.

Caninae: The Dog roses are nearly all European, several native to Britain. *R. canina* has hips rich in vitamin C, and *R. eglanteria* is the 'Sweet Briar'. *R. rubrifolia* has plum-coloured leaves.

Carolinae: All seven of these come from North America. *R. foliosa* has willowy leaves; those of *R. nitida* are small and polished; *R. palustris* grows in swamps. The most beautiful of them is *R. virginiana*, a pink shrub.

Cinnamomeae: A large section with many beauties, especially a group including *R. macrophylla* and *R. moyesii* which are greatly prized for their long red hips. Two species have pale, almost white leaves, namely *R. beggeriana* and *R. fedtschenkoana*. *R. acicularis* is the 'Arctic Rose', growing in northern Asia, Europe and America. Some beautiful fern-like leaves are to be seen on *R. multibracteata*, *R. willmottiae* and *R. webbiana* which all bear pink flowers. *R. pendulina* is almost thornless and *R. rugosa* is noted for its tough, wrinkled leaves, which are almost impervious to blackspot, as well as for its long flowering season.

How to identify a rose

A rose is a flowering plant.

Its seeds are enclosed in a receptacle called the hip.

The seedlings germinate with two seed leaves.

The rose has perfect flowers, which in part means that a flower can set seed without outside help, for it contains both sexes.

The flowers are regular, i.e. its petals are all approximately the same size. The other parts of the flower, for example sepals and stamens, are evenly matched in size.

The rose in its original wild state is pentamerous, i.e. it has five petals and five sepals.

Its leaves are placed alternately on the stem.

It is a shrub or climber and generally prickly.

The leaves are sub-divided into leaflets, always of an odd number.

Each leafstalk bears stipules – a pair of small leafy growths at its base.

The flower has many stamens and pistils.

The hips are fleshy.

The seeds of the rose are like miniature nuts.

The First Hybrids

The first man-made hybrids arose in three main areas of civilization, but so long ago that no records exist to prove how the work was done. Before human beings came on the scene, nature had a million years or more to make her own hybrids.

Nature's hybrids arise when a wild rose, instead of pollinating itself, receives pollen from another species. This may easily happen with roses because the female part of the flower is usually receptive before the male pollen is ready. During this interval, wind or insects may introduce pollen from a rose of a different species.

Hybrids and sports

Once such a conception occurs, the resultant seed has half its chromosomes from one species and half from another. In most wild roses this means seven from each parent. Each chromosome is equipped with an unknown number of particles called genes which determine the characteristics of the seedling. When two different species are so united, their different genes will show varying degrees of dominance. A gene from one parent may dominate the corresponding gene from the other parent, or a compromise may be reached. The seedling will therefore be different from the plant which bore the seed.

Many such hybrids are sterile. Some are fertile and when they in turn set seed their genes will play the same game so that the seedlings are again different from their parents. Should more foreign pollen fertilize a hybrid, then the possibilities of variation are increased by the arrival of new genes. It commonly happens that some genes wait many generations before they show. It cannot be doubted that natural hybrids occurred freely before the age of man; many wild roses are in fact hybrids and not true species. These have established themselves in character owing to an unusually settled dominance of certain genes.

Below
'Versicolor', a sport of *R. gallica*, has flowers streaked with crimson, white and pink. It is also known as 'Rosa Mundi'.

Nature also provided another source of variation by freak changes which are called sports, or mutations. These arise from irregularities of the growth processes, possibly induced by outside influences in some cases, or sheer chance in others. The most obvious are changes in colour or in doubleness; in the latter case, stamens have usually grown into petals. Probably the earliest intervention by mankind was to collect some of these unusual variations. Once people began to grow such roses in proximity and sow their seed, rose breeding had begun.

The ancient Chinese

Many of humanity's basic skills are said to have originated in China. As this country was more richly endowed than any other with beautiful wild roses, the chances are that rose breeding started in China too. Certainly the modern rose owes more to the ancient Chinese than to any other people.

An example of bringing home natural variations is clearly shown by the Banksian roses: they were originally white and single, but the Chinese either found or made them yellow and double. The greatest achievements of the Chinese were the 'China Rose' and the 'Tea Rose', raised, so far as can be judged, from *R. chinensis* and *R. gigantea*.

When western traders were permitted to enter Chinese ports in the eighteenth century, they saw extraordinary roses growing in Chinese gardens and nurseries. These roses were remarkable for flowering again and again during the same season, for their smart, bright leaves, for the touch of buff yellow in some of them, and for their delicate scent. The important roses sent to Europe at this time were 'Old Blush', 'Hume's Tea-scented China', 'Park's Yellow Tea-scented China' and 'Slater's Crimson China'.

Early western hybrids

Returning to antiquity, but this time in the west, it appears that roses were grown in the area now known as Iraq – the cradle of western civilization. These roses were taken westwards with successive civilizations: Minoan, Mycenean, Egyptian, Greek, Roman and western European. By the seventeenth century the west had its own roses, largely descended from *R. gallica*. The chief European roses were Gallicas, Damasks and Albas, with Centifolias arriving late on the scene. They usually flowered, pink, white, or dull red, only once in the summer.

The yellow roses of Asia

The third area appears to have been central Asia, particularly Iran. It is from here that a great contribution came, offered neither by China nor the west, namely bright yellow roses. The Persians undoubtedly knew the ancient roses of the west, but it was not until the sixteenth century that the west became aware that yellow roses were being cultivated in the Ottoman Empire.

For some centuries Muslims and Christians had avoided one another's territories, unless well-armed, out of a surely mistaken belief that the other was inhabited by barbarians of the utmost cruelty and ferocity. Needless to say, each set of barbarians contained rose breeders. From the Muslims came 'Austrian Yellow' in about 1560 and *R. hemisphaerica*, the 'Sulphur Rose', about 1600. In the early 1800s, 'Austrian Yellow' was bred with Scotch roses to produce some double yellow hybrids. *R. foetida persiana* ('Persian Yellow') was introduced to England from Tehran in about 1837. This bright, double yellow rose from Iran was thus ready to join the roses of China and the roses of Europe to glorify the gardens of the twentieth century.

petal

anthers
stamens
stigmas
pistil

ovules

sepal

Top
The early flowering, double yellow flowers of *R. banksiae lutea*. The original species has white, single blooms.

Above
'Old Blush', one of the first roses taken from China to the west in the 18th century.

Right
A cross-section of the rose flower. The female organs, each consisting of an ovule, stigma and style, are surrounded by the stamens, or male organs, with their pollen-bearing anthers.

Old Cultivated Roses in Europe

Before considering the influence of Chinese and Iranian roses on the west, the story of the old garden roses of Europe must be told. These roses would have been familiar to Nero, Robert Burns and Napoleon, not that all three of them would have seen the same varieties. Each generation raised its own varieties, with what differences it is impossible to tell. The old garden roses existing today were raised mainly in the nineteenth century. It may be assumed, from old descriptions and paintings and from the genetical material that was available, that the general character of the old roses was fairly similar.

The Gallicas and Damasks

The 'French Rose', *R. gallica*, was the European prototype though in fact it grows more commonly east of France through southern Europe into Asia. It varies from light pink to red, with the occasional increase of petals by chance to semi-double or double. Thus a wide range of varieties was possible. This was increased by a tendency of *R. gallica* to change towards purple as the flower aged and to produce sports which were speckled or striped.

It is assumed that *R. gallica* hybridized itself with another wild rose in western Asia, possibly *R. phoenicia*, to produce the Damask roses. These were marked by a tendency to grow as open bushes with long arching shoots, and they had pale colours: white or pink. Both these characteristics could have come from *R. phoenicia*, which is a white climber, a member of the Synstylae and closely related to the 'Musk Rose', *R. moschata*.

Both Gallicas and Damasks flower only in summer, with one very interesting and unaccountable exception. This is a Damask called 'Quatre Saisons', or 'Autumn Damask', which is to some degree remontant. It has caused some speculation as to whether it could have been the rose of Paestum, a town in Italy which was famous for roses, and where, as the poet Virgil said, the rose gardens flowered twice in a season. However, Virgil may have been taken in, as many expert horticultural judges have been, by the skill of the cultivators. One can lengthen the flowering period by forcing some plants into bloom early and pruning others to make them late, but the individual bushes flower only for their natural length of time.

Albas and Centifolias

The third class, probably of similar antiquity, is the Alba roses. They have a completely different character, being much more handsome in their growth and leaves than either the Gallicas or Damasks. Their place and time of origin are quite unknown. Their appearance has led students to suppose that they originated as a hybrid between one of the Dog roses, either *R. canina* or *R. corymbifera*, and a Damask.

After these three grand originals came the Centifolias, probably in the second half of the sixteenth century. They were also known as Cabbage roses. It seems likely that they were raised first in Holland, but this is not certain because one claim gives credit to the south of France. Centifolias are upright growers, usually with many petals as their name implies. The theory of their origin is that the Damask 'Quatre Saisons' was one parent and that the other was either an Alba or a Gallica.

Both the Damask 'Quatre Saisons' and subsequently many of the Centifolias gave rise to remarkable sports called Moss roses. Their name came from small glandular extensions to the hairs on their sepals and seed pods, which looked like little pieces of moss.

These old garden roses are still greatly treasured and grown today. They only flower in summer (except for 'Quatre Saisons')

Above
'Celestial', an Alba shrub. The delicate pink flowers are borne on a spreading bush.

on old wood. Therefore they are not pruned hard like modern roses, otherwise the flowering wood would be cut off. They are usually pruned by shortening their side shoots and reducing the new main shoots by cutting off the top third of their length. They are prone to mildew, especially after flowering. Among the favourite varieties are:

Gallicas

Belle de Crécy: Pink, turning to mauve-pink as the flower ages.
Camaieux: Rosy purple, heavily marked with blush-white splashes and stripes. The old flowers are greyish-purple.
Cardinal de Richelieu: A deep, rich purple, very double and striking.
Charles de Mills: Dark red, changing to purple-red. The buds look too short but they open well enough. The petals are crinkled.

Top
The Gallica shrub 'Cardinal de Richelieu'.
Above
'Mme. Hardy', a Damask.
Left
The purple Moss rose 'William Lobb'.

Gloire de France: Pink, changing to lilac-pink.
Président de Sèze: Purple-red at the centre, the outer petals being lilac-pink.
Tuscany (also 'Tuscany Superb'): Dark maroon-red; upright growth.

Damasks
Celsiana: Pink, changing to white. Fragrant, low-centred blooms.
Mme. Hardy: A beautiful white rose with wide, flat flowers, very double and intricately petalled.
Quatre Saisons ('The Autumn Damask'): Light pink and fragrant.

Albas
Celestial: Spreading bush, delicate pink flowers.
Félicité Parmentier: Blush and white, very pretty formation.
Königin von Dänemark: Pink and handsome, but not typical of the class. Very fragrant.
Maiden's Blush: Pale blush, turning white. Vigorous.
Mme. Legras de St Germain: Beautiful white flowers of charming form and fragrance.
Semi-plena: Semi-double white; very vigorous. The only one with good hips.

Centifolias
Bullata: Pink, with leaves crinkled like a lettuce. The flowers are very double with low, round centres.
Chapeau de Napoléon: Pink. This is also known as 'Crested Moss'. It has unusual long fronds on its sepals.
Petite de Hollande: Bright pink, with many small 'rosettes'.
Spong: Bright pink, like a short, compact 'Petite de Hollande'.
Tour de Malakoff: A large shrub with flowers which change from magenta to light greyish-pink.

Moss roses
Blanche Moreau: White, with dark bristly moss.
Common Moss: Pink; the best for attractive green moss.
William Lobb: A bold purple colour, but the moss is not always well pronounced.

Old Cultivated Roses: the Chinese Influence

Portland roses

When the China roses were taken to the west they quickly made their influence felt over a wide geographical area. The speed owed nothing to the work of breeders but to chance hybridization within twenty years of their general distribution.

Their geographical spread was probably influenced by climate and very soon embraced Italy, the United States, the island of Réunion and France. In about 1800 a red rose called 'Paestana' arrived in Italy. It was re-named 'Duchess of Portland' in France and gave its name to a class known as Portland roses. The striking thing about this red rose to contemporary rosarians was that it proved remontant, or at least partly so, by producing some flowers in the autumn after its summer flush. The assumption is that it was a chance hybrid between 'Quatre Saisons' (the 'Autumn Damask') and a red China rose. The Portlands did not develop into a significant class, but 'Duchess of Portland' had contributions to make in the future.

The Noisettes

Of more interest were the Noisettes, which started life in the garden of a farmer called John Champney who lived in Charleston, South Carolina. He had a plant of the 'Musk Rose' (*R. moschata*)

growing near 'Old Blush', a China rose. In about 1802 Champney collected a seed pod from one of these two plants and raised from it a climber, which he introduced as 'Champney's Pink Cluster'.

Philippe Noisette, a nurseryman from Charleston, raised seeds from 'Champney's Pink Cluster' and found among the seedlings a light-coloured shrub rose which flowered both in summer and autumn. This was a greatly valued characteristic. His rose, 'Blush Noisette', soon became popular in France and England. From it, with the help of 'Park's Yellow Tea-scented China' in particular, came a beautiful race of roses known as Noisettes. They were mostly climbers and showed the soft yellow of the Chinese roses to superb effect, particularly in the well-known 'Maréchal Niel'. Other famous Noisettes were 'Gloire de Dijon', 'Mme. Alfred Carrière' and 'William Allen Richardson'.

Introduction of the Bourbons

About 1818 a significant discovery was made in Réunion, a remote island in the Indian Ocean, governed by France. A man called Périchon was planting a rose hedge with 'Duchess of Portland' and the China rose 'Old Blush'. Among the plants was an obvious stranger to both varieties. He planted it in his garden and after it had flowered a botanist on the island sent seeds to France.

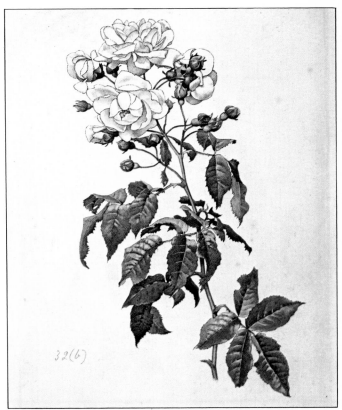

Above
A water-colour by Alfred Parsons of 'Aimée Vibert', a white Noisette climber.

Left
The pink blooms of the Hybrid Perpetual 'Mrs John Laing'.

Opposite page
'Zéphirine Drouhin', a fragrant Bourbon climber with thornless stems and semi-double carmine-pink flowers.

When these seeds were grown and cultivated, they gave rise to a new class. The class became known as Bourbon roses because the name of Réunion at that time was Ile de Bourbon. The improved flowers of the Bourbons were a step on the way to modern roses. The China rose had infused more of its habit of growth and its remontancy into 'Duchess of Portland'. Some of the outstanding Bourbons were 'Boule de Neige', 'Gloire des Rosomanes', 'Mme. Pierre Oger', 'Mme. Isaac Pereire', 'Souvenir de la Malmaison' and 'Zéphirine Drouhin'.

In 1812, an important rose called 'Rose du Roi' appeared in France. It was red and remontant, and considered of great excellence. The British called it 'Crimson Perpetual'. Most probably it was a Portland rose, but already the differences between classes were becoming difficult to distinguish. The growers in those days solved this problem by classing every variety which bore flowers in the autumn as Perpetuals.

Hybrid Perpetuals and Tea roses
Bourbons were soon grown among the Perpetuals and their seed gave rise to a new class of large-flowered remontant roses which became known as Hybrid Perpetuals. The first variety of note was 'Princess Hélène' in 1837.

Hybrid Perpetuals were the delight of Victorian rosarians and thousands of different varieties were introduced. Among the most famous Hybrid Perpetuals were 'Général Jacqueminot', 'Victor Verdier', 'Ulrich Brunner', 'Mrs John Laing', 'Frau Karl Druschki' and 'Hugh Dickson'.

Shortly after the introduction of 'Rose du Roi', another development started in France which led to the Tea roses. Together with the Hybrid Perpetuals, this class gave great pleasure and joy to Victorian rosarians. The China rose 'Old

Blush' had been mainly responsible for the classes referred to so far. However the Tea roses owed much of their creation to the influence of 'Park's Yellow Tea-scented China' on the Noisettes. It was not only this rose, but also 'Hume's Blush Tea-scented China', which gave to the Teas a look of aristocratic delicacy. Beside them the Hybrid Perpetuals looked bigger and stronger, but also coarser.

The first Tea rose was introduced about 1830. As with the Hybrid Perpetuals, thousands of varieties followed but unfortunately many were not hardy enough to survive during winter. Towards the close of the century, some particularly hard winters almost wiped them out. Some of the more familiar names are 'Safrano', 'Niphetos', 'Devoniensis', 'Catherine Mermet', 'Général Schablikine', 'Maman Cochet' and 'Lady Hillingdon'.

The first hybrid teas
The delicate Tea roses were eventually married to the tough Hybrid Perpetuals in order to put beauty and strength together. The result, as every gardener knows today, was the hybrid teas, starting with 'La France' in 1867. By the end of the nineteenth century the first famous hybrid teas had arrived: 'Lady Mary Fitzwilliam', 'Mme. Caroline Testout' and 'Mme. Abel Chatenay'. While they were in their infancy the hybrid teas received a present from Persia – the colour yellow.

Old Cultivated Roses: the Persian Influence

By the late nineteenth century the rose had changed completely from what it had been when the century started. It had turned from a mid-summer flowering plant into one that could bloom well into winter. The rose began to force geraniums out of prime display positions, whereas before it had been confined to the rosery. However, one major factor was still lacking: the colour yellow.

The light yellow received from the Chinese nurseries many years before had never been satisfactorily bred into bush roses. Only the lovely climber 'Maréchal Niel' had really shone with yellow. This rose grew so early in spring that it needed the protection of a glasshouse, otherwise the early growth was damaged by spring frosts.

Although the yellow of 'Austrian Yellow' was bred into the Scotch roses, a remontant bush rose with this colour had not been produced. The breeders turned to 'Persian Yellow', otherwise known as *R. foetida persiana*. By this time breeders had learned a lot about their task. The research with 'Persian Yellow' was made in the light of knowledge and purpose which had not been available to rose breeders before.

Ancestry of the Persian roses

The yellow roses of Persia, as Iran was then known, are a fascinating mystery. The species involved is *R. foetida* ('Austrian Yellow') which despite its name came from Asia, not Austria. One double yellow variety, *R. hemisphaerica*, had been taken to Europe from Turkey. It is, so far as experience goes, completely sterile. But the Persians had another rose, 'Persian Yellow', which was much brighter and easier to grow.

Neither of these two double roses appears to be a simple mutation of 'Austrian Yellow'; therefore they are presumably hybrids. In searching for their other parent, the inquirer comes to a blank wall. A likely candidate does not appear to exist. One can only assume that they arose as chance seedlings of 'Austrian Yellow' and were preserved through many years by skilful propagation in Persia, for they are not easy to propagate, particularly *R. hemisphaerica*.

This theory involves a strange fact about 'Austrian Yellow'. Although it is thought to be a wild rose, it does not bear many seeds. One is forced to ask whether the mystery goes back even further to the origin of that rose. Was it also a hybrid, raised from who-knows-what by the ancient Persians? If so, the possibility of variation in its seedlings would be the greater.

The introduction of 'Soleil d'Or'

Serious breeding with 'Persian Yellow' was conducted by at least three rose breeders in the late nineteenth century. The Englishman Henry Bennett is said to have sown hundreds of hips with no result. Another breeder was Dr Franz Müller in Germany. Despite his intelligent approach, the best he raised was a light yellow bush with only about ten petals, named 'Gottfried Keller'.

The third breeder was Joseph Pernet-Ducher of France, and he was the lucky one. He used the pollen of 'Persian Yellow' to fertilize a red Hybrid Perpetual named 'Antoine Ducher'.

No doubt the reason that Bennett and Müller had failed was that 'Persian Yellow' is almost sterile. It bears no viable seed and very little viable pollen. Instead of having 98 grains out of 100 capable of fusing with the female cell, as the 'Scotch Rose' has, 'Persian Yellow' has very few. Pernet-Ducher succeeded in raising some seedlings from his cross but they were not immediately exciting. One objection was that they followed 'Persian Yellow' in

flowering only in summer. This is, in fact, normal in the first generation if one of the parents is a rose that flowers only in summer. Remontancy does not appear until the second generation or later.

Pernet-Ducher left his young plants growing for two or three years. One of them set seed and grew. It was only when a friend asked to see the interesting offspring of 'Persian Yellow' that Pernet-Ducher noticed the self-set seedling with its flowers of orange-yellow and red. Every rose breeder needs some luck with his work, but of all the astounding strokes of good fortune few can have equalled Pernet-Ducher's. However, he was one of the most skilful and successful rose breeders and luck is said to favour the bold.

The seedling was propagated. In 1898 it was shown at Lyon where it created a sensation. It was named 'Soleil d'Or' and introduced in 1900. This rose was not pure yellow but it was the means of introducing the brilliant yellow of Persian roses into modern garden roses. In hybrid teas, floribundas, miniatures and many climbers, the yellow they now flaunt so boldly has all stemmed from 'Soleil d'Or'.

Thus in one century the prize roses of China, Persia and Europe had been fused together to create roses more beautiful than any that mankind had seen before. Millions of years of evolution and thousands of years of man's cherishing had suddenly been brought to a climax. What would the twentieth century bring?

Opposite page
A water-colour by Alfred
Parsons of *R. hemisphaerica*.

Right
'Persian Yellow', an
illustration from *Flores des
Serres et des Jardins de
l'Europe*, published in 1848.

Off. lith. & pict. in Horto Van Houtteano.

A Brief History of Rose Gardens

Above
The rose was a popular plant with medieval gardeners.

The history of early rose gardens is not well documented and we often have an inaccurate picture of the gardens of the past. For instance we are led to believe that the Greeks and Romans lived much out of doors, dining in splendour on sun-drenched patios amid bowers of roses that appeared to be perpetually in flower. However, it is well known that the rose was a popular flower in medieval Europe. It was used as an emblem and constantly appeared as a decorative device on costumes and in paintings of the period.

The rose has been a popular subject to plant from the dawn of history, although the genus is not mentioned in early literature as frequently as some would have us believe. The rose is referred to only once in the Bible, so one can presume that it was not particularly popular in the eastern Mediterranean area at that time. In fact, the garden rose as it is planted today did not exist until 175 years ago. Before 1800 the varieties available were derivatives of the large old garden rose groups: the Albas, Centifolias, Damasks and Gallicas. They were large informal shrubs, one or two possessing vigour enough to climb, but the majority were summer flowering, coloured white, pink or red, and seldom fragrant. The exquisite Elizabethan knot garden did not include the rose, which was relegated to the large informal mixed shrub border. The great landscape gardeners of the eighteenth century, such as Capability Brown, did not consider the flower garden to be an important element in their planting schemes.

Introduction of the formal rose garden

It was not until well into the nineteenth century that the formal rose garden came into its own. The introduction of the Hybrid Perpetuals provided the necessary material for the geometrical garden designs beloved of the Victorians.

The availability of cheap and abundant labour made these gardens possible, for the small circular, rectangular and triangular beds enclosed by box hedges were difficult to maintain and were a positive haven for every predator and disease imaginable. Standards (tree roses) were *de rigueur*; the gardeners in *Alice in Wonderland* had a terrible time with them! The Victorians liked to cultivate the rose on its own, and to this day many formal rose gardens are to be found in solitary isolation away from the rest of an estate.

The student of garden history will find very little evidence of the detailed and intricate formal rose gardens that were so popular in the nineteenth century. Some country houses still possess a formal garden that appears totally alien in style to the rest of the planting scheme – distinguished, perhaps, by the liberal planting of small box hedges. But today very few gardeners have the patience to maintain such a relic of a more splendid era.

The modern rose garden

Two world wars and a radical change in our social structure have made the pretensions of our forefathers outmoded. Today the rose is a plant that anyone can grow. Rose breeders have developed a subject tolerant of the most outrageous abuse from the least green-fingered beginner. The rose today demands none of the high horticultural skills of a hundred years ago.

Rose gardens have also changed radically. The majority are designed and planted with one overriding aim – the elimination of costly maintenance routines. One effect of this is that in the bigger gardens machinery can be used to carry out precise spraying programmes, including the application of herbicides, to reduce intensive labour. Rose beds are designed in such a way as to enable large lawn-mowing equipment to be used, and plants are no longer used as edging material.

In small gardens similar economic considerations must prevail. Very few people can afford a gardener. Thus design must aim to minimize the time-consuming jobs such as edging rose beds and lawns and there is an increasing tendency for large areas of the garden to be covered by paving stones and slabs.

Not everything has changed. Climbing roses still have to be given support and the design of arches and pillars has altered very little. However, the plant material we use has been rationalized. For example, the more rampant old ramblers, so heavy on labour maintenance costs, have been virtually eliminated. Basic design factors have changed very little. Every good garden should have a focal point or points. The use of water is as popular now as ever, for it lends the garden an air of tranquility.

The introduction of the swimming pool has possibly altered the design of gardens more radically than any other factor. Unless it is well-sited, it can dominate any garden scheme. The miniature rose has introduced a new dimension to the design of many areas of the modern garden. Its great popularity has increased the use of slabs and patio tiles.

The rose has been used since time immemorial to enhance the quality of life. It has adapted itself with the aid of man to fulfil the functions expected of it, and today has a wider appeal than any other genus. The rose is universally regarded as one of the essential ingredients of attractive gardens.

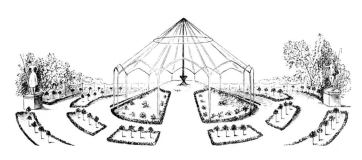

Above
A colonnade of climbing roses from *Roses et Rosiers*, 1872.
Above left
An illustration from *The Rose Garden* by William Paul, 1888, showing a design for a rose shrubbery.
Left
A plan for a rose garden designed by William Paul in 1878. Each bed was planted with roses of the same colour except for the centre bed which was mixed.
Below
A formal design from *Roses Cultivées à l'Hay*, 1902.

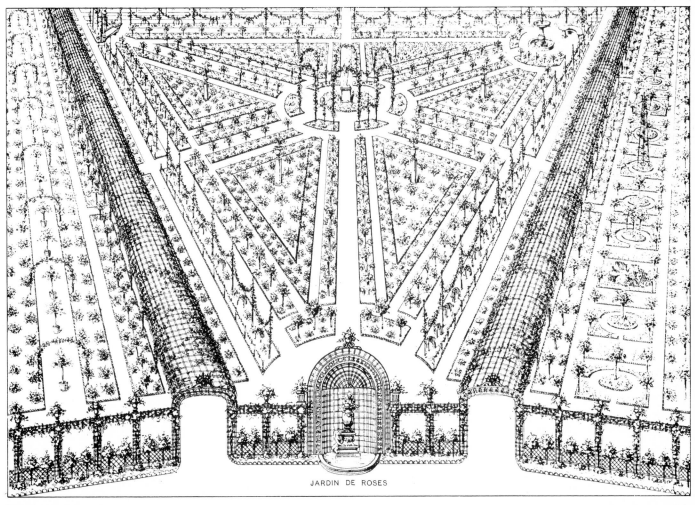

JARDIN DE ROSES

The Rose in the Formal Garden

Right
Miniature roses planted in raised beds.

Below
Formal rose beds and a pond in a town garden.

Opposite page, left
A country rose garden with a sundial.

Opposite page, above right
Geometric rose beds bordered by small hedges.

Opposite page, below left
Massed rose beds in a public garden.

Modern architecture has posed problems for the horticulturist and garden designer which would have been inconceivable 50 years ago. Vast areas of glass and coloured panels also offer greater challenge to the landscape gardener of today. Rose breeders themselves have hardly helped, since the introduction of vivid vermilions and bright yellows, to the detriment of more subtle colours, has narrowed the selection of varieties. Pink roses, which suffered by comparison with modern colours, are only just coming back into favour.

The design of modern housing estates has encouraged open planning and the absence of large fences and hedges in some respects is a great help. Narrow passages and draughty corners are disastrous to any variety of rose.

The term 'formal garden' suggests an area that has been designed for a specific function as, for example, the Victorian and Edwardian rose garden. Today the term is more relevant to large-scale municipal plantings. Modern domestic gardens are often too small for traditional formal designs but patios and confined areas may be laid out in a formal or geometric style. Thus there are three types of formal garden to consider: the traditional rose garden, big public planting schemes and small, town house gardens.

The traditional rose garden
The rose gardens beloved of our late-nineteenth and early-twentieth century ancestors were the product of a tremendous development in the cultivation and availability of a wide range of roses suitable for planting in formal rose beds. There was the added novelty that a single genus, the rose, could be planted with the hope that colour would be provided continually throughout the summer months. William Paul, the great rosarian of the late 1800s, wrote at considerable length about the design and mainten-ance of such rose gardens.

Today the inheritors of these gardens have tremendous pro-blems of maintenance, particularly when plants need to be replaced, or when an entire garden needs to be resited.

Soil in rose gardens can get stale or exhausted. Such a problem in an old rose garden is called 'rose sickness' – the soil is just tired of growing roses. No amount of feeding or plant husbandry will remedy the situation; the soil itself must be dealt with. The average life of a well-maintained bush rose is about 15 years but it can still look garden worthy after 20 or 25 years. The problem arises when a formal rose bed has to be replaced, for young maiden plants will not thrive in the same soil as established plants.

There are two solutions in treating large gardens with 'rose sickness'. The first consists of grassing over the old rose beds and replanting in fresh soil in another part of the garden. The other solution is to remove the soil from the old site to a depth of about 30cm (12in) and replace it with fresh soil from a rose-free environment.

Public planting schemes

Some 10 to 15 years ago, research into the basic cost of maintaining lawns in urban areas compared with the upkeep of similar areas of rose beds, revealed the astonishing fact that a large rose bed is cheaper to maintain than a similar area of grass. This statistic has given considerable encouragement to local authorities who wish to beautify town centres. The towns and cities of northern European countries have benefited from this fact and the major proportion of roses produced goes to meet this demand. In the United Kingdom, the United States of America and Australasia, however, city authorities are only just beginning to plant in this way.

There are relatively few difficulties in big plantings. Roses must be chosen to meet the needs of a particular site in terms of hardiness, compatibility and colour. Generally speaking, the medium-sized free-flowering floribundas are admirably suited to these situations. The central reservations of urban motorways are improved by colourful roses. Litter presents a problem and care must be taken to select varieties that are relatively smooth wooded and do not accumulate rubbish round their stems. Varieties to be avoided are vigorous bushes such as the 'Queen Elizabeth' rose and varieties whose continued flowering is dependent on constant maintenance such as dead-heading and frequent disease control.

In America types of *R. multiflora* seedlings have been used as crash barriers on motorways. The space needed for shrubs of this size is probably too costly elsewhere. Ground-cover plants massed in large numbers are used in Europe but, although easy to plant and maintain, they are not very colourful.

Formal town gardens

The small, private garden calls for specialized plants and the rose has much to contribute in this respect. Town gardens are often divided these days into patio and lawn, with a notable absence of colour. The shorter-growing floribundas and miniature roses can be a great asset here, especially the free-flowering varieties.

Patios are generally built on a base of builders' rubble and care must be taken to clear the planting areas of rubbish and improve the soil with good garden compost. The addition of extra peat or other moisture-retaining media in such areas will ensure that the freshly planted bushes do not suffer from excessive drought in the first season before they become established.

The Informal Rose Garden

Fashions in gardening, as in any other sphere, come and go, influenced by technical developments and by reaction against these same developments. Until the end of the eighteenth century the rose was a totally informal subject for the plantsman. The large sprawling shrub roses – the Damasks, Centifolias, Albas and Gallicas – lent themselves to magnificent plantings on a grand scale. The formal rose garden did not exist for the very simple reason that the varieties then available were capable of providing colour for only a relatively brief period during the summer months and deliberate planting in stylized beds was not possible. By the 1880s breeders had improved the quality of the rose to a degree where it was possible to plant the formal rose gardens so popular in the late nineteenth and early twentieth centuries.

From this development arose the fallacy that roses should be grown in their own environment with no competition from any other plant. Even today debate rages as to the desirability of mixing roses with other plants.

Economic and sociological factors have quashed this notion to a considerable extent and the rose has regained its proper place as an integral part of the whole planting scheme of any garden, however small is the space it is allowed.

The informal rose may be used in two ways: as a complement to other shrubs, or as a single plant in its own right.

Roses in the shrub border

The idea of recommending roses to complement a shrub border would have been considered a heresy until it was realized that the old herbaceous borders were extremely time-consuming in terms of labour and propagation and so were usually beyond the scope of the weekend gardener. The introduction of container-grown shrubs has enabled gardeners to acquire plants easily, to cut down on their maintenance and to replace worn-out sections of a herbaceous border with ease.

The varieties available may be divided into two distinct groups. The true shrub roses, summer-flowering or recurrent, contribute colour in foliage, flower and fruit at the appropriate season of the year. However, some varieties have their shortcomings and one must take these into consideration when planting them. The Albas and Gallicas, together with the Damasks, can be planted in groups or singly, and will brighten a dull border in mid-summer with

Opposite page
A corner of the garden at Sissinghurst Castle created by the late Victoria Sackville-West.

Left
An informal border using roses in combination with other plants.

Below left
An archway of climbing roses in full bloom.

Below centre
Shrub roses and climbers in an old country garden.

Below
Informal shrub roses bordering a lawn.

large falls of flower. Their foliage and fruit, however, are of little value. Centifolias and Moss roses have beautiful flowers that will give great pleasure for a short period, usually in mid-summer, although the foliage is poor.

The species roses may be used in a variety of ways. The early-flowering types such as *R. hugonis* and *R. xanthina* 'Canary Bird' are a delight in early summer. They have such an abundance of colour that for a brief period they can dominate even very careful planting. Both these roses have attractive fern-like foliage. The majority have small flowers, sometimes insignificant, but often delicate and pretty, and the most common colour is pink. These shrubs do contribute to the architectural composition of the garden however and they produce worthwhile fruits in the autumn. The rose as an informal plant is most effective in providing splashes of colour in large shrub borders or in hiding architectural eyesores.

The more vigorous floribundas can be planted very effectively among other shrubs, despite lingering prejudices to the contrary. Groups of five or seven bushes planted roughly 60–90cm (2–3ft) apart provide a pleasing break. A solitary bush, unless of an extremely vigorous nature, lacks significance in a shrub border. It must be remembered that irrespective of the site and variety, the rose requires a lot of light, particularly in late spring and early summer, and needs basic maintenance and feeding.

Climbing and rambling roses

The more vigorous shrubs, together with climbers and ramblers, can be used to give height and informality and to break up dull areas of the garden. The rampant old Wichuraianas and sub-species ramblers are ideal for this but care must be taken to ensure that they are well supported, especially during windy weather.

Wooden trellises and screens provide good supports and are more successfully used in the United Kingdom and the United States than metal structures. Metal pergolas are very common on the European continent and are used most effectively there.

The rose in its wild state is a very informal plant which provides an abundance of flower for very long periods. Given basic maintenance and good, sound feeding it will generally produce pleasure and beauty for a longer period in the summer than any other genus of plant.

Great Rose Gardens of Today

The modern rose is a highly sophisticated product of the plant breeder's art. It can be seen at its very best in some of the most beautiful gardens in the world today which are devoted to the cultivation of this genus. Economic factors necessarily limit the number of these gardens and today the wealthier horticultural societies and local authorities are the chief sponsors of such enterprises.

Gardens devoted entirely to roses are usually created with two aims in mind, the first being the creation of rose museums which can demonstrate and perpetuate a living history of the genus. Secondly, there is the endeavour to promote the future well-being of the rose by conducting rose trials for the introduction of new varieties. In many cases these gardens also have spectacular plantings of modern hybrid teas and floribundas. In addition, some of the largest rose nurseries in many parts of the world have demonstration areas and gardens that are well worth visiting.

The United Kingdom

One of the finest rose gardens of recent origin is to be found in England. The garden of the Royal National Rose Society at St Albans is a feast for the discerning rose lover and the amateur gardener alike. Here one can see and compare whole families of old roses planted together, and trace the history of the rose through to the modern hybrids grown in beautifully maintained beds which are interspersed with large pergolas supporting rampant, old-fashioned ramblers. There are large collections of the rarer species of the genus and a trial ground internationally famous for its excellence of cultivation. This is probably the most comprehensive rose garden anywhere in the world.

Three other gardens are worthy of mention. The Royal Horticultural Society's garden at Wisley has fine rose borders and a large rose garden recently renovated to allow space for some of the newest roses. Queen Mary's Rose Gardens at Regent's Park in London are the epitome of grand design, a welcome oasis in the middle of the city. Recently the British Association of Rose Breeders, at the invitation of the Springfields garden in Spalding, Lincolnshire, has contributed a large number of roses to enable the famous bulb garden to blossom in the summer also.

Many municipal gardens in the United Kingdom have large plantings and a few have demonstrations of varieties which have recently received trial certificates. The City of Belfast, in association with the Rose Society of Northern Ireland, run their own international trials at the Sir Thomas and Lady Dixon Park. The trial area is surrounded by magnificent plantings of both old garden roses and modern varieties.

The Netherlands

Although traditionally considered to be the home of horticulture, more particularly of bulbous plants, the Netherlands is not famous for its roses. Nevertheless, the rose garden in Westbroek Park at the Hague is very colourful. The large plantings in natural settings have an air of informality, and there are some modern in-

Above right
The Skansen rose garden at Stockholm, Sweden.
Centre right
A mass of bush roses at the Royal Horticultural Society's garden at Wisley, England.
Below right
A view of the Royal National Rose Society's garden at St Albans, England.
Opposite page
The International Rose Test garden at Portland, Oregon, USA.

troductions also. The soil appears almost arid and the production of excellent blooms reflects the ability of the director.

Spain
The Municipal Rose Gardens in Madrid have been described as the most beautiful rose gardens in Europe. Originally planted in 1956, they have now reached a high degree of maturity. The large specimens of climbers are unique and well worth a visit.

France
Paris can boast two major rose gardens: Bagatelle and La Roseraie de l'Hay-les-Roses. They have contributed much to the preservation of the history of the rose, although both suffered neglect and destruction during the last war. Nevertheless they are now restored to their former glory. In addition, the municipalities of Lyon and Orléans have large, beautiful gardens which are magnificently designed and maintained.

Germany
In northern and central Europe massed roses seem to have been planted at every bend in the road. While it is true that the rose in Germany is used to a larger extent than elsewhere, large gardens are the exception rather than the rule. There are, however, three famous rosariums worthy of mention. In East Germany the magnificent rosarium at Sangerhausen contains probably the largest and most comprehensive living museum of old garden roses in the world. West Germany similarly boasts a famous garden at Baden-Baden and, owing to the inaccessibility of Sangerhausen to West Germans, a new garden has been developed at Dortmund.

The United States
The United States can probably boast the largest number of rose gardens. Two are especially notable. The oldest and best maintained is at Portland, Oregon, and the other is a newcomer – the Hershey Rose Gardens at Harrisburg, Pennsylvania.

Above
An entire rose bloom, showing the stigmas (female) surrounded by the stamens (male).

Left
The petals of the bloom have been removed, exposing the stamens and stigmas.

Early rose breeding

In practice, rose breeding is absurdly simple: use the pollen of one variety to fertilize another variety and then grow the resulting seeds. Each will prove to be a new variety (although probably not a good one), for among hybrid roses twins are about as common as they are in the human race.

A good example of early rose breeding may be found in the 'Scotch Rose'. In 1793, a nurseryman from Perth dug up some wild specimens slightly different from the normal 'Scotch Rose', which is white with five petals. He sowed seed from them and selected the more interesting seedlings for further breeding. By 1803, only ten years later, he had introduced eight double varieties. This is an example of selection. The 'Scotch Rose' is an amenable species for this purpose. Other nurserymen followed suit and within a few years there were hundreds of varieties.

During the nineteenth century, France was the centre of rose breeding. The French breeders gathered whatever hips nature had given them in the autumn. The seeds were sown very often without a label and therefore their parentage was unknown. The quantities were enormous: one breeder called Laffay was said to have between two and three hundred thousand seedlings. It would be reasonable to suppose that a few of these were worthwhile.

In 1832 Thomas Rivers published his *Rose Amateur's Guide*, suggesting that the best method of obtaining a hybrid between two particular roses was to plant them side by side. In 1848 William

Paul published his *Rose Garden*, in which he suggested conveying the pollen from one rose to the stigmas of the other by hand. So far as can be ascertained, this advice was not generally taken for many years. A Frenchman, Jean Sisley, repeated it in 1877.

The father of modern rose breeding

A Wiltshire farmer named Henry Bennett proved William Paul's point. Having been a cattle breeder, Henry Bennett was professionally aware of the need to keep bulls and cows segregated, and of the virtues of a stud book. In 1878 he announced the forthcoming introduction of ten 'Pedigree Hybrids of the Tea Rose'. The word 'pedigree' was challenged, but in reply Bennett could quote the parents of each of his roses. It rapidly became clear to the rose world that his methods made sense. Henry Bennett is taken by many people to be the father of rose breeding; but it may seem astounding that so obvious a practice was not generally adopted much sooner.

The methods of modern breeders

The pedigree of a rose cannot be established unless the seed-bearing parent is prevented from fertilizing itself with its own pollen. Therefore the stamens are removed from the seed parent before they begin to shed pollen. This may be done with tweezers or a pair of small scissors. The correct time for removing the stamens varies with different varieties and is only learned from

Centre
The female, or seed parent. The stamens have been removed before they begin to shed pollen.

Near left
Pollination of the seed parent. The pollen from the chosen male parent is placed on the stigmas by hand or with a fine brush.

Below
The ripening hips after successful fertilization.

experience of working with a variety. Single roses usually shed pollen before the petals open but in some cases double flowers open quite a long way before their pollen is released. The stamens can be removed with less injury and difficulty the nearer the parts of the flower are to maturity. The petals have to be removed first in order to get at the stamens.

If this operation takes place in the open air, the remains of the flower must be covered to keep out pollen brought by insects or wind. A paper cone was often used for this purpose. One method was to enclose the male parent upside down at the top of the cone with all its petals removed and the stamens facing the stigmas of the female parent. Thus the pollen would fall where it was wanted over the next two or three days, without any need to remove the paper cone.

Most rose breeders in cool climates prefer to work under glass to be sure of good conditions for pollination and adequate time for ripening the seed. With this method it is unusual to cover the flowers prepared for fertilization because the risk of natural fertilization is quite small (providing that no rose in the same glasshouse is allowed to shed pollen at the same time). Pollen parents are normally grown in a separate house or compartment, or immature stamens taken from the seed parent may be kept a day or two and their pollen then applied to a different variety.

When the flower has been pollinated it is labelled, usually in some code or abbreviation containing the names of both parents.

Some crosses are not successful, owing either to inefficient work or to the incompatibility of the parents chosen. Others may be lost through diseases such as botrytis. This may be prevented by keeping the greenhouse adequately ventilated.

Crosses which succeed are harvested in autumn. The hips are shelled out and the seed stored until sowing time. In cool countries such as Britain, the seeds should be sown under glass. The results are seen much sooner and more effectively in a greenhouse than out of doors. The time to sow under glass is late winter. Heat is not necessary – in fact rose seeds germinate better at a quite cool temperature rather than a warm one. A small stove may be kept in reserve for use during a very frosty spell before summer. The method for growing roses from seed is described on pages 120–121.

The importance of selection

The seeds sown in late winter under this regime will flower in early summer, when the first culling should take place. The continuing process of selection, both on the seed bench and in future years as the seedlings are propagated out of doors, is one of the most important for the rose breeder.

If he has no eye for selection the breeder will waste a lot of time, money and work. Thanks to Henry Bennett's example, rose breeders can conduct their work with more economy than was possible with the random ways of old.

The Rose Breeders: Examples of Success

When the rose breeder goes to work, he needs an aim and a good eye for roses; in other words imagination, observation and knowledge. Alec Cocker and Sam McGredy are two breeders who showed all three of these qualities in the way they bred 'Silver Jubilee' and 'Priscilla Burton' respectively.

Jack Harkness

E. B. LeGrice

The award-winning 'Silver Jubilee'

Alec Cocker's aim was to breed healthy hybrid teas. He asked himself 'which is the healthiest rose likely to be compatible?' Rugosas would give the health but not the compatibility. However there is a compatible hybrid between *R. rugosa* and *R. wichuraiana*, two types remarkable for health. That hybrid is *R. kordesii*. Therefore Mr Cocker chose to work with a Kordesii hybrid, a climber called 'Parkdirektor Riggers'. He crossed it with the hybrid tea 'Piccadilly'.

Alec Cocker knew most of the seedlings would be climbers, some of them only summer-flowering. All he wanted from the cross was a bush which flowered in summer and in autumn. He was not interested in selling the bush; he wanted it purely for breeding. And he got it: an ugly, dull red, double-flowered bush, no good for anything at a casual glance.

From the next generation he wanted another bush, preferably more handsome, but anything would do provided it was perfectly healthy and would set seed. This plant would not be for sale either; he hoped it would be the parent of many of his future introductions. From a great number of crosses with his ugly duckling he produced a seedling which answered his requirements. Its leaves glistened and shone, its growth was abundant and its colour was brilliant orange-scarlet. The fact that the flowers were small and semi-double did not trouble him. Within its cells were the genes of 'Piccadilly' and he was quite confident that given another hybrid tea as mate, the ensuing seedlings would include some of hybrid tea character.

Alec Cocker crossed this plant with many hybrid teas and had many failures. But in the eighth year since he had first put pollen from 'Piccadilly' on to 'Parkdirektor Riggers' he found in his seed bench a lovely long-petalled rose, pink and creamy, with shades of orange. It had come from the pollen of 'Mischief' and was introduced five years later as 'Silver Jubilee'. It won the highest British award for new roses and was quickly accepted as one of the finest hybrid teas in existence.

Sam McGredy's 'hand painted' roses

Sam McGredy's aim was quite different. On looking at the shrub rose 'Frühlingsmorgen' he saw a large cherry pink flower, composed only of five petals. At the base of each petal was a large creamy area, so that the centre of the flower appeared to have a big creamy eye. He began to ask himself whether broken colours and patterns could be bred into modern roses. Here was 'Frühlingsmorgen' as a starting point, with the disadvantages of dull foliage, shrubby growth and few flowers after summer. The obvious first move was to mate it to a variety with brilliant leaves, compact growth and good remontancy. The partner he chose was 'Orange Sweetheart'. The seedling he wanted for more breeding was a remontant bush, preferably showing the large eye.

Most of the seedlings were shrubby and a number were not remontant. Nearly all had foliage even worse than that of 'Frühlingsmorgen'. But Sam McGredy decided to persevere with the few which were dwarf and remontant. His next step was to put their pollen on to 'Evelyn Fison', leaving the genes of 'Frühlingsmorgen' to determine the pattern and trusting modern roses to

improve the foliage and growth, which at first sight were so bad that many a breeder would have given up there and then.

At the third generation a cross on to 'Marlena' gave him a rose with a novel pattern of white upon its carmine petals. He named it 'Picasso' and described it as his 'hand painted' rose; but the foliage was still too reminiscent of 'Frühlingsmorgen'. He then played his trump card. He used as a seed parent a remarkably healthy seedling to which shrub roses, climbers and floribundas had contributed. This at last enabled him to introduce 'hand painted' roses in which the pattern of 'Frühlingsmorgen' was improved and developed, while the faults of 'Frühlingsmorgen' were gradually lost. In another generation or two, Sam McGredy successfully introduced 'Priscilla Burton'.

Rose breeders with different aims

These two examples have shown how breeders work. Every good breeder sets himself an aim, for there is no satisfaction in crossing roses randomly in the hope that something will turn up. Most breeders find what they are looking for. Alain Meilland wanted to breed roses for the cut flower growers and succeeded with names such as 'Sweet Promise' (syn. 'Sonia Meilland'), 'Visa' and 'Alpha'. Pat Dickson wanted to put red hybrid teas on to strong, well-leaved plants and produced 'Red Devil', 'Red Planet' and 'Precious Platinum'. Edward LeGrice experimented for years to find the right mate for 'Goldilocks'. He tried many and when an experiment suggested that 'Ellinor LeGrice' was the answer, he raised many seedlings from that cross, including 'Allgold'.

Right
'Priscilla Burton', one of the 'hand painted' roses descended from 'Frühlingsmorgen'.

Below
The shrub rose 'Frühlingsmorgen', with its large creamy eye.

Herbert C. Swim

Mathias Tantau

Alain Meilland

Sam McGredy

Cutting Roses for Arrangement

Cutting roses for indoor arrangement is a question of timing. Many people leave their roses in the garden until they are almost fully open, then decide to cut and bring them indoors. It is no wonder that they do not last long in the house because they were almost at the end of their life when they were cut.

When and how to cut roses
To enjoy roses in the house as well as the garden, try to cut them late in the evening or early morning when transpiration is at its lowest. Do not wait for them to be fully open but pick or cut some in bud and some half open; like this you will have a variation of form when they are arranged.

Cut just above a leaf joint when cutting from the garden; this will allow another shoot to grow. Try to study the shape and size of the bush when cutting, i.e. cut one or two roses if the bush is new or small, although you could cut a third of the bush if it is large and well-established. Most roses last well in water but do not pick them when they are past their prime. If the tips of the stamens of open roses are brown or dry, it usually means the bees have pollinated them, which in turn means they will begin to fade as their role in life has been fulfilled. Hybrid tea roses and the Garnette type of rose last very well when cut and it was noticed that the milk chocolate parchment-brown rose 'Julia Rose' lasted another week when taken home after five days on show at the Royal Horticultural Society's Chelsea Flower Show. Although wide open, the petals did not seem to drop.

Floribunda roses are excellent for arranging but the cluster heads do need to be thinned out. Try to cut out the more fully opened blooms, leaving room for the buds to open or expand as they grow. The blooms that are removed need not be wasted, for they can be used in small table decorations or floated in a shallow dish of water, held up by their own leaves.

Preparing roses before arranging
After cutting, remove the lower leaves and scrape off the thorns with the sharp blade of a knife. This will make positioning the rose in the decoration easier. Next split the stem ends with a knife and stand them in deep, tepid water for some hours or overnight if possible, adding some sugar (a teaspoonful to each pint of water). This long drink will fully charge the stems with water and so help them to remain turgid and strong in the vase. There are several quite effective products on the market now for lengthening the life of flowers. If cut roses start to droop at the head, recut the stem ends and stand in very hot water, making sure the steam does not reach the flower head. This removes any air locks and some say it swells the wood, so allowing for a quicker intake of water.

Colour schemes and containers
The colour of the roses you use depends upon personal choice or the occasion for which they are used. Many people do not accept the trend towards blue roses and others abhor the browny, grey, parchment and lilac colourings, referring to them as insipid. It all depends on whether you need a strong colour impact in the garden or a display of subtle colour in home decoration. However, for decorators a great deal will depend upon the lasting quality of the roses. A list of suitable roses is given below. In addition to these there are several attractive bi-coloured, shrub and climber roses.

The choice of containers for rose arrangements much depends on the setting and the style of home in which the roses are to be seen. There was a time not so many years ago when it was said that roses should only be arranged in silver or glass vases. That view of course is far too rigid. Silver, glass, porcelain dishes and fine china are ideal for a formal setting but wood, chunky pottery, steel and rough china containers are more appropriate for a modern atmosphere. In all cases it is better not to use a container which has a highly patterned surface for this will conflict with the roses.

Not everyone has access to garden roses and have to buy them from a florist. Some growers concentrate on producing roses that will cut, pack and last well on their long journey from the nursery to the purchaser. For those who buy roses from the florist, these are long lasting: 'Baccara' and 'Illona' (red); 'Sonia' and 'Bridal Pink' (pink); 'Golden Times' and 'Dr A. J. Verhage' (yellow); 'Orange Belinda' (orange) and 'Jack Frost' and 'Rose Landia' (creamy white).

Suitable roses for cutting

Hybrid Teas

Yellow and cream
Grandpa Dickson
Peace
Sutter's Gold
Young Quinn
Diorama
Sunsilk
Pascali (white)

Orange or tangerine/flame
Whisky Mac
Doris Tysterman
Bettina
Just Joey
Sir Lancelot
Cheshire Life (orange-vermilion)
Korp

Red
National Trust
Alec's Red
Stanley Gibbons

Fragrant Cloud
Mme. Louis Laperrière
Super Star (orange-red)

Pink
Blessings
Ballet
Prima Ballerina
Lady Seton (deep pink)
Criterion
Mischief (salmon)
Helen Traubel (coral)

Floribundas

Pink
Pink Parfait
Queen Elizabeth
Dearest
Paddy McGredy (pinky-red)
Fleur Cowles (cream/pink)

Salmon/coral/orange/flame
Pineapple Poll
Woburn Abbey
Joseph's Coat
Elizabeth of Glamis

Deep and light red
Rob Roy
Lilli Marlene
Anne Cocker
Evelyn Fison
Rosemary Rose
Marlena
City of Belfast

Yellow
Arthur Bell
Allgold
Golden Delight

Cream and white
Iceberg
Moon Maiden
White Spray
Penelope

Unusual colours

News (purple-red)
Lilac Charm (lilac-mauve)
Ripples (wavy petalled, mauve)
Silver Charm (lilac)
Grey Dawn (soft grey)
Jocelyn (mahogany)
Tom Brown (two-toned brown)
Café (coffee-cream/brown)
Amberlight (golden brown)
Julia Rose (chocolate/parchment)

Right
A graceful arrangement of large pink roses and green foliage in a classical setting.

Arranging Roses: Basic Techniques

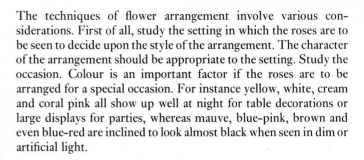

The techniques of flower arrangement involve various considerations. First of all, study the setting in which the roses are to be seen to decide upon the style of the arrangement. The character of the arrangement should be appropriate to the setting. Study the occasion. Colour is an important factor if the roses are to be arranged for a special occasion. For instance yellow, white, cream and coral pink all show up well at night for table decorations or large displays for parties, whereas mauve, blue-pink, brown and even blue-red are inclined to look almost black when seen in dim or artificial light.

Three styles of arrangement
Having prepared the cut roses as described in the previous chapter, let us look at the formal style. This is usually made in the shape of a triangle. It can be a tall triangle if the rooms are high or if the arrangement is for a pedestal group, or it can be a low triangle for a side table, dinner table or a shelf.

There are two methods of holding the stems firmly in place. Use either crumpled wire netting placed in the vase, or floral foam, a plastic type of foam block available from the florist. If you use the former method, fill your container with 5cm (2in) mesh crumpled wire netting, making sure the wire reaches about 3cm or an inch or two above the rim of the container. To keep the wire secure tie it down to the vase with reel wire or string which can be removed after the arrangement is made, or hitch some of the cut edges of the wire over the rim of the container. Some find it helpful to place a pinholder in the base of the container, underneath the wire netting, to hold the central stems very firmly. In all cases do have tepid water in the vase before starting the arranging as this will prevent the stems from becoming dry at the ends. If you use a block of floral foam you can secure this by pressing it on to a heavy pinholder or by using sellotape or florist's tape pressed on to the vase then taken across the foam and pressed down the other side. The foam should be well soaked in water before starting. Always leave a space at the back of the vase for water to be added each day. Start a formal, triangular arrangement by:
1 Establishing the height of the design (a fair guideline is one and a half times the height of the vase) and the width (about two thirds the height) to make your outline or pattern.
2 Emphasize the centre with bigger or more opened roses, cutting the stems to different lengths so that no two blooms stand level. Make sure that the lower flowers tilt forward to avoid a flat effect.
3 Fill in with more roses, never going beyond the established height and width but placing some flowers further forward than others to avoid an even surface. Always aim each stem towards the centre so that the arrangement seems to radiate from a central point near the rim beneath the tallest stem. Any leaves that have been removed can be tucked in around the centre to unify all the stems and some should flow forward over the rim low in the front.

The modern style is appropriate for tall pottery containers or low dishes. A pinholder is nearly always used to hold the stems firmly in place. When using a shallow dish the pinholder can be hidden by a piece of bark or root wood, stones or leaves. Space is one of the essential factors in modern design, so fewer flowers are used. These can be placed at the base of tall branches or tucked behind driftwood. They can be used with shells, stones or pieces of bark or chunky glass; in fact there are no restrictions, as long as the finished effect is uncluttered and original. Don't be afraid of heights, for tall designs can look more modern than squat ones, and do resist the temptation to fill in the spaces.

The informal style allows you to create a casual arrangement.

The container could be a jug, a basket, or any attractive holder and the blooms can be of any colour or type. The flowers are placed in chicken wire or foam and arranged for your pleasure.

Table arrangements
Roses for the table can become a conversation piece. The colours used can echo those of the room or the china, or can contrast or complement the tablecloth. The can be arranged low, flanked by two tall candlesticks, or you can create a tall, thin arrangement balanced on each side by a low placement. A low, long triangular design can be made if the table is long, or a round arrangement would appear better if the table is round. No matter what style you choose, follow the advice given for the formal style arrangement, only making it much lower. Remember that however you fill in the front, turn the container round and fill in the back in a similar fashion so that the arrangement can be seen equally well from all angles.

Heavily scented roses are not always the best choice for a formal dinner party, as the fragrance might interfere with the aroma of the food, but an original scheme of roses with matching or contrasting table linen can make a dinner party memorable. Many cloths can be dyed to match the roses for special occasions. Try a green cloth with white roses for a summer luncheon party, or a gold lamé cloth with gold coloured roses for a golden wedding party. Pink roses with ribbon stretching over the length of a deeper pink cloth look lovely for a girl's birthday party. The ideas are endless. You could place a tall candlestick on a plate, surrounding it with short roses of the same colour inserted into pieces of floral foam. Remember always to condition the flowers with a long, deep drink before arranging them, then add water daily as roses are always thirsty.

Top
A low table arrangement featuring Fleur Cowles' with decorative foliage, flanked by tall, pink candles.
Above
Red and white old roses are mixed casually in this informal arrangement.
Left
An arrangement in the modern style using white roses and driftwood in a simple pottery container.

Opposite page
Pink roses and decorative foliage arranged in the traditional style. The height and width are carefully balanced.

The Modern Rose

Top
The serrated petals of 'Just Joey'.
Above
'Peace', the world's favourite rose.
Right
'Troika', the healthiest of the copper roses.
Opposite page, above
The popular white bedding rose, 'Pascali'
Opposite page, below
The full, red blooms of 'National Trust'.

The history of horticulture and the evolution of sophisticated plants is exemplified in the development of the hybrid tea bush rose. The modern rose has classically shaped blooms and a stem length suitable for arrangement or exhibition. Above all, the plant produces a continuity of flower unparalleled in any other genus, together with a range of colour that is unique in modern floriculture. This has been achieved in the comparatively recent past.

Advent of the hybrid tea

The year 1867 saw the birth of the first modern hybrid tea. It was the product of a cross between the Hybrid Perpetuals and the Tea roses. The Hybrid Perpetuals, then the mainstay of formal plantings, were coarse in habit, gross in presentation and (contrary to modern assumptions) abysmally lacking in scent. The Tea roses were, conversely, frail and pleasantly perfumed but unfortunately only semi-hardy. Gardening manuals of that time devoted a considerable amount of space to various methods of protection during the long, wet, cold winters of northern Europe.

These two great families were crossed to produce the modern hybrid tea, relatively short in stature, averaging about a metre (3ft) in height, the majority pleasantly scented, but above all producing the classic shape we are so familiar with today on a hardy bush. The colours ranged from deep crimson through pinks to pastel yellows and whites. The gaudy bicolours and brilliant yellows of today were unknown at that time. In fact 30 years elapsed before a French hybridist used the progeny of *R. foetida* and *R. foetida bicolor* ('Austrian Yellow' and 'Austrian Copper') to broaden the spectrum of available colours in hybrid teas.

'Peace'

Two more recent developments brought the hybrid tea rose to the perfection we are familiar with today. 'Peace', bred in the 1930s but not introduced until 1946, astonished the rose world with its vigour, abundance of flower and subtle gradations of colour. Fifteen years later, in 1950, Kordes of West Germany broke the colour barrier with the introduction of the first of the brilliant, almost luminous, vermilion roses that dominate the red spectrum in roses today. 'Super Star', 'Alexander' and many others would not have been possible until this colour break occurred. The modern rose now possesses a range of colour unsurpassed by any

other garden plant growing in extremes of temperature, with a majority of varieties having at least a modicum of scent.

A hybrid tea, by definition, is a rose plant producing large, well-formed blooms singly rather than in clusters. The size of flower is no criterion but rather the freedom of flower on the individual stem. To enhance the quality of these big blooms, the lateral growths, or side buds, may be removed by a process called disbudding. This is usually done at an immature stage when the buds are young and brittle. Removal when they are in a semi-mature condition causes damage to the fabric of the plant and does not affect the eventual size of the bloom.

Hybridists have developed the hybrid tea bloom to the most extraordinary dimensions. The result is an accent on shape and form rather than garden worthiness. Care must be taken therefore when choosing varieties to plant. Amateur exhibitors at the much publicized big rose shows tend to grow this type of exhibition rose which has little in common with the free-flowering bush which is so popular in rose gardens throughout the world. Plants grown to such sophistication produce undesirable weaknesses. The most common fault is that the petals rot before the bloom develops. This is called balling and usually occurs in varieties with a large number of petals, growing in damp conditions, or where extremes of temperature occur. There is no remedy except to grow your roses 'harder' i.e., to cut down on the available nitrogen and feed more potash. Alternatively one can grow the more decorative varieties and consult a nurseryman who should be able to help in their proper selection.

Planting

Hybrid tea bush roses vary in both breadth and height, but with very few exceptions, e.g. 'Peace' and 'Alexander', may be planted when bedding out at 45–60cm (18in–2ft) apart. This distance will enable the weekend gardener to maintain a high degree of weed control, cultivation and, of paramount importance, pest and disease control.

The vexed question of planting one variety per rose bed or mixing varieties is a matter of personal taste. A mixture causes problems of distance, comparative heights, uniformity of growth and visual effect. On the other hand, a small garden can be overwhelmed by the predominance of one colour and variety.

A modern hybrid tea is tolerant of most soils and situations, but draught is an important hazard and is to be avoided. Rose plants are grown commercially in open, windswept fields without detriment. These same plants however will not thrive when subjected to a sharp wind blowing down a draughty garden where survival is a fight for light, fertility and attention.

Soil environments in a wide geological spectrum will be tolerated provided good drainage and a reasonable degree of cultivation is maintained. Yellow roses did have a history of failure on some light, sandy soils. This was true 50 years ago but today these varieties have been eliminated. Similarly, some of the copper-yellows were more disease-prone, but recent introductions are tougher. Highly calcareous (chalky) soils still present a problem and it is safer to select the basic pinks and reds for success in these conditions.

Neighbours can offer very useful advice on choosing plants. Roses are known by variety to favour certain areas. This knowledge is available at your doorstep and is certainly an asset.

The hybrid tea today is the finest example of man's ability to manipulate plants to a degree of sophistication inconceivable only a century ago.

Hybrid Tea Bush Roses: A-Z

Adolph Horstmann
The deep yellow blooms are edged with pink and have a pale bronze effect. Tall, upright bush. Roses in this colour range are slightly subject to disease but this one is an outstanding exception. The flowers possess a slight fragrance, are generously borne singly and last well as cut flowers.
Raised by W. Kordes Sohne, West Germany, 1972
Parentage: 'Dr. A. J. Verhage' × 'Colour Wonder'
Available: Canada, Eire, Europe, UK, USA
Royal National Rose Society Trial Ground Certificate

Alec's Red
A very popular scarlet cherry-red. The large, almost outsize blooms have tremendous fragrance. The foliage is luxuriant and large and the bush vigorous and free. The most widely grown red hybrid tea today, it appears to have few defects and is an asset to any garden. Good for cutting and exhibition. Alec Cocker, the breeder, was at a loss to name this very successful rose and adopted the nickname bestowed on it by his fellow rose growers.
Raised by James Cocker and Sons, Scotland, 1970
Parentage: 'Fragrant Cloud' × 'Dame de Coeur'
Available: Worldwide, but not happy in excessive heat when it tends to blow quickly
Royal National Rose Society President's Trophy Winner and Gold Medal; Henry Edland Memorial Medal for Fragrance; Gold Medal and Award for Fragrance, Belfast

Alexander (Syn. 'Harkness Alexander')
Rose breeding has made great advances with the introduction of orange-vermilion colours. 'Alexander' is considered a vast improvement on 'Super Star', which was so popular 15 years ago. The long, pointed flowers are borne in abundance on very long stems. Extremely vigorous.
Raised by R. Harkness and Co., England, 1972
Parentage: 'Super Star' × ('Ann Elizabeth' × 'Allgold')
Available: Worldwide
Royal National Rose Society Certificate of Merit

Blessings
Considered by many rose growers to be the ideal bedding rose. The growth of medium height supports beautiful coral-pink fragrant blooms. The freedom of flower caused it to be classified as a floribunda when introduced, but after reclassification it is now a hybrid tea. Healthy and vigorous, the first flush of bloom is very early.
Raised by C. Gregory and Son, England, 1967
Parentage: 'Queen Elizabeth' × unnamed seedling
Available: Eire, Europe, UK
Royal National Rose Society Certificate of Merit; Baden-Baden Gold Medal

Blue Moon (Syns. 'Mainzer Fastnacht', 'Sissi')
So-called blue roses have only recently become popular although ramblers in this shade have been grown for some years. 'Blue Moon' is quite the most successful in this colour range. Grown throughout the rose-growing world, the lilac-lavender blooms possess a delicate fragrance. This is the nearest yet to a blue rose. The bushes are moderately vigorous and healthy. Good for cutting.
Raised by M. Tantau, West Germany, 1964
Parentage: Unnamed seedling × 'Sterling Silver'
Available: Worldwide
Royal National Rose Society Certificate of Merit; Rome Gold Medal

Bobby Charlton
The large, deep pink blooms with a silvery reverse are produced freely on strong, upright, very healthy bushes which come into flower much later than most cultivars in this colour range.
Raised by Fryers Nurseries Ltd., England, 1974
Parentage: 'Queen Elizabeth' seedling
Available: Canada, Eire, UK, USA

Champion
Giant-sized blooms of creamy gold. Very fragrant. A rose for the exhibitor, but free enough to merit garden use. The bushes are vigorous and healthy, with glossy foliage.
Raised by Fryers Nurseries Ltd., England, 1977
Parentage: 'Grandpa Dickson' × 'Whisky Mac'
Available: Canada, Eire, UK, USA

Chivalry (Syn. 'Macpow')
A tall, free-flowering bicolour with tremendous vigour, about 1.5m (5ft) tall. The flamboyant, long-lasting blooms of red and ivory are produced on long stems clothed in dark, glossy green foliage.
Raised by S. McGredy International, New Zealand, 1977
Parentage: 'Peer Gynt' × 'Brasilia'
Available: Eire, Europe, UK

Colour Wonder (Syns. 'Königin der Rosen', 'Queen of Roses')
Low-growing plant with free-flowering, globular blooms of orange-salmon with pale yellow reverse. A variety which comes into production late, but is consistent, colourful and fragrant.
Raised by W. Kordes Sohne, West Germany, 1964
Parentage: 'Perfecta' × 'Super Star'
Available: Worldwide

Dekorat (Syn. 'Freude')
A vigorous late-flowering variety with fragrant blooms of cherry red shot with tinges of pale gold. A new strain of hybrid tea which, if pruned lightly, will develop into a shrub about 1.2m (4ft) tall. Very hardy and free-flowering.
Raised by W. Kordes Sohne, West Germany, 1977
Parentage: Unknown
Available: Australia, Eire, Europe, New Zealand, UK

Diorama
The large apricot-yellow blooms are the first to flower in this colour range. Somewhat short of petals, it has had a reputation for blowing (coming out too quickly). Nevertheless, the fragrant flowers, supported on a bushy plant of medium height, are very beautiful and make this an excellent bedding variety.
Raised by G. de Ruiter, Netherlands, 1965
Parentage; 'Peace' × 'Beauté'
Available: Eire, Europe, UK
Royal National Rose Society Trial Ground Certificate

Double Delight
The fragrant, well-shaped blooms are a blend of strawberry and vanilla. Altogether quite a remarkable rose of medium height, bushy and free-flowering.
Raised by Armstrong Nurseries, USA, 1976
Parentage: 'Grenada' × 'Garden Party'
Available: Canada, Eire, UK, USA
All-America Rose Selections Award

Duke of Windsor (Syn. 'Herzog von Windsor')
A very popular orange-salmon flower. The

short compact bushes, 75cm (2ft 6in) high, are very thorny and produce an abundance of relatively small, fragrant blooms. Lately it has shown a tendency to mildew and rust which has given rise to its nickname 'Duke of Mildew'.
Raised by M. Tantau, West Germany, 1968
Parentage: 'Prima Ballerina' × seedling
Available: Worldwide
Royal National Rose Society Certificate of Merit; Henry Edland Memorial Medal for Fragrance

Elizabeth Harkness
A remarkably free-flowering, creamy buff rose which appears to improve in its flowering ability as it is more widely grown. The large, perfectly formed blooms are a most welcome addition to this colour range, and are borne on a healthy bush of medium height.
Raised by R. Harkness and Co., England, 1969
Parentage: 'Red Dandy' × 'Piccadilly'
Available: Australia, Canada, Eire, most of Europe, New Zealand, UK, USA

Evening Star
A tall, strong plant of recent introduction, which produces the most beautiful, fragrant white/cream roses.
Raised by Jackson and Perkins Co., USA, 1971
Parentage: 'Saratoga' × 'White Masterpiece'
Available: Canada, Eire, Europe, UK, USA
Has won acclaim and numerous awards in Europe and America

Fragrant Cloud (Syns. 'Duftwolke', 'Nuage Parfumé)
The large, coral-scarlet blooms possess a fragrance that quashes the notion that modern roses possess no scent. One of the earliest to flower, and grown wherever roses are to be found. The scent is quite unforgettable, and the dark green foliage complements one of the most popular garden varieties today.
Raised by M. Tantau, West Germany, 1964
Parentage: Seedling × 'Prima Ballerina'
Available: Worldwide
Royal National Rose Society's President's International Trophy and Gold Medal

Fragrant Hour
The large, salmon-pink blooms are supported by healthy foliage. The fragrance

matches the beauty of the flower. Tall, upright plant.
Raised by S. McGredy International, New Zealand, 1973
Parentage: 'Arthur Bell' × ('Spartan' × 'Grand Gala')
Available: Canada, Eire, UK, USA

Gavotte
Large blooms of rose-pink and silver are perfectly formed and make this an almost obligatory flower for the keen exhibitor. The bush is vigorous, of medium height but straggly, and the flowers must be heavily disbudded and protected in inclement weather conditions.
Raised by John Sanday (Roses) Ltd., England, 1963
Parentage: 'Ethel Sanday' × 'Lady Sylvia'
Available: Australia, Eire, New Zealand, UK
Royal National Rose Society Certificate of Merit

Grandpa Dickson (Syn. 'Irish Gold')
The pure lemon-yellow, fragrant flowers are of classical pointed shape and have a hint of green in the bud stage. One of the most popular roses flowering throughout the season. The pale green foliage complements this beautiful rose. Named after one of the most famous rose growers from Northern Ireland. Healthy, floriferous, and can be grown to exhibition size.
Raised by Dicksons Roses, Northern Ireland, 1966
Parentage: ('Kordes Perfecta' × 'Governador Braga da Cruz') × 'Piccadilly'
Available: Worldwide
Has won awards in Australia, Europe, UK and USA

John Waterer
Large, rich crimson blooms that tend to dull with age. A tall erect grower, very healthy deep green foliage and slightly fragrant flowers.
Raised by S. McGredy International, New Zealand, 1970
Parentage: 'King of Hearts' × 'Hanne'
Available: Canada, Eire, UK, USA
Royal National Rose Society Certificate of Merit

Josephine Bruce
Dark crimson roses are always very popular and 'Josephine Bruce' is no exception. The velvety blooms sometimes have a hint of scarlet and, like so many in this colour range, the young growth is quickly attacked by mildew. A sprawling bush with fragrant

flowers.
Raised by Bees Ltd., England, 1949
Parentage: 'Crimson Glory' × 'Madge Whipp'
Available: Eire, UK
Royal National Rose Society Trial Ground Certificate

Just Joey
Coppery-orange veined with red, paling at the edges with slightly serrated outer petals. A rose unique in its colouring, very free-flowering and fragrant. Dark green foliage on a healthy bush of medium height.
Raised by Cants of Colchester, England, 1973
Parentage: 'Fragrant Cloud' × 'Dr. A. J. Verhage'
Available: Eire, Europe, UK
Royal National Rose Society Trial Ground Certificate

King's Ransom
A pure yellow, highly pointed bloom makes 'King's Ransom' a reliable, profuse plant in most gardens, although calcareous (chalky) conditions do not appear to favour it. The dark green foliage supports a medium sized bush but mildew tends to attack the young growth in the autumn. An abundance of bloom from early in the season.
Raised by D. Morey, USA, 1961
Parentage: 'Golden Masterpiece' × 'Lydia'
Available: Worldwide
All-America Rose Selections Award

Korp (Syn. 'Prominent')
Sometimes listed as a floribunda. The perfect rose for the button-hole. The medium sized blooms of classical shape, signal red in colour, are borne singly on large inflorescences on a vigorous, compact bush with medium green, healthy foliage. The long stems make this variety equally useful in the garden or for flower arrangement.
Raised by W. Kordes Sohne, West Germany, 1971
Parentage: 'Königin der Rosen' × 'Zorina'
Available: Worldwide
Royal National Rose Society Certificate of Merit

Kronenbourg (Syn. 'Flaming Peace')
A sport (mutation) from 'Peace', which it resembles in habit and foliage. The blooms of scarlet-crimson, with an old-gold reverse, need dead-heading early as they discolour badly. A similar sport exists called 'Chicago Peace' but this does not

possess the brilliance of colour shown by 'Kronenbourg'.
Discovered by S. McGredy International, New Zealand, 1965
Parentage: 'Peace' sport
Available: Canada, Eire, Europe, UK, USA
Royal National Rose Society Trial Ground Certificate

Lady Seton

The sweetly scented, deep rose-pink, full flowers are plentifully borne on a bushy plant of medium height.
Raised by S. McGredy International, New Zealand, 1966
Parentage: 'Ma Perkins' × 'Mischief'
Available: Eire, UK
Royal National Rose Society Certificate of Merit

Litakor (Syns. 'Lolita', 'Korlita')

Pure copper-gold blooms on long stems. The colour, so fashionable these days, is an asset to any garden. The dark green foliage is remarkably disease free and the flowers last well when cut.
Raised by W. Kordes Sohne, West Germany, 1973
Parentage: 'Colour Wonder' × seedling
Available: Canada, Eire, Europe, UK, USA

Mme. Butterfly

In the 1930s every bride was married with a bouquet of roses in the fashionable colour of flesh pink. 'Ophelia' produced a multitude of sports, of which 'Lady Sylvia' and 'Mme. Butterfly' were the most notable. 'Mme. Butterfly', although considered by many to almost qualify as an old garden rose, is still to be found in many catalogues. The pale pink blooms with a hint of yellow at the base of the petals have retained their charm together with a pronounced fragrance. The plants of medium height are very free and will require disbudding.
Discovered by E. G. Hill & Co., USA, 1918
Parentage: 'Ophelia' sport
Available: Worldwide.

Mischief

Very fragrant blooms of coral-salmon. The deep green foliage on stout stems makes this a very good bedding rose. May need fungicide protection in areas where rust is prevalent.
Raised by S. McGredy International, New Zealand, 1960
Parentage: 'Peace' × 'Spartan'

Available: Worldwide
Royal National Rose Society President's International Trophy and Gold Medal

Mister Lincoln

A rich, dark crimson rose with abundant scent; the healthiest of the dark reds, with strong upright growth. A variety which has never gained the recognition it deserves.
Raised by Swim and Weeks, USA, 1964
Parentage: 'Chrysler Imperial' × 'Charles Mallerin'
Available: Australia, Canada, Eire, New Zealand, UK, USA
All-America Rose Selections Award

Mullard Jubilee (Syn. 'Electron')

A strong, bushy grower bearing large well-shaped fragrant blooms of deep rose-pink. Very free-flowering and a first class bedding rose. The stems are very thorny and the foliage may require protection from mildew.
Raised by S. McGredy International, New Zealand, 1970
Parentage: 'Paddy McGredy' × 'Prima Ballerina'
Available: Most countries
Royal National Rose Society Gold Medal; The Hague Gold Medal

National Trust

A compact, bushy grower bearing beautifully formed scarlet-crimson blooms of medium size. Very good as a bedder, the foliage is remarkably healthy, but unfortunately the flowers have very little scent.
Raised by S. McGredy International, New Zealand, 1969
Parentage: 'Evelyn Fison' × 'King of Hearts'
Available: Eire, Europe, UK
Royal National Rose Society Trial Ground Certificate

Papa Meilland

A plant of moderate growth with foliage extremely prone to mildew. It bears the darkest red hybrid tea rose with the most exquisite scent. For the perfectionist it can be grown under glass, but it is a shy producer of flower.
Raised by Meilland, France, 1963
Parentage: 'Chrysler Imperial' × 'Charles Mallerin'
Available: Most countries

Pascali

The best white bedding rose today. White roses are not particularly popular because of weather damage, disease and unfashion-

able colour. However, 'Pascali' seems to surmount these problems and is very widely grown.
Raised by Louis Lens, Belgium, 1963
Parentage: 'Queen Elizabeth' × 'White Butterfly'
Available: Worldwide
Royal National Rose Society Certificate of Merit; The Hague Gold Medal

Peace (Syns. 'Gloria Dei', 'Gioia', 'Mme. A. Meilland')

Variously described as the rose of the century, or the world's favourite rose. Although 'Peace' was bred in France in 1937 it did not go into commerce until almost ten years later. In the meantime World War II intervened. Budwood of this variety was smuggled out in a diplomatic bag when the German invasion of France was almost complete in 1940. Its real potential was not immediately recognized (one grower in America threw it out) but eventually at a United Nations meeting in San Francisco in 1945 it was duly christened 'Peace'.

The plant possesses more vigour than the average bush and care must be taken in positioning it in the garden. The large flowers are yellow, flushed with pink as the blooms age. Careful, light pruning will produce a shrub about 1.5m (5ft) tall, but early shoots are sometimes blind.
Raised by Meilland, France. Introduced 1945
Parentage: [('George Dickson' × 'Souvenir de Claudius Pernet') × ('Joanna Hill' × 'Charles P. Kilham')] × 'Margaret McGredy'
Available: Worldwide
Gold Medals in almost every rose growing country in the world

Peer Gynt

A large, free-flowering plant. The tall, sturdy stems bear large canary yellow flowers which age to a pretty peach at the edges and are sometimes frilled. Can be grown singly if disbudded to produce large exhibition blooms, or in large inflorescences if grown naturally without disbudding. Has become prone to mildew of late, but is very hardy.
Raised by W. Kordes Sohne, West Germany, 1968
Parentage: 'Königen der Rosen' × 'Golden Giant'
Available: Australia, Eire, Europe, New Zealand, UK
Royal National Rose Society Certificate of Merit

Piccadilly
Bicolours have long held a fascination for many rose growers, although detested by some. 'Piccadilly', with an abundance of flower, is probably the most popular variety in this colour range. The scarlet and gold blooms are borne on a medium-sized plant clothed with dark green, glossy foliage. Remarkably free-flowering from early in the season, it is a splendid bedding variety which will do equally well as a standard.
Raised by S. McGredy International, New Zealand, 1959
Parentage: 'McGredy's Yellow' × 'Karl Herbst'
Available: Worldwide
Royal National Rose Society Certificate of Merit; Madrid and Rome Gold Medals

Pink Favourite
The very large rose-pink flowers are produced freely on strong stems with healthy, glossy foliage. Although a late starter, it is a consistent producer of quality blooms for the exhibitor or for the garden. It enjoys the reputation of being the most disease-proof bush today. Its vigour in America and Australia is such that it is excluded from exhibition classes as a hybrid tea, but in Europe it conforms to acceptable bedding standards.
Raised by F. Von Abrams, USA, 1956
Parentage: 'Juno' × ('Georg Arends' × 'New Dawn')
Available: Worldwide

Precious Platinum (Syn. 'Opa Potschke')
Pat Dickson has been described as the 'king of the red roses' by his brother hybridizers and 'Precious Platinum' fully justifies his title. The fragrant, bright crimson blooms of medium size are weather hardy, and the bright green foliage is disease resistant on a vigorous medium-sized bush. The name is derived from the platinum industry which commissioned the title to promote the value of the metal.
Raised by Dicksons Roses, Northern Ireland, 1974
Parentage: 'Red Planet' × 'Franklin Engelmann'
Available: Worldwide

Prima Ballerina (Syn. 'Première Ballerine')
A cherry-pink rose of medium height. Rather more famous to aficionados as a prolific parent, it nevertheless is a good, reliable bedding variety in its own right. The scent is very sweet. Has become prone to mildew recently.
Raised by M. Tantau, West Germany, 1957
Parentage: Seedling × 'Peace'
Available: Australia, Canada, Eire, Europe, New Zealand, UK, USA
Royal National Rose Society Trial Ground Certificate

Red Devil (Syn. 'Coeur d'Amour')
Probably the most perfectly formed red rose today. The high centre and classical shape make it obligatory on any show bench. The robust, vigorous plant, with bronze-green foliage, supports enormous blooms which are equally suitable for garden purposes. The fragrant, bright scarlet blooms, with a slightly paler reverse, are not very tolerant of rain and are damaged badly unless protected.
Raised by Dicksons Roses, Northern Ireland, 1967
Parentage: 'Silver Lining' × 'Prima Ballerina'
Available: Worldwide
Royal National Rose Society Certificate of Merit; Gold Medal, City of Belfast; Gold Medal Japan

Rose Gaujard
'Peace' is well known for its inability to produce in its progeny the same luxuriant growth and vigour but this variety makes a gallant effort. The large, fragrant carmine blooms flushed with white have an annoying habit of becoming split. However, well-formed examples have been produced for the show bench. Very healthy but late flowering.
Raised by J. Gaujard, France, 1958
Parentage: 'Peace' × 'Opera' seedling
Available: Worldwide
Royal National Rose Society Gold Medal

Silver Jubilee
Medium-sized blooms of coppery salmon-pink with peach shadings. The dense, glossy green foliage supports a multitude of well-shaped, slightly fragrant flowers on a disease-free bush. It was named by permission of H. M. Queen Elizabeth II, to commemorate her Silver Jubilee.
Raised by James Cocker and Sons, Scotland, 1978
Parentage: [('Parkdirektor Riggers' × 'Piccadilly') × ('Highlight' × 'Colour Wonder')] × 'Mischief'
Available: Eire, UK
Royal National Rose Society President's International Trophy and Gold Medal

Super Star (Syn. 'Tropicana')
The first of the brilliant vermilion, luminous red roses which heralded a completely new break in rose breeding and created a big sensation when it was introduced. Lately the plant has shown a tendency towards mildew but it is still worth growing in disease-free areas. The bushes are of medium height, free-flowering but late.
Raised by M. Tantau, West Germany, 1960
Parentage: (Seedling × 'Peace') × (Seedling × 'Alpine Glow').
Available: Worldwide
It vies with 'Peace' in the number of awards it has received around the world

Sutter's Gold
The light orange-yellow blooms are flushed pink with scarlet veining. Generally accepted as the sweetest-scented yellow rose today. The elegant flowers are disease resistant and borne on long stems with medium-green foliage.
Raised by Swim and Weeks, USA, 1950
Parentage: 'Charlotte Armstrong' × 'Signora'
Available: Australia, Canada, Eire, Europe, New Zealand, UK, USA

Troika (Syn. 'Royal Dane')
A first-class bedding rose. The medium-sized bushes clothed with deep green, luxuriant foliage support early blooms of orange-bronze with red shadings. The healthiest of the copper roses, and tolerant of extremes of temperature and soil which have been the bugbear of older varieties in this colour range.
Raised by D. T. Poulsen, Denmark, 1972
Parentage: Unknown
Available: Canada, Eire, Europe, UK, USA
Royal National Rose Society Certificate of Merit

Wendy Cussons
The cerise-scarlet (rose red) large blooms are produced from early in the season with a heavy fragrance likened to a Damask rose. The foliage is dark green and healthy and the flowers are weather resistant.
Raised by C. Gregory and Son, England, 1959
Parentage: 'Independence' × 'Eden Rose'
Available: Worldwide
Royal National Rose Society President's International Trophy; The Hague Gold Medal; Gold Medals: Portland (USA) and Rome

Floribunda Bush Roses: Introduction

Left
The fragrant, unfading blooms of 'Korresia'.
Below, far left
'Iceberg' bears large clusters of pure white blooms.
Below left
'Bonfire Night', a floribunda-hybrid tea-type rose.
Bottom
The vivid, scarlet blooms of 'Trumpeter'.
Below
'Matangi', an extraordinary blend of orange and vermilion, has a silvery eye and reverse.
Opposite page
The clear pink blooms of 'Queen Elizabeth'.

Rose breeders, fired by the successful introduction of the modern hybrid tea, dreamed of a rose plant that would produce the continual abundance of flower usually associated with some bedding plants or even chrysanthemums and dahlias. This rose would have to flower from early summer through to the autumn, require very little maintenance, be hardy, disease-free and tolerant of a wide variety of environments.

Such a plant was first envisaged by a Danish breeder, Poulsen, when he used *R. multiflora* blood in a dwarf form called polyanthas, crossed with some of the early hybrid teas in 1920. The result was a family of Poulsen roses or hybrid polyanthas, all named after his daughters. 'Else', 'Karen', 'Kirsten' and 'Anne Poulsen' were famous names in the 1930s, planted in great bedding schemes but unfortunately lacking in variety of colour (they were either pink or red).

The name hybrid polyantha was changed in the 1950s and today all roses flowering naturally in clusters in a bush form are called floribundas. Such was the lack of colour and the total absence of scent of these early Poulsen roses, that even when newer colours were introduced these defects did not encourage enthusiastic cultivation.

Important introductions
Like the hybrid tea, the floribunda's development can be traced by a series of important introductions. 'Frensham', raised in the United Kingdom in 1945, was the first cluster rose to inherit the true classical shape in its bud form, although the mildew-riddled specimens seen today are but a mockery of the plants grown 30 years ago.

'Masquerade' was the first really big breakthrough in contributing novelty, freedom of flower and popularity to the floribundas. The large clusters of flower, yellow in youth and turning in sunlight through pink into scarlet, were startling. More importantly, unlike 'Frensham', it proved a most remarkable parent and produced seedlings by the thousand. About this time the vermilion colour introduced by Kordes was used to produce the hundreds of new bright reds, vermilions and oranges which have dominated the nurserymen's catalogues for so many years. It is a curious fact that the introduction of this colour range virtually eliminated the softer pink varieties which were then just becoming popular.

'Queen Elizabeth' was introduced in 1955. Its vigour and popularity can only be likened to 'Peace'. Although used as a parent, it has never been as popular as 'Masquerade'. The salmon floribundas can be traced to 'Spartan', introduced in 1954. 'Elizabeth of Glamis' is the most famous example, although 'Mary Sumner', only just on the market, will soon supersede it. The most significant advance in the breeding of floribundas is the introduction of the 'Picasso' strain from Sam McGredy. For many years he felt that the fusion of new blood from species of rose not used so far in the development of the modern plant might produce new concepts of plant form and colour. 'Picasso', with a conventional parent on one side but *R. spinosissima* offspring and other forms on the other, has produced a completely novel form. The flower is scarlet with a white eye and a silver reverse and the edge of the petals is pale pink. This variety together with its progeny has contributed a frilled effect and heralds the advance and improvement of one of the most widely grown genus of plants today.

Since the early, heady days of novelty the floribunda has gone from strength to strength. The average-size bloom has grown out of all recognition and we now have two new sections: the floribunda-hybrid tea type and the grandiflora. The first of these two is self explanatory – a bush producing large clusters of flowers – but the blooms themselves are of a quality to match the more decorative hybrid teas. The grandifloras form a group because of their size and vigour and are epitomized by the 'Queen Elizabeth' rose. They are in fact floribundas with unusual zeal in growth. They average 1.2–1.5m (4–5ft) in height but as they are very upright in character they should not be likened to a more open-growing shrub rose.

Planting and pruning
Floribundas add a new dimension to gardening. Their continuity of flower ensures that the annual laborious exercise of bedding out plants in the late spring is but a memory to many of us. With ever increasing labour costs and the demand for a smaller capital outlay in planning and maintaining gardens, a planting subject such as this is invaluable.

Bush roses, either hybrid teas or floribundas, require very little maintenance; this applies more to the latter. Apart from the annual exercise of pruning, a spring feed followed by a booster in mid-summer is all that is required. Dead-heading will ensure a continuity of bloom, especially with varieties that are 'Masquerade' seedlings. They are so fertile that to allow hips to develop will practically stop all further growth.

The sight of a large bed of a modern floribunda in full flower must contribute to the theory that planting by variety is more rewarding. If the garden is small, a mixture of two, or at the most three, varieties is quite pleasing. Alternatively, groups planted in mixed herbaceous borders will add colour and interest and provide flowers in mid-summer when many other plants have finished blooming.

Floribundas are hardier, more tolerant of difficult positions, not so prone to disease and obviously freer flowering than hybrid teas. They do not suffer the weather damage encountered by hybrid teas but, except for the floribunda-hybrid tea type, many do not make good subjects for cutting. The abundance of flower from 'Iceberg', the healthiness of 'Mary Sumner' and the amazing vigour of 'Queen Elizabeth' must in some ways compensate for this and make any garden an enjoyable and brilliant place in mid-summer.

Floribunda Bush Roses: A-Z

Allgold
Very bright buttercup-yellow. For many years this variety reigned supreme as the best yellow floribunda. Newer introductions recently have ousted it from its distinguished position. The bushes of moderate height and vigour have large clusters of fragrant yellow flowers with disease-free, bright green foliage.
Raised by E. B. LeGrice, England, 1956
Parentage: 'Goldilocks' × 'Ellinor LeGrice'
Available: Worldwide
Royal National Rose Society Gold Medal

Ann Aberconway
A very strong-growing apricot-yellow with an abundance of fragrant flowers borne on robust stems with dark, healthy foliage. It is named after the wife of the President of the Royal Horticultural Society, Lord Aberconway.
Raised by J. Mattock Ltd., England, 1976
Parentage: 'Arthur Bell' seedling
Available: Eire, UK

Arthur Bell
Grows in large clusters of bright yellow which have a delicate fragrance. The bushes are vigorous and upright and well furnished with glossy, green foliage. One of the earliest floribundas to flower; the colour tends to fade as it ages.
Raised by S. McGredy International, New Zealand, 1965
Parentage: 'Cläre Grammerstorf' × 'Piccadilly'
Available: Canada, Eire, Europe, UK, USA
Royal National Rose Society Certificate of Merit

Bonfire Night (Syn. 'Bonfire')
Probably the most sophisticated of the 'Masquerade' family. It is a floribunda – hybrid tea type. Large clusters of beautifully formed, pale orange-yellow flowers that turn scarlet and have a lighter reverse. The growth is bushy, upright and compact; the foliage a semi-glossy deep green.
Raised by S. McGredy International, New Zealand, 1971
Parentage: 'Tiki' × 'Variety Club'
Available: Australia, Canada, Eire, Europe, New Zealand, UK, USA
Royal National Rose Society Trial Ground Certificate

Chinatown (Syn. 'Ville de Chine')
A bush with tremendous vigour that may suggest it is really a shrub. The deep yellow clusters of flower, with a suggestion of pink edging, pale quickly and are produced on stems 1.5m (5ft) tall. The foliage is a medium green. Is best used in mixed borders planted in groups of three or five.
Raised by D. T. Poulsen, Denmark, 1963
Parentage: 'Columbine' × 'Cläre Grammerstorf'
Available: Canada, Eire, Europe, UK, USA
Royal National Rose Society Gold Medal

City of Belfast
A bedding rose possessing great continuity of flower. A bush grower 75cm (2½ft) high, the trusses of medium-sized vermilion-scarlet blooms are an asset in a small garden where size of plant is most important.
Raised by S. McGredy International, New Zealand, 1968
Parentage: 'Evelyn Fison' × ('Circus' × 'Korona')
Available: Australia, Canada, Eire, Europe, New Zealand, UK, USA
Royal National Rose Society President's International Trophy Winner and Gold Medal

City of Leeds
Rich salmon-pink blooms which appear to appreciate cool, northern climates. The bushes are upright with semi-glossy, dark green foliage. The well-formed blooms are very good for floral art. Sometimes prone to rust disease.
Raised by S. McGredy International, New Zealand, 1966
Parentage: 'Evelyn Fison' × ('Spartan' × 'Red Favourite')
Available: Australia, Canada, Eire, New Zealand, UK, USA
Royal National Rose Society Gold Medal

Dame of Sark
A vigorous and upright grower with glossy, medium green foliage. The large blooms, gold flushed with scarlet, give a hint of its 'Masquerade' ancestry but the quality of flower shows considerable advance in this prolific line of breeding.
Raised by R. Harkness and Co., England, 1976
Parentage: ('Pink Parfait' × 'Masquerade') × 'Tabler's Choice'
Available: Eire, UK
Royal National Rose Society Trial Ground Certificate

Dearest
The advent of the bright vermilion colours has seen a decline in the use of 'Dearest', for many years the standard pink bedding floribunda. Still considered a very good medium-sized plant; the salmon-pink flowers have a pleasant scent but do not like wet weather. The dark green foliage may need protection from black spot fungus.
Raised by Dicksons Roses, Northern Ireland, 1960
Parentage: Seedling × 'Spartan'
Available: Australia, Canada, Eire, New Zealand, UK, USA

Elizabeth of Glamis (Syn. 'Irish Beauty')
The large clusters of fragrant double flowers of coral-salmon are set off by a vigorous plant with medium green, semi-glossy foliage. Recently 'Elizabeth of Glamis' has shown a dislike of cold, heavy soils and in such situations is not weather hardy. Nevertheless, it is still a great compliment to a very gracious lady, the Queen Mother.
Raised by S. McGredy International, New Zealand, 1964
Parentage: 'Spartan' × 'Highlight'
Available: Australia, Canada, Eire, New Zealand, UK, USA
Royal National Rose Society President's International Trophy and Gold Medal and Henry Edland Memorial Medal for Fragrance

Escapade
The semi-double blooms of lilac-rose with a white centre have a slight fragrance and are produced in large clusters. The plant is vigorous and tall, 1.2m (4ft), with glossy, light green foliage.
Raised by R. Harkness and Co., England, 1967
Parentage: 'Pink Parfait' × 'Baby Faurax'
Available: Eire, UK
Royal National Rose Society Certificate of Merit; Baden-Baden Gold Medal; Gold Medal, City of Belfast

Evelyn Fison (Syn. 'Irish Wonder')
A highly weather-resistant vivid red. The large clusters of flower are produced on a vigorous bush with medium green foliage. A good bedding variety.
Raised by S. McGredy International, New Zealand, 1961
Parentage: 'Moulin Rouge' × 'Korona'
Available: Australia, Canada, Eire, New Zealand, UK, USA
Royal National Rose Society Gold Medal

Eye Paint
A truly remarkable free-flowering plant. The single blooms of scarlet, edged with

pink, have a distinct white eye and are produced in large clusters. Although catalogued as a floribunda, with light pruning it will produce an admirable shrub 1.2m (4ft) tall. A member of the very popular 'Picasso' family.
Raised by S. McGredy International, New Zealand, 1976
Parentage: (('Little Darling' × 'Goldilocks) × ['Evelyn Fison' × ('Coryana' × 'Tantau's Triumph')]) × 'Picasso'
Available: Canada, Eire, Europe, UK, USA
Royal National Rose Society Trial Ground Certificate

Frensham

For many years the most popular red floribunda, used for hedges and bedding. The deep scarlet-crimson medium-sized flowers are produced on large trusses. Unfortunately it has become a victim of mildew but is still widely grown, particularly as a shrub. It was raised by A. Norman, a diamond cutter by profession, whose hobby was rose growing and breeding. In a short space of time he produced two outstanding roses – 'Ena Harkness' and 'Frensham'. His achievement is even more noteworthy as the parents he used, 'Crimson Glory' and 'Southport', had been used by his professional counterparts with little success.
Raised by A. Norman, England, 1946
Parentage: Seedling × 'Crimson Glory'
Available: Australia, Eire, New Zealand, UK
Royal National Rose Society Gold Medal

Iceberg (Syns. 'Schneewittchen')

Seldom has a rose been bred with the floriferousness of 'Iceberg'. Large clusters of pure white flowers, moderately full but opening flat, appear from early in the season. The outer petals assume a faint pink tinge especially in damp weather or in the autumn. The vigour of the plant suggests that it may be a shrub. Nevertheless, if pruned with moderation it will produce a fine bedding plant about 1.1m (3ft 6in) tall. Prone to mildew late in the season.
Raised by W. Kordes Sohne, West Germany, 1958
Parentage: 'Robin Hood' × 'Virgo'
Available: Worldwide
Royal National Rose Society Gold Medal

Iced Ginger

A beautiful apricot-buff with tints of pure copper. An upright grower of the floribunda-hybrid tea type, with fragrant blooms which last well in water. The colour has been likened to the very popular climber 'Schoolgirl'.
Raised by Dicksons Roses, Northern Ireland, 1971
Parentage: 'Anne Watkins' seedling
Available: Australia, Canada, Eire, New Zealand, UK, USA

Irish Mist

The slightly fragrant, perfectly shaped blooms of orange-salmon appear early in the season. The plant is bushy with semi-glossy, dark green foliage. In some cases the wood appears brittle and is easily damaged in summer gales. It must therefore be planted in sheltered areas or be given protection from winds.
Raised by S. McGredy International, New Zealand, 1967
Parentage: 'Orangeade' × 'Mischief'
Available: Eire, Europe, UK
Royal National Rose Society Certificate of Merit

Isis

This variety has an outstanding spicy scent. The large, white hybrid tea type blooms are produced in small clusters on a moderately sized bush about 60cm (2ft) tall with deep green foliage.
Raised by J. Mattock, Ltd., England, 1973
Parentage: 'Shepherdess' × 'Vera Dalton'
Available: Eire, Europe, UK

Kerryman

An unusual pink floribunda of the hybrid tea type; the outer petals deepen in colour with age. The flowers of medium size are borne in large clusters on a medium-sized bush with glossy foliage.
Raised by S. McGredy International, New Zealand, 1970
Parentage: 'Paddy McGredy' × ('Mme Léon Cuny' × 'Columbine')
Available: Canada, Eire, UK, USA
Royal National Rose Society Certificate of Merit

Kiskadee

The golden-yellow flowers are of a high quality but lack the intensity of colour associated with this spectrum (see 'Korresia'). Nevertheless, some gardeners prefer subtle shades. A profuse plant of medium height with deep green foliage.
Raised by S. McGredy International, New Zealand, 1973
Parentage: Unknown
Available: Eire, UK

Korresia (Syn. 'Fresia')

Yellow floribundas have had a chequered history and 'Korresia' is no exception. Introduced almost unnoticed only four years ago, it is now the most popular yellow floribunda and is widely grown throughout the world. A by-product of Kordes's forced rose breeding programme, it nevertheless quickly ousted its nearest rival 'Allgold'. The brilliant, unfading yellow flowers are produced in large clusters. They are well-shaped and have a pronounced fragrance. The bushes are moderate in height, well-clothed with medium green foliage and the bloom is almost continuous.
Raised by W. Kordes' Sohne, West Germany, 1973
Parentage: Unknown
Available: Australia, Canada, Eire, Europe, New Zealand, UK, USA

Lilli Marlene (Syn. 'Lilli Marleen')

A most reliable and consistent dark red bush. The large clusters of flower are produced in profusion from early in the season but may require protection from mildew in the autumn. Legend has it that it was named, at a particularly inebriated party of rose breeders, after the song which often brings tears to the eyes of participants at such festivities.
Raised by W. Kordes Sohne, West Germany, 1959
Parentage: ('Our Princess' × 'Rudolph Timm') × 'Ama'
Available: Worldwide
Royal National Rose Society Certificate of Merit; The Hague Gold Medal

Margot Koster

The newcomer to rose growing would be astonished at the small number of floribundas available before 1939. Until then the biggest bedding varieties (apart from the new Poulsen roses) were dwarf polyanthas. About 60cm (2ft) high, they produced large clusters of small flowers about 3.7cm (1½in) in diameter. Their greatest asset was freedom of flower. However, they lacked a range of colour – whites, pinks and reds were their limit and they were very prone to mildew in the autumn. 'Margot Koster' has survived because of its freedom from disease. The flowers are globular, salmon in colour, and the bushes are about 45cm (18in) high. The 'Koster' strain is still grown for forcing as a pot rose.
Discovered by D. A. Koster, Netherlands, 1931
Parentage: A 'Dick Koster' sport
Available: Worldwide

Floribunda Bush Roses: A-Z

Marlena

A low, compact grower about 45cm (18in) high. The short, free-flowering bushes are covered in crimson-scarlet clusters of flower. Could well be called a dwarf 'Lilli Marlene'.
Raised by W. Kordes Sohne, West Germany, 1964
Parentage: 'Gertrud Westphal' × 'Lilli Marlene'
Available: Australia, Eire, Europe, New Zealand, UK
City of Belfast Gold Medal

Mary Sumner

Slightly fragrant, orange-salmon blooms are produced in large clusters on a vigorous bush about 1m (3ft) tall. The foliage is a glossy, deep green and very healthy. Named after the founder of the Mothers' Union.
Raised by S. McGredy International, New Zealand, 1975
Parentage: ('Orangeade' × 'Margot Fonteyn') × ['Elizabeth of Glamis' × ('Little Darling' × 'Goldilocks')]
Available: Eire, UK
Royal National Rose Society Certificate of Merit

Masquerade

The phenomenon of a rose petal turning colour as it ages in sunlight is not new, but the introduction of 'Masquerade' caused considerable astonishment. The slightly fragrant, perfectly shaped yellow blooms quickly change through salmon pink to dark red – but only in sunlight. This rose has produced a large number of well-known seedlings. Because of their fecundity the flowers must be dead-headed, otherwise few blooms will appear in the autumn.
Raised by Boerner, Jackson and Perkins, USA, 1950
Parentage: 'Goldilocks' × 'Holiday'
Available: Worldwide
Royal National Rose Society Gold Medal

Matangi

Considered by many rose breeders to be the finest 'Picasso' seedling Sam McGredy has produced. Orange-vermilion with a silver eye and reverse, the slightly fragrant blooms are borne either singly or several together on a bush of medium height with glossy, dark green foliage.
Raised by S. McGredy International, New Zealand, 1974
Parentage: (('Little Darling' × 'Goldilocks') × ['Evelyn Fison' × ('Coryana' × 'Tantau's Triumph')]) × 'Picasso'
Available: Australia, Canada, Eire, Europe, New Zealand, UK, USA
Royal National Rose Society President's International Trophy and Gold Medal

Memento (Syn. 'Dicbar')

A cerise-pink rose with a reverse of carmine. Has tremendous floriferousness which can be likened to the productivity of 'Iceberg'. The medium-sized bush is extremely weather resistant.
Raised by Dicksons Roses, Northern Ireland, 1978
Parentage: 'Bangor' × 'Korbell'
Available: Eire, Europe, UK
Royal National Rose Society Trial Ground Certificate

Molly McGredy

An upright, bushy floribunda-hybrid tea type. The perfect blooms of cherry-red with a silver reverse are produced in medium sized clusters. The effect is spectacular. The foliage is very disease-free.
Raised by S. McGredy International, New Zealand, 1969
Parentage: 'Paddy McGredy' × ('Mme. Léon Cuny' × 'Columbine')
Available: Canada, Eire, UK, USA
Royal National Rose Society President's International Trophy Winner and Gold Medal

News

The large, flat blooms are beetroot-red turning to deep purple, complemented by golden-yellow anthers. Very free-flowering.
Raised by E. B. LeGrice, England, 1969
Parentage: 'Lilac Charm' × 'Tuscany Superb'
Available: Australia, Eire, Europe, New Zealand, UK
Royal National Rose Society Gold Medal

Old Master

Deep carmine-purple with silver eye and reverse. Slightly fragrant blooms. The glossy green foliage is outstanding on a bush of medium height.
Raised by S. McGredy International, New Zealand, 1973
Parentage: [('Evelyn Fison' × ('Tantau's Triumph' × 'Coryana')) × ('Hamburger Phoenix' × 'Danse du Feu')] × ['Evelyn Fison' × ('Orange Sweetheart' × 'Fruhlings-morgen')
Available: Canada, Eire, Europe, UK, USA
Royal National Rose Trial Ground Certificate

Pernille Poulsen

One of the few scented pink floribundas, always in flower and very healthy. A great tribute to the fourth generation of Danish rose breeders who introduced the first hybrid polyanthas to the garden.
Raised by D. T. Poulsen, Denmark, 1965
Parentage: 'Ma Perkins' × 'Columbine'
Available: Eire, Europe, UK
Royal National Rose Society Trial Ground Certificate

Picasso

The original 'hand painted' rose. A unique introduction that is the forerunner of a completely new concept in rose colours, inconceivable ten years ago. The medium-sized blooms are pink, irregularly splashed with crimson, and have a white 'eye'. The edge of the petals and reverse are a lighter shade. The plant is short, very free-flowering, and the stems and foliage slender but freely produced.
Raised by S. McGredy International, New Zealand, 1971
Parentage: 'Marlena' × ['Evelyn Fison' × ('Orange Sweetheart' × 'Frühlings-morgen')]
Available: Australia, Canada, Eire, Europe, New Zealand, UK, USA
Royal National Rose Society Certificate of Merit

Priscilla Burton (Syn. 'Macrat')

A vigorous, upright plant. The medium-sized clusters of flower are silvery white, splashed with carmine, reminiscent of a latter day 'Rosa Mundi'. The dark, glossy green foliage is an outstanding feature.
Raised by S. McGredy International, New Zealand, 1978
Parentage: 'Maxi' × ['Evelyn Fison' × ('Orange Sweetheart' × 'Frühlings-morgen')]
Available: Eire, Europe, UK
Royal National Rose Society President's International Trophy Winner and Gold Medal

Queen Elizabeth

There is no doubt that 'Queen Elizabeth' is one of the milestones of rose breeding. The soft, clear pink blooms, borne on bushes of considerable height and magnificence, are a feature of many gardens in rose growing areas round the world. The vigour of this variety (an unpruned plant can grow to about 3m (10ft)) precludes it from formal planting, but it enhances shrub borders and can also be grown as a shrub. The large stems are apt to look bare at the base and

therefore care must be taken to camouflage this. 'Dearest' will blend in well to do a good covering act. The early stems sometimes go blind but produce bloom eventually.
Raised by W. L. Lammerts, Armstrong Nurseries, USA, 1956
Parentage: 'Charlotte Armstrong' × 'Floradora'
Available: Worldwide
The list of awards can only be equalled by 'Peace'.

Rosemary Rose
A unique variety. The full, double flowers are rosette shaped, currant-red in colour and borne on vigorous bushes with beautiful coppery-red foliage. A splendid subject to add colour to a mixed border, but unfortunately very subject to mildew.
Raised by G. de Ruiter, Netherlands, 1954
Parentage: 'Gruss an Teplitz' × seedling
Available: Eire, Europe, UK
Royal National Rose Society Gold Medal; Rome Gold Medal

Scarlet Queen Elizabeth
The clear, medium-sized scarlet flowers are produced in small clusters on a vigorous plant about 1.2m (4ft) high. Not to be compared in size to its pink namesake but nevertheless taller than the average floribunda. It therefore requires careful placing in the garden, coming into flower later than most varieties.
Raised by Dicksons Roses, Northern Ireland, 1963
Parentage: 'Korona' seedling × 'Queen Elizabeth'
Available: Australia, Eire, New Zealand, UK
Royal National Rose Society Trial Ground Certificate

Scented Air
A bushy grower whose large, deep salmon-pink flowers possess an outstanding fragrance. The deep green, luxuriant foliage is remarkably disease-free.
Raised by Dicksons Roses, Northern Ireland, 1967
Parentage: 'Spartan' seedling × 'Queen Elizabeth'
Available: Eire, Europe, UK
Royal National Rose Society Certificate of Merit and Henry Edland Memorial Medal for Fragrance

Sea Pearl (Syn. 'Flower Girl')
A very free-flowering salmon-pink with beautiful peach shadings. The hybrid tea sized flowers are well-shaped and reminis-cent of a cut flower variety. Suitable as a medium-sized plant but prone to mildew.
Raised by Dicksons Roses, Northern Ireland, 1964
Parentage: 'Kordes Perfecta' × 'Montezuma'
Available: Australia, Canada, Eire, New Zealand, UK, USA
Royal National Rose Society Certificate of Merit

Shepherdess
The large, soft-gold flowers are edged with carmine reminiscent of 'Peace'. The bushes are of medium height, free-flowering and healthy, with deep, glossy bronze-tinted foliage.
Raised by J. Mattock Ltd., England, 1967
Parentage: 'Allgold' × 'Peace'
Available: Eire, UK
Royal National Rose Society Trial Ground Certificate

Southampton
The apricot flowers have a slight fragrance and the bushes have unusual vigour – 1.2m (4ft). It has a freedom from disease which is rare in this colour range.
Raised by R. Harkness and Co., England, 1969
Parentage: ('Ann Elizabeth' × 'Allgold') × 'Yellow Cushion'
Available: Eire, Europe, UK
Royal National Rose Society Trial Ground Certificate

Sunsilk
The lemon-yellow blooms have the purity of colour associated with 'Grandpa Dickson'. Medium-sized blooms are borne on an upright bush of medium height.
Raised by Fryers Nurseries Ltd., England, 1974
Parentage: 'Pink Parfait' × 'Red Gold'
Available: Eire, Europe, UK
Royal National Rose Society Trial Ground Certificate

The Sun
Clusters of medium-sized, soft orange-salmon double blooms. They flower in great profusion on an upright, sturdy bush of average height. The foliage is dark green and healthy.
Raised by S. McGredy International, New Zealand, 1974
Parentage: ('Little Darling' × 'Goldilocks') × 'Irish Mist'
Available: Eire, Europe, UK
Royal National Rose Society Certificate of Merit

Tiptop
Like Topsi, a product of the demand for smaller plants. The clusters of salmon-pink flowers have a delicate fragrance and the growth is stout, bushy and healthy.
Raised by M. Tantau, West Germany, 1963
Parentage: Unknown
Available: Eire, Europe, UK

Tony Jacklin
The coral-pink blooms possess a vibrancy which distinguish them from 'City of Leeds'. Very similar in habit but healthier, especially in warmer climates.
Raised by S. McGredy International, New Zealand, 1972
Parentage: 'City of Leeds' × 'Irish Mist'
Available: Australia, Eire, New Zealand, UK

Topsi
The advent of the small patio garden has encouraged tailor-made small plants for situations where the natural vigour of the modern floribunda is too great. 'Topsi' is such a product. The short, 45cm (18in) high, free-flowering plants bear a profusion of bright vermilion flowers.
Raised by M. Tantau, West Germany, 1972
Parentage: 'Fragrant Cloud' × 'Fire Signal'
Available: Canada, Eire, Europe, UK, USA
Royal National Rose Society President's International Trophy Winner and Gold Medal

Trumpeter (Syn. 'Mactru')
A new, vibrant scarlet bedding rose. A consistant and continuous flowering plant. The handsome, deep green foliage is remarkably disease-free.
Raised by S. McGredy International, New Zealand, 1978
Parentage: 'Satchmo' × seedling
Available: Australia, Eire, Europe, New Zealand, UK
Royal National Rose Society Trial Ground Certificate

Yvonne Rabier
A survivor of bygone days. Technically a polyantha rose, 'Yvonne Rabier' is a true delight in an informal border. The pure white small blooms, very double, are borne in large clusters and are very fragrant.
Raised by F. Turbat and Co., France, 1910
Parentage: 'R. wichuraiana' × a polyantha
Available: Eire, Europe, UK

Modern Shrub Roses: Introduction

It is very difficult to define the criteria for classifying a rose as a shrub rather than a bush. For example, could one put a date on when old garden roses ceased and modern shrub roses began? It seems reasonable to use 1900 as the base year for this classification, the exceptions being the Rugosas and the Hybrid Musks.

It is true to say that many modern bush roses will develop into the most magnificent shrubs. 'Queen Elizabeth' and 'Frensham' come quickly to mind. It is also true that some of the modern recurrent flowering climbers, if lightly pruned and controlled, do an equally splendid job in the garden. A shrub rose can be defined as a plant that will develop, with the right amount of pruning, into a specimen plant which is free flowering and produces quality blooms. Such a plant is an important complement to a shrubbery or mixed border. The Royal National Rose Society of Great Britain has defined shrub roses as 'usually taller and/or possibly wider than Bush Roses and particularly suitable for use as specimen plants'.

The shrub as a hedge

Many questions are asked by gardeners when planting shrub roses. How far apart? How big? What is their flowering period? What is their use in a modern garden?

The most useful role that shrub roses can play in a small garden is that of a hedge. A decorative display of scented flowers supported by deep, luxurious growth creates interest in the garden without the monotony of dull cypress or laurel. A hedge of flowers can be used to create divisions between pleasure and kitchen gardens or to provide a screen round unsightly features such as compost heaps or tool sheds.

The Rugosas provide ample material for such positions and the majority of the species require very little in the way of maintenance. They are for the main part disease free, require no pruning, and four of them produce beautiful large hips in the autumn. The rose is a deciduous plant and this fact must be borne in mind when planning a garden. Complete privacy can be obtained with an evergreen hedge, but often at the expense of colour in the garden. A rose hedge will provide variety but will lose its leaves in the winter.

Specimen plants give a diversity of shape and colour when planted singly or in clumps. Such plantings can look most effective in lawns, but care must be taken to select the appropriate varieties. They can also add interest to an orchard or wild garden. The Pemberton Hybrid Musks will provide just this with an immense amount of heavily scented bloom in early summer, followed by a satisfactory second flush early in the autumn. They have the added advantage of requiring little maintenance.

Shrubberies and ground cover

Shrub roses, by their very nature and name, must be appropriate in shrubberies. Grouped in clusters of three or five they will create splashes of colour in the summer and, with the majority of varieties, again in the early autumn when colour is so scarce.

The rose, as a genus, is a plant that needs light. It does not necessarily require full sunlight but, at the least, freedom from the heavy shade of plants in a border. Care should therefore be taken to plant shrub roses where they will respond to this preferential treatment, more especially in the early spring when the light factor is most critical.

The rose being used for ground cover is a relatively recent horticultural practice. The economics of big municipal planting have called for inexpensive but adequate material which the rose has supplied. Several varieties are now propagated by the thousand to provide material for landscaping projects.

Planting and maintenance

The average shrub rose received from the nursery is disproportionate in size to its eventual development. Modern packaging requires a standard plant about 37–60cm (15in–2ft) high. It will require, like any rose, good planting conditions although it is the toughest of all types of rose. No staking should be required,

certainly not for the first year or two. Eventually some of the bigger specimens will require support but this should be unobtrusive and not consist of ugly great poles sticking up through the bush. Three posts planted 1.5–1.8m (5–6ft) apart, approximately 1.2m (4ft) high, supporting a triangle of heavy wood, will help control the more vigorous varieties. A 'Nevada' in all its glory comfortably supported by such a triangular arrangement adds beauty and serenity to the garden.

There are about 250 shrub roses available and they all require pruning by different methods. Trim rather than prune; develop the plant so that it achieves its maximum effect in a natural way. Never cut back strong young growths. Allow shrub roses their natural freedom and they will produce an abundance of flower. It is better to control a plant, particularly a vigorous specimen, by thinning out old wood, so giving access to sunlight at the base. This will also encourage a continuity of young growth that should create the quality and abundance of flower expected.

Shrub roses are divided into recurrent and non-recurrent flowering groups. Beyond that one must discuss them by families associated with their original habit of growth. They are not by nature particularly fastidious and require very little in the way of pest and disease control. Plant for plant they are the most rewarding of all the rose family and always give great pleasure.

Above, far left
'Ballerina' has large clusters of white-eyed pink blooms.
Above centre
The pink flowers of 'Yesterday' turn lavender as they age.
Above
'Fountain' is a vigorous shrub with large, blood-red blooms.
Far left
'Nevada' produces large, creamy-white flowers.
Left
'Golden Wings' has creamy-yellow flowers set off by stamens of buff-yellow.
Opposite page
Throughout the summer 'Cornelia' carries clusters of small, fragrant pink flowers.

Modern Shrub Roses: A-Z

Note: The availability of shrub roses is not well-documented. Local and national rose societies may be able to offer advice on the availability of these varieties in particular areas.

Recurrent shrub roses
Hybrid Musks
The Rev. Joseph Pemberton was a famous rosarian who resigned his living to devote his life to roses. When he died early in this century, he left a legacy of splendid Hybrid Musk shrubs. They are characterized by an abundance of sweet-smelling blooms produced in large clusters on a tidy plant which, in maturity, is about 1.2–1.5m (4–5ft) high and as wide. These roses require very little maintenance apart from heavy dead-heading. It is advisable to give a boost of fertilizer in mid-summer to produce a flush of bloom in the autumn. These shrubs are available from specialist nurseries in the temperate zones.

Cornelia
Clusters of small apricot-pink flowers, very double, are produced throughout the summer on a vigorous shrub about 1.8m (6ft) in height. The blooms have a pleasing fragrance.
Raised by the Rev. J. H. Pemberton, United Kingdom, 1925
Parentage: Unknown

Felicia
Apricot-pink flowers in clusters turn to a silvery pink. The most productive and floriferous of all the roses in this section. Very useful as specimen plants or as a hedge, but lacking in scent.
Raised by the Rev. J. H. Pemberton, United Kingdom, 1928
Parentage: 'Trier' × 'Ophelia'
Royal National Rose Society Certificate of Merit

Penelope
Light pink clusters of flower with a hint of salmon-apricot pink. The most popular in this section, the open blooms have a beautiful scent and the foliage is a handsome green.
Raised by the Rev. J. H. Pemberton, United Kingdom, 1924
Parentage: 'Ophelia' × seedling
Royal National Rose Society Gold Medal

Trier
Clusters of small, sweetly scented, creamy-white double flowers are produced on a shrub about 1.2m (4ft) high. Pemberton

used this cultivar as the basis of his breeding programme to develop this section.
Raised by P. Lambert, Germany, 1904
Parentage: 'Aglaia' × seedling

Rugosas and Rugosa hybrids
The Rugosa family has more claim to the title 'ornamental shrub' than any other species. The stems are covered in densely packed, sharp bristly thorns. The thick, dark green foliage, totally resistant to disease, contributes to a nicely rounded plant ranging from 90cm–1.8m (3–6ft) high. The blooms have a splendid scent and are followed, in the majority of varieties, by an abundance of large, round red hips which are spectacular. The group is exceedingly tough and, as a native of heathland areas, will survive the roughest of treatment. On ageing the plants tend to grow unkempt and straggly. Pruning in the conventional manner is not recommended – it will encourage ugly top growth. If the shrub gets out of hand, reduce the plant to within 30cm (12in) of the ground during mid-winter. New growth will produce a rehabilitated plant the following summer. These shrubs grow very easily from cuttings, but such propagation will encourage suckering and undisciplined growth. It is better to plant budded material.

Blanc Double de Coubert
A fast growing tall shrub 1.8m (6ft) with very heavily scented, large double white flowers. Not a plant for the small garden.
Raised by Cochet-Cochet, France, 1892
Parentage: Probably *R. rugosa* 'Alba' × 'Sombreuil'

Frau Dagmar Hastrup (Syn. 'Frau Dagmar Hartopp')
The prettiest of all in this group. The delicate, single pink flowers are produced in abundance from early in the season. The hips produced in the autumn are an equally splendid delight. The plant is neat and compact, rarely growing to more than a metre (3ft). It is ideal in a small garden.
Origin and date of introduction unknown

F. J. Grootendorst (Syns. 'Grootendorst', 'Nelkenrose')
Unique in appearance, with clusters of small, bright crimson flowers with a distinct frill to the petals. A useful plant, but possessing no scent or hips. Small, wrinkled leaves.
Raised by De Goey, Netherlands, 1918
Parentage: *R. rugosa typica* × 'Baby Rambler'

A feature of this variety is its ability to sport and produce lateral growths of pale red and pink. One of these, 'Pink Grootendorst', has been stabilized and was introduced by Grootendorst in 1923.

R. rugosa 'Alba'
The large, single, fragrant pure white flowers are followed by bright scarlet hips that would do justice as small tomatoes. A shrub growing to about 1.5m (5ft) with dense green, typically disease-resistant *R. rugosa* foliage.
Discovered in Japan. Origin and parents unknown.

R. rugosa 'Rubra'
Identical in flowering habit but slightly more vigorous than 'Alba'. The large, single, mauve-pink flowers are complemented by distinctive yellow stamens.
Origin and parents unknown

R. rugosa 'Scabrosa'
A slightly smaller form of 'Rubra' which will proliferate from cuttings in an astonishing way. The fragrant blooms are pinker and the hips smaller.
Origin and parents unknown

Roseraie de l'Haÿ
The finest shrub rose in the Rugosas. The large, double, crimson-purple flowers are produced on a vigorous shrub about 1.8m (6ft) tall. The heavy scent fills the garden. The blooms are continuous but do not bear hips. Must not be confused with 'Parfum de l'Haÿ' which is a much inferior semi-climber.
Raised by Cochet-Cochet, France, 1901
Parentage: *R. rugosa rosea* sport

Schneezwerg
Has sometimes been called a miniature 'Blanc Double de Coubert', which is not quite true. The plants are as vigorous but the white flowers are small and lighter, possessing the same heavy fragrance and producing myriads of small, bright red hips in autumn.
Raised by P. Lambert, Germany, 1912
Parentage: Probably *R. rugosa* × *R. bracteata* or a white Polyantha

Recurrent modern shrub roses
Certain types of rose cannot be pigeonholed and placed in tight botanical groups. The criteria for selecting the following varieties are their recurrent nature and garden worthiness.

Ballerina

A dense plant producing large clusters of round, pink flowers with a white centre remarkably similar to phlox. It grows to about 60cm–1.2m (2–4ft) in height and the small, light green foliage is produced in abundance. Probably bred by the Rev. J. H. Pemberton, but attributed to Bentall who introduced so many of the Reverend's seedlings after his death. A similar variety bred by Lambert in Germany is called 'Mozart'. Since its introduction in 1937 hybridists have attempted to improve this novel shrub. The most successful to date has been Harkness with 'Marjorie Fair', a red form with white eye, 1978.
Parentage unknown

Fountain

A vigorous, long-flowering shrub with large, deep blood-red flowers produced in large clusters. The plants usually grow to about 1.5m (5ft) and are healthy and well-clothed with dark green foliage, but some of the more vigorous shoots are brittle and tend to blow out in summer gales.
Raised by M. Tantau, West Germany, 1972
Parentage: Unknown
Royal National Rose Society President's International Trophy Winner and Gold Medal

Fred Loads

A very vigorous, upright grower up to 2.4m (8ft) high, reminiscent of 'Queen Elizabeth'. The large flowers, borne in well-formed trusses, are bright vermilion.
Raised by R. A. Holmes, United Kingdom, 1967
Parentage: 'Orange Sensation' × 'Dorothy Wheatcroft'
Royal National Rose Society Gold Medal and Certificate of Merit

Golden Wings

One of the best flowering shrubs available today. The creamy-yellow, single flowers have a beautiful centre of buff-yellow stamens not unlike 'Mermaid'. The foliage is light green and dense, about 3m (10ft) high.
Raised by R. Shepherd, USA, 1956
Parentage: 'Soeur Thérèse' × (R. spinosissima altaica × 'Ormiston Roy')

Kathleen Ferrier

A free-flowering plant with large clusters of deep salmon-pink flowers with a pleasant fragrance. Spreading habit, about 1.5m (5ft) in height, with deep bronze-green foliage. Suitable for hedges, particularly when lightly pruned.
Raised by G. A. H. Buisman, Netherlands, 1955
Parentage: 'Gartenstolz' × 'Shot Silk'
Royal National Rose Society Trial Ground Certificate

Lavender Lassie

Extremely fragrant, pale lavender clusters of flower on upright growth similar to a large floribunda. In Europe it will grow to about 1.5m (5ft) but has been known to grow to 2.4m (8ft) in the United States.
Raised by W. Kordes Sohne, West Germany, 1959
Parentage: Unknown
Royal National Rose Society Trial Ground Certificate

Nevada

The most vigorous modern shrub today. The large arching sprays, 3–4.5m (10–15ft), are clothed in large, open flowers of creamy-white. Its true character is lost if these are shortened in the spring. The flush of flower in early summer is an astonishing sight and is followed by intermittent flowers for the rest of the summer. A plant for a big garden, but it may get black spot in some areas.
Raised by P. Dot, Spain, 1927
Parentage: Reputed to be 'La Giralda' × R. moyesii
There is a pink sport which occurred simultaneously in three nurseries but is attributed to T. Hilling, England, 1959.

The Fairy

The large clusters of small, pink flowers suggest a polyantha rose, in which category it used to be catalogued. When lightly pruned it will produce a very dense shrub about 90cm–1.2m (3–4ft) tall, late to commence flowering but continuous and healthy.
Discovered by J. A. Bentall, England, 1932
Parentage: A sport of 'Lady Godiva'

Yesterday

Unusual, short-growing small pink flowers are produced in large clusters that turn a pretty lavender as they age. Will grow to about 1.2m (4ft) and is very healthy and fragrant.
Raised by R. Harkness and Co., England, 1974
Parentage: ('Phyllis Bide' × 'Shepherd's Delight') × 'Ballerina'
Royal National Rose Society Certificate of Merit

Non-recurrent modern shrub roses

Horticulturally, it would appear slightly anachronistic for a modern rose to be non-recurrent. Nevertheless, some very valuable plants with this characteristic have recently been bred. These are generally available in the United Kingdom and Europe.

Constance Spry

A vigorous, sprawling shrub with large cup-shaped, fragrant pink blooms flowering early in the season.
Raised by D. Austin, England, 1961
Parentage: 'Belle Isis' × 'Dainty Maid'

Fritz Nobis

The perfectly shaped blooms, of a form similar to a hybrid tea, are produced in small clusters on a large sprawling shrub. The salmon-pink blooms turn to a soft creamy-pink as they age. Considered to be the most beautiful of the modern summer-flowering shrubs.
Raised by W. Kordes Sohne, West Germany, 1940
Parentage: 'Joanna Hill' × R. rubiginosa 'Magnifica'

Frühlingsgold

W. Kordes was a breeder with tremendous depth of knowledge and wisdom. His contribution to the development of the modern rose is phenomenal. In the course of his search for hardiness he produced (using R. spinosissima) a series of very vigorous shrubs of which 'Frühlingsgold' is considered the most successful. Large, arching branches 3m (10ft) high are covered early every summer with large, creamy-yellow, single flowers with a heavy fragrance.
Raised by W. Kordes Sohne, West Germany, 1937
Parentage: 'Joanna Hill' × R. spinosissima 'Hispida'

Ground cover shrub roses

Ground cover plants are fashionable today. They are used in thousands in new town landscaping. They can be equally useful for covering rough areas, unsightly manhole covers or even river banks. 'Max Graf' is probably the most successful, with clusters of bright pink flowers produced in early summer, followed by colourful, dense green foliage with beautiful autumn colouring. Others that are widely used are R. paulii (white) and R. paulii rosea (pink). Hybridists are busy improving this type of plant.

Climbers and Ramblers: Introduction

A hundred and fifty years ago most rose arbours and the like were planted with the more vigorous forms of the old garden roses. True climbers and ramblers were introduced with the discovery of *R. odorata* and *R. chinensis*. They were crossed with forms of *R. arvensis* and *R. moschata* to produce the earliest modern climbers. Similarly *R. multiflora* and *R. wichuraiana*, again used with some of the old garden roses, produced the large family of pendulous, exotic, rampant rambler roses.

Throughout the development of the early ramblers and climbers, one factor dominated the scene. The genetic characteristic ensuring the continuity of the flowering season was completely absent. Consequently, practically all the roses that possessed any pretensions to clothing pergolas or walls were summer flowering only. A peculiarity was the fact that even the freest flowering hybrid tea roses occasionally mutated to produce climbing sports. These were very easy to stabilize when propagated vegetatively (budded) but they all produced only one flush of flower. The big break occurred when hybridizers, principally Kordes and Mc-Gredy, through patient research and not a little luck, bred what we now know as remontant or recurrent flowering climbers. But before discussing this advance, we must define the distinctions between ramblers and climbers.

Differences between climbers and ramblers

A rambler is a variety whose growth is lax. Generally speaking ramblers flower in clusters and, if they are *R. wichuraiana* or *R. multiflora* in origin, produce magnificent displays of bloom relatively early in the summer, with possibly a slight flush of flower in a freak season very late in the autumn. Because of their pendulous growth they are more suitable for pergolas or arches which give support. They require very careful pruning in the early autumn because they make rapid new growth immediately after flowering in the summer. The new growth must be preserved to the almost total exclusion of the old flowering wood, for it is the new wood which produces the major flush of flower in the following season. This fact alone has meant that with smaller gardens, the high cost of labour and the expertise required, this section has almost disappeared from current rose lists.

A climbing rose is stronger in stature, upright in habit and generally produces large flowers, although this last factor is no criterion for classification. The majority of the older climbers were sports of contemporary bush varieties. Although these were mainly hybrid teas, the occasional floribunda sported with its clusters of small blooms. These, with very few exceptions, were summer flowering. Although they did not require the time-consuming and expert pruning of the ramblers, the absence of colour in the autumn detracted from their appeal and the majority have now disappeared.

This has now changed radically. The majority of available plants suitable for growing on walls and trellises or arches are recurrent in their flowering habits and so a change of classification has occurred. The old, strict divisions based on habit of growth have been replaced by frequency and profuseness of flower. To sum up, these varieties can be divided thus:

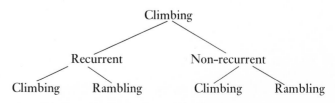

For a brief period the phrase 'continuous flowering' was used instead of recurrent; but this is inaccurate and botanically impossible. Nevertheless, it would be true to say that the productivity of the most recent introductions in the recurrent section is beyond the dreams of the most optimistic breeder of 30 years ago.

Climbers and ramblers for the modern garden

Few generalizations can be made about modern climbers or ramblers; however there are a few salient points to remember when planning a rose garden. The older types are very vigorous, require ample support and must be placed in aspects that will truly benefit them. Many respond to very hot, dry conditions; some are perfectly happy on shady walls; all are gross feeders. The young growths that are made immediately after the summer flush grow with astonishing rapidity and are in the main very brittle. Consequently they must be secured as soon as is practicable. The majority are relatively pest resistant (aphids are probably their biggest enemy) but mildew is persistent in cultivars with Bourbons in their ancestry, e.g. 'Zéphirine Drouhin', and in the *R. wichuraiana/multiflora* seedlings such as 'Dorothy Perkins'. The modern recurrent climbers, because of their ability to produce flower in the autumn, are relatively slower growing. There is complete absence of the coarse summer growth and the maintenance problem is reduced.

Those with *R. kordesii* in their ancestry are very hardy and without exception can be grown in the most difficult positions, to the point where they may be called sub-zero temperature roses. Their maintenance requires only that they be heavily dead-headed, nothing more. Their climbing habit is much slower and every bit of available wood must be preserved to build a fabric of good coverage. Many of the McGredy climbers, with the exception of 'Schoolgirl', are useful as pillar roses. All make decorative large shrubs.

Two alternative uses in the garden may be mentioned for the old ramblers. The *wichuraianas*, such as 'Albéric Barbier', are used to produce weeping standard or umbrella roses. Their lax, informal growth is admirably suited for propagation on a stem about 1.5–1.8m (5–6ft) tall. The use of trainers or umbrellas is not to be recommended and is usually an indication that the wrong variety is being used for this purpose. A weeping standard (tree rose) should appear naturally pendulous and not be confined or trained by artificial means. Ramblers may also be used as ground cover material. The spectacle of rambling roses gracing the edge of a lake, pond or river is possibly one of the most beautiful and natural sights of the wild garden.

Climbing and rambling roses are tough and tolerant, but possibly require more care than other types of rose. However, they can be more rewarding, both culturally and aesthetically, than any other group in the genus *Rosa*.

Above, far left
'Danse du Feu', a bright orange-scarlet climber.
Above, centre
'Schoolgirl' bears hybrid tea sized blooms of apricot-orange with a heavy fragrance.
Above
The remarkable 'Mermaid', a rose with open, sulphur-yellow flowers and amber stamens. The luxuriant foliage is almost evergreen.
Below left
The cream and pink blooms of 'Handel'.
Left
'Pink Perpêtue' has bright pink flowers with a carmine reverse which are produced in large clusters.
Opposite page
'Compassion' is free flowering and healthy. Its fragrant, orange-salmon blooms are in small clusters.

Climbers and Ramblers: A-Z

This section has been divided in broad terms according to habit of growth and flowering potential. The plants are not necessarily identical in their characteristics, but these divisions will help when planning a garden.

Recurrent flowering ramblers
The majority of these are derived from *R. kordesii* seedlings. They are relatively lax in growth, very hardy and all have a delightful scent.

Coral Dawn
The deep coral-pink blooms have a most pleasing scent and are large, borne in clusters on a moderately vigorous plant of about 3m (10ft). Hardy but will benefit from a warm position.
Raised by Jackson and Perkins Co., USA, 1952
Parentage: ('New Dawn' seedling × unnamed yellow) × unnamed polyantha
Available: Canada, Eire, Europe, UK, USA

Dortmund
A true *R. kordesii* climber/rambler. The large clusters of single flowers are crimson-red with a white eye. Growing to about 2.4m (8ft), the glossy green foliage is very disease resistant. If the flowers are not dead-headed large clusters of bright red hips are borne in the autumn but will curtail late flowering. Suitable for all aspects but thrives on a shady wall.
Raised by W. Kordes Sohne, West Germany, 1955
Parentage: Seedling × *R. kordesii*
Available: Australia, Eire, Europe, New Zealand, UK

Hamburger Phoenix
The very healthy, dark green foliage compliments clusters of dark crimson-scarlet flowers with a slight scent. Like 'Dortmund', it produces a multitude of hips if not dead-headed. Will grow to 3m (10ft).
Raised by W. Kordes Sohne, West Germany, 1954
Parentage: *R. kordesii* × seedling
Available: Eire, Europe, UK
Royal National Rose Society Trial Ground Certificate

Leverkusen
A moderately vigorous plant that will grow to about 3m (10ft). The creamy-yellow flowers in clusters of three or four have a delicate scent and the foliage is a medium green. The closest yet to a rambler with recurrent flowering characteristics.

Raised by W. Kordes Sohne, West Germany, 1954
Parentage: *R. kordesii* × 'Golden Glow'
Available: Australia, Eire, Europe, New Zealand, UK

New Dawn
A plant which can justifiably be said to have been born before its time. The very pale, silvery-pink flowers have a powerful scent and are produced in clusters throughout the summer. Although slow growing it will eventually go to 3.6m (12ft). Has been used as a valuable parent in breeding.
Introduced by H. A. Dreer, USA, 1930
Parentage: 'Dr. W. van Fleet' sport
Available: Worldwide but particularly popular in northern Europe where its hardiness excels.

Parkdirektor Riggers
One of the most widely grown of the *kordesii* family, it is nevertheless the most disappointing. Very vigorous, 4.5m (15ft) tall, the clusters of large single scarlet flowers are produced on large stems with deep green, glossy foliage which has now become subject to mildew and black spot.
Raised by W. Kordes Sohne, West Germany, 1957
Parentage: *R. kordesii* × 'Our Princess'
Available: Australia, Eire, Europe, New Zealand, UK

Recurrent flowering climbers
This group consists of the most widely grown climbing plants today. They are ideally suited to small, modern gardens because of their smaller stature and plentiful supply of bloom. Many of them are equally suitable for clothing wattle fencing 1.8m (6ft) high or as pillar roses 2.4m (8ft) high. The varieties with these limited characteristics are listed first. With a minimum of support and judicious annual pruning to 1.2m (4ft), they all make splendid shrubs.

Bantry Bay
Light rose-pink clusters of semi-double flowers almost like the 'Dog Rose' in appearance. Vigorous and free with glossy, deep green, healthy foliage.
Raised by S. McGredy International, New Zealand, 1967
Parentage: 'New Dawn' × 'Korona'
Available: Canada, Eire, UK, USA
Royal National Rose Society Certificate of Merit

Compassion
The most successful English-bred climber

to date. The medium-sized, very fragrant blooms of pale orange-salmon have a lighter reverse and are produced in small clusters. Moderate in growth 2.4m (8ft) but free flowering and healthy.
Raised by R. Harkness and Co., England, 1973
Parentage: 'White Cockade' × 'Prima Ballerina'
Available: Canada, Eire, Europe, UK, USA
Royal National Rose Society Trial Ground Certificate; Henry Edland Memorial Medal for Fragrance

Copenhagen
The most beautiful scarlet flowers in this range. The blooms are fragrant and shapely with large, handsome foliage.
Raised by D. T. Poulsen, Denmark, 1964
Parentage: Seedling × 'Ena Harkness'
Available: Canada, Eire, Europe, UK, USA
Royal National Rose Society Certificate of Merit

Danse du Feu (Syn. 'Spectacular')
A bright orange-scarlet climber with an abundance of bloom early in the season followed by limited recurrent flowering.
Raised by Mallerin, France, 1954
Parentage: 'Paul's Scarlet Climber' × *R. multiflora* seedling
Available: Australia, Eire, Europe, New Zealand, UK
Royal National Rose Society Certificate of Merit

Golden Showers
The most popular of all yellow climbers. Slow to start but magnificent in its production of flower. The golden-yellow, pointed flowers are produced in small clusters.
Raised by: Dr. W. L. Lammerts, 1956
Parentage: 'Charlotte Armstrong' × 'Capt. Thomas'
Available: Australia, Canada, Eire, Europe, New Zealand, UK, USA
Portland Gold Medal, Oregon, USA, and All America Rose Selections Award

Handel
A beautiful cream with the edge of the petals flushed deep pink, producing an almost theatrical effect. Very similar in growth to 'Golden Showers'.
Raised by S. McGredy International, New Zealand, 1965
Parentage: 'Columbine' × 'Heidelberg'
Available: Australia, Canada, Eire,

Europe, New Zealand, UK, USA
Royal National Rose Society Trial Ground
Certificate

Joseph's Coat
Could well be described as a climbing
'Masquerade', to which it is remarkably
similar. The semi-double, bright yellow
flowers turning orange and cherry-red are
produced in large clusters on a plant of
moderate growth.
Raised by Armstrong and Swim, USA,
1964
Parentage: 'Buccaneer' × 'Circus'
Available: Canada, Eire, UK, USA
Royal National Rose Society Certificate of
Merit; Bagatelle Gold Medal, Paris

Pink Perpêtue
A moderate grower producing large clus-
ters of bright rose-pink flowers with a
carmine reverse. A good second crop of
flowers.
Raised by C. Gregory and Son, England,
1965
Parentage: 'Danse du Feu' × 'New Dawn'
Available: Australia, Eire, Europe, New
Zealand, UK
Royal National Rose Society Certificate of
Merit; Bagatelle Gold Medal, Paris

Royal Gold
Quite the deepest golden-yellow in climbing roses. The large well-formed flowers,
produced in small clusters, are astonish-
ingly vivid. The plant is, however, prone to
frost damage and must be grown on a warm
wall.
Raised by D. Morey, USA, 1957
Parentage: 'Climbing Goldilocks' × 'Lydia'
Available: Australia, Canada, Eire, New
Zealand, UK, USA

Zéphirine Drouhin
A very famous semi-climber, technically a
Bourbon. The cerise-carmine flowers with
a strong scent are produced continuously
from mid-summer. The smooth wood has
given rise to its name of 'the thornless rose'.
Grows to 3.6m (12ft) or more. Very prone
to black spot and mildew like so many with
Bourbon origins. There is a pale pink sport,
'Kathleen Harrop' introduced by Dickson,
Northern Ireland in 1919.
Raised by Bizot, France, 1868
Parentage: Unknown
Available: Worldwide

To complete this section four more varieties are included which are similar but
much more vigorous in habit.

Altissimo
An astonishing blood-red. The very large,
single flowers have a central feature of
bright golden stamens. It is long lasting
and weather resistant.
Raised by Delbard-Chabert, France, 1967
Parentage: 'Tenor' × seedling
Available: Australia, Canada, Eire,
Europe, New Zealand, UK, USA
Royal National Rose Society Certificate of
Merit

Dreaming Spires
A vigorous bright golden-yellow, hardy
and prolific. The medium-sized blooms are
slightly scented. Dark green foliage.
Raised by John Mattock, Ltd., England,
1973
Parentage: 'Buccaneer' × 'Arthur Bell'
Available: Eire, Europe, UK
City of Belfast Gold Medal

Mermaid
The open, sulphur-yellow flowers with
amber stamens are a truly memorable
sight. A connoisseur's rose. An established
plant will grow 9–12m high (30–40ft), with
luxuriant, glossy green foliage which is
retained on the climbers to give an almost
evergreen effect. It is somewhat tempera-
mental and will stand moribund for a
season before going into growth. In warm
areas it will grace a shady wall but has been
known to be cut down by frost in a severe
winter.
Raised by W. Paul, England, 1918
Parentage: *R. bracteata* × double yellow
Tea rose
Available: Most parts of the world with the
exclusion of the colder temperate zones.
Royal National Rose Society Gold Medal

Schoolgirl
A fast-growing climber in the fashionable
colours of apricot-orange. The large hybrid
tea-sized blooms have a heavy fragrance.
The stems are liable to go bare at the base
unless properly pruned and trained.
Raised by S. McGredy International, New
Zealand, 1964
Parentage: 'Coral Dawn' × 'Belle Blonde'
Available: Canada, Eire, UK, USA

Summer-flowering climbers
The majority of these are mutations or
climbing sports of well-known bush roses.
The blooms are generally bigger than their
dwarf counterparts, and they possess an
astonishing vigour, growing to 6 or 9m
(20–30ft). They are generally available
throughout the world.

Clmbg Ena Harkness: Scarlet crimson;
fragrant
Clmbg Etoile de Hollande: Deep crimson; fragrant
Clmbg Iceberg: White
Clmbg Masquerade: Yellow/pink/red
Clmbg Mrs Sam McGredy: Copper/
orange/bronze
These are worth growing for the magnificent flush of flower early in the season,
but are apt to look dreary in late summer.
Their vigour precludes them from all but
the largest gardens. They require little in
the way of maintenance other than a
tedious pruning in late autumn or early
winter. The young growths should be tied
back carefully and the flowering wood cut
back to within 5cm (2in) of the main stem.

Summer-flowering ramblers
The memory of Victorian pergolas and
arbours clothed in a profusion of rose buds
is revived with these vigorous examples of
the *R. wichuraiana* and *R. multiflora* seedlings. They fall into three sections because
of their slightly different habits. These
varieties are generally available.

The *wichuraianas* are fast-growing,
beautifully furnished plants with glossy
foliage. The blooms are small in size and
pleasantly scented. Examples of these
include:

Albéric Barbier: Creamy-yellow
Albertine: Soft salmon and coppery-pink
buds
Crimson Shower: A modern scarlet with
clusters of flowers that appear later than
most of this type.
Dorothy Perkins: An old pink favourite
which is now prone to mildew.
Emily Gray: Rich golden-yellow
François Juranville: Salmon-pink

The *multiflora* seedlings possess an even
greater vigour, require a vast amount of
space and are quite capable of climbing
12–15m (40–50ft) into old trees or over
buildings where they can gain support.
Amethyste: Amethyst-purple
Bobby James: White
The Garland: White, lightly tinged pink
Wedding Day: Pale yellow fading to white

Two varieties, very similar in character
to the *multiflora* group, are botanically
species in their own right. Both produce
large clusters of small, bright red hips in
the autumn.
R. filipes 'Kiftsgate': Creamy-white
R. longiscuspis: White

Miniature Roses: Introduction and A-Z

Even the most assiduous botanical scholar would have to admit that the origin of the miniature rose is obscure. We know that when the first *R. chinensis* species and their cultivars were introduced to western civilizations, a form of *R. chinensis* 'Minima' did exist. We also know that it was unfortunately a misnomer and modern research suggests that the seedling in question was a miniature form of *R. chinensis* 'Semperflorens'. The fact remains that certain types of dwarf rose were beloved of the Victorians, who propagated them by seed and cuttings to produce a wide range of roses for culture in pots.

Towards the end of the nineteenth century this fashion had run its course. Miniatures had almost disappeared when, in 1918, an observant Swiss army officer, Major Roulet, found a form of double pink miniature rose grown in pots in a Swiss village. A local plantsman 'on information received' rescued this plant and promptly introduced it as *R. roulettii*.

The modern miniature rose owes its existence to this remarkable piece of observation and opportunism. Since then hybridists have used *R. roulettii* as the base from which to develop miniatures into the wide selection available today. The popularity of these plants, especially in small town gardens where their size is appropriate, is quite phenomenal and has developed only in the last ten years. Ironically, as recently as 1971 a famous rosarian remarked that the miniature rose was 'not really part of the general garden scene'.

Miniature roses need the same attention as an ordinary garden bush rose. They are not alpines or rockery plants – they require good, deep soil, regular feeding and pruning. Their position in the garden is relative to their dwarf habit. The ideal place for them is on the edges of borders and in clumps on restricted pathways. They enhance raised beds on walls and will grow admirably in pots and troughs.

These roses must not be treated as house plants. Nevertheless, a container of miniature roses brought into the conservatory or living area will bring great joy when the plants are in flower. After blooming they should be trimmed to encourage new growth and they will need a spell outside before being brought indoors once more. Miniature roses are usually propagated from cuttings or grafted, and will retain their dwarf stature with these methods. Some of the modern varieties have extra vigour and could well be called patio roses.

The miniature roses listed here are a small selection of the vast number being marketed at present. Unfortunately many miniature roses have a variety of synonyms causing confusion and reducing the numbers catalogued. Mention should be made of the tremendous work being done by the celebrated American hybridist Ralph Moore. He has succeeded in producing miniature Moss roses with marked success, but unfortunately they are susceptible to disease and in cool climates may not be weather hardy. The varieties available are:

Dresden Doll: Double pink, 1977
Fairy Moss: Rose red, 1969
Kara: Single pink, 1976
Paint Brush: Buff yellow, 1977

Angela Rippon (Syns. 'Ocaru', 'Ocarina')
A compact modern plant with dainty double blooms of salmon-pink, about 30cm (12in) high.
Raised by G. de Ruiter, Netherlands, 1978
Parentage: 'Rosy Jervel' × 'Zorina'
Available: Eire, Europe, UK

Baby Gold Star (Syn. 'Estrellita de Oro')
A popular miniature whose deep golden-yellow blooms fading to cream have a slight scent. If grown on its own roots it will remain compact, but grafted or budded plants can grow to 45cm (18in).
Raised by P. Dot, Spain, 1935. Not introduced until 1940
Parentage: 'Eduardo Toda' × *R. roulettii*
Available: Canada, Eire, Europe, UK, USA

Baby Masquerade (Syns. 'Baby Carnaval', 'Baby Maskerade')
A most prolific plant, bearing in miniature the characteristics of the floribunda 'Masquerade'. The yellow blooms, turning pink and scarlet, are freely produced on a stout plant about 30cm (12in) high. Needs dead-heading to look neat.
Raised by M. Tantau, West Germany, 1956
Parentage: 'Peon' (Syn. 'Tom Thumb') ×

Above left
'Royal Salute', a vigorous miniature or patio rose which blooms almost continuously.
Above right
'Baby Masquerade' is a prolific plant bearing yellow flowers that turn to pink and scarlet.
Left
The beautifully shaped miniature blooms of 'Pour Toi' are white, tinted yellow at the base.

'Masquerade'
Available: Worldwide

Colibre

A delightful, vivid orange-yellow edged with coral. The plant is bushy with glossy green foliage and grows tidily to about 30cm (12in).
Raised by Meilland, France, 1958
Parentage: 'Goldilocks' × 'Perla de Montserrat'
Available: Australia, Canada, Eire, Europe, New Zealand, UK, USA
Golden Rose of the Hague

Darling Flame (Syn. 'Minuetto')

A free-flowering vermilion-orange with a good bushy habit, about 30cm (12in) high. Has slight fragrance and vigorous growth.
Raised by Meilland, France, 1971
Parentage: ('Rimosa' × 'Rosina') × 'Zambra'
Available: Canada, Eire, Europe, UK, USA

Frosty

Clusters of small, white flowers with a green eye. The compact bush has a spreading habit to suggest a miniature ground cover plant.
Raised by R. Moore, USA, 1953
Parentage: *R. wichuraiana* × unnamed seedling
Available: Canada, Eire, UK, USA

Little Sunset

Small, double flowers of salmon orange-pink with yellow shading. About 25cm (10in) high.
Raised by W. Kordes Sohne, West Germany, 1967
Parentage: Seedling × 'Tom Thumb'
Available: Australia, Canada, Eire, Europe, New Zealand, UK, USA

Mon Trésor (Syns. 'Red Imp', 'Maid Marion')

A true miniature about 22cm (9in) high with flat, slightly fragrant blooms of scarlet-crimson.
Raised by J. de Vink, Netherlands, 1951
Parentage: 'Ellen Poulsen' × 'Tom Thumb'
Available: Australia, Canada, Eire, Europe, New Zealand, UK, USA

New Penny

Small, semi-double flowers of coppery salmon-pink freely produced with a slight fragrance – about 25cm (10in) high.
Raised by R. Moore, USA, 1962

Parentage: (*R. wichuraiana* × 'Floradora') × unnamed seedling
Available: Canada, Eire, UK, USA

Perla de Alcanada (Syns. 'Baby Crimson', 'Pearl of Canada', 'Titania', 'Wheatcroft's Baby Crimson')

A tough, free-flowering plant with dark glossy foliage. The clusters of reddish-carmine blooms are touched with white at the base. 30cm (12in) high.
Raised by P. Dot, Spain, 1944
Parentage: 'Perle des Rouges' × *R. roulettii*
Available: Canada, Eire, Europe, UK, USA

Pour Toi (Syns. 'Para Ti', 'For You', 'Wendy')

Beautifully formed, almost perfectly produced, miniature blooms of cream turning white. A favourite miniature with a vigorous, free-flowering habit about 30–45cm (12–18in) in height.
Raised by P. Dot, Spain, 1946
Parentage: 'Eduardo Toda' × 'Pompon de Paris'
Available: Worldwide

R. roulettii

A dainty plant with clusters of rose-pink flowers about 25cm (10in) high. Considered the forebear of the miniature rose. Genetically the dwarfing habit is dominant and has remained so in the evolution of the modern miniature.
Discovered by Major Roulet, Switzerland, 1918
Parentage: Unknown
Available: Worldwide

Rosina (Syns. 'Josephine Wheatcroft', 'Yellow Sweetheart')

Similar in habit and growth to 'Pour Toi'. The bright yellow flowers have a slight fragrance. Not the easiest to propagate from cuttings but it will make a plant about 30–45cm (12–18in) high on a grafted stock.
Raised by P. Dot, Spain. Introduced 1951 (but raised in 1936)
Parentage: 'Eduardo Toda' × *R. roulettii*
Available: Worldwide

Rosmarin

Clusters of soft, light-pink, large flowers with a darker reverse. A fine bushy grower about 30cm (12in) high.
Raised by W. Kordes Sohne, West Germany, 1965
Parentage: 'Tom Thumb' × 'Dacapo'

Available: Australia, Eire, Europe, New Zealand, UK

Royal Salute

A strong-growing, miniature/patio rose about 30–45cm (12–18in) in height. The blooms of rose-pink have a little fragrance and are almost continuous in their production. Such is the popularity of miniatures that in 1977 33,000 of this variety were sold to raise funds for the Queen's Silver Jubilee Appeal in Great Britain.
Raised by S. McGredy International, New Zealand, 1977
Parentage: 'New Penny' × 'Marlena'
Available: Canada, Eire, UK, USA

Scarlet Gem (Syn. 'Scarlet Pimpernel')

Small, bright scarlet flowers are produced on a compact bush about 25cm (10in) high. The foliage is dark and glossy.
Raised by Meilland, France, 1961
Parentage: ('Moulin Rouge' × 'Fashion') × ('Perla de Montserrat' × 'Perla de Alcanada')
Available: Australia, Canada, Eire, Europe, New Zealand, UK, USA

Starina

A vivid orange-scarlet about 25cm (10in) tall. The plant is free and bushy but it appears to be hard to propagate in some countries.
Raised by Meilland, France, 1965
Parentage: ('Dany Robin' × 'Fire King') × 'Perla de Montserrat'
Available: Australia, Canada, Eire, Europe, New Zealand, UK, USA

Sweet Fairy

The beautiful appleblossom-pink flowers are very double with pointed petals and a slight fragrance. A sturdy free-flowering bush about 25cm (10in) high.
Raised by J. de Vink, Netherlands, 1946
Parentage: 'Peon' (Syn. 'Tom Thumb') × unnamed seedling
Available: Worldwide

Wee Man

A stout plant with fragrant crimson-scarlet flowers freely produced on a bush about 30cm (12in) high. Sometimes prone to black spot.
Raised by S. McGredy International, New Zealand, 1974
Parentage: 'Little Flirt' × 'Marlena'
Available: Canada, Eire, Europe, UK, USA
Royal National Rose Society Certificate of Merit

The Rose in Your Garden

Life Cycle of the Garden Rose

A rose is no sooner alive than it is divided into two parts, the roots and the shoots. Both parts are joined at a point near ground level. The division is evident where the bark changes its nature from that of root to shoot.

The root system

The main purpose of the roots is to anchor the plant. This being accomplished, they absorb water from the soil through pores on their surface. The water contains such minerals in solution as the plant needs for its growth. Roots need the soil to be closely packed around them. For this reason they do not like to be loosened by gardeners digging in the rose bed.

When the roots are growing freely they split into many small sub-divisions known as rootlets. Their young growths are soft and pale in colour and are called root hairs. Occasionally the roots produce aerial shoots called suckers. This is a survival technique in case the plant above the ground should be destroyed.

The shoots and leaves

The shoots are more complex because they have many different parts. The shoot consists of pith at the centre, gradually hardening into wood. Just underneath the bark are the routes by which food supplies are carried in the stem. These are where the water, minerals and chemicals are moved, so one must be careful not to damage stems with careless blows from tools.

The stems are adorned with prickles and leaves. The prickles have two purposes, one being to deter animals which threaten damage, the other to gain some support from the surrounding vegetation. This is especially valuable to climbing and trailing roses in their native habitat; prickles may very well be the reason that roses started to climb at all.

Leaves are the lungs and factory of the plant. They absorb gases from the air, moisture and minerals from the water that falls on them, and most important of all, sunlight. It is the sun which makes the green particles within the leaf move. From this movement comes the manufacture of carbohydrates which are transported about the plant, undergoing chemical reactions as they move and turning into food, wood, colour, scent or whatever else the plant needs. If the leaves are taken away, all this activity comes to a halt.

The leaves of a rose are pinnate, that is, instead of being a single leaf, they are split into leaflets (always of an odd number), arranged two by two along the leafstalk, with one at the end. Roses have from three to 19 leaflets but the usual numbers on garden roses are five or seven.

Where the leafstalk meets the stem it bears a small piece of leaf on each side. These two fragments are called stipules. Just above the place where the stipule-clad leafstalk joins the stem, there is almost invariably an eye which is a dormant growth bud capable of becoming a shoot in its own right. These eyes are of importance in both pruning and propagation.

A shoot arising from the base of the plant is called a basal shoot. A very prominent shoot is known as a main shoot. When one of the eyes on a shoot grows outwards and becomes a shoot in its own right, it is known as a lateral or side shoot. Shoots growing from a side shoot are known as sub-laterals.

The rose flower

The purpose of the roots and shoots is to crown the latter with flowers and eventually seeds. The stalk bearing a flower bud is called the pedicel. Each flower bud is protected by a leafy covering

Parts of the Rose

1	Rootstock	16	Lateral or side shoot
2	Roots	17	Sub-lateral
3	Rootlets	18	Pedicel
4	Root hairs	19	Calyx
5	Sucker	20	Sepal
6	Shoot	21	Petal
7	Bark	22	Stamen
8	Prickles	23	Anther
9	Leaf	24	Pollen
10	Leaflet	25	Pistil
11	Leafstalk	26	Stigma
12	Stipule	27	Seed pod
13	Eye	28	Hip
14	Basal shoot	29	Flower cluster
15	Main shoot		

called the calyx which unfolds into five segments called sepals, thereby revealing the petals. When the petals in turn open, the stamens can be seen standing in a ring. The pollen is found on the anthers at the top of the stamens. The pollen is intended to fall on the pistils, which compose the very centre of the flower. Each pistil has a sticky top, known as the stigma, to receive the pollen. The pollen grows down the style or stem of the pistil to fuse with the egg cell in the seed pod below the flower. When the seed pod matures it is called a hip.

Most roses produce many flowers together in a head called a cluster. Some produce their flowers one to a stem, or singly. A rose of five petals is called single; up to about fifteen, semi-double; and with more petals, provided they hold together for a reasonable time, double.

Roses have two quite different habits of flowering. Some produce a flower on the end of nearly every shoot. If they continue growing through the season they are remontant, that is they flower twice or more often in a season. Other roses, including most of the world's wild roses, do not flower at the end of every shoot. They grow a shoot with no blooms on it at all and in the following year they bear flowers on laterals borne on that shoot. The result of this habit is usually to give only one season of bloom, usually in summer or late spring.

Growth and regeneration

Such is the blueprint of a rose, or rather the outline, for a living plant hides many complexities within itself. A rose is designed for a life in competition with many other plants. It cannot lift its head out of danger, like a tree, but must survive the perils of its natural environment, of which the most frequent are fire, frost and being eaten. The rose's response to these dangers is regeneration from the base of the plant or even from the roots.

Therefore rose shoots are not designed to live to a great age – they grow and hastily ripen before winter. Once their wood is hard they should be safe from frost. In time, they become more woody and the bark suffers the injuries of the years until the channel under the bark is no longer a free-flowing canal for supplies. The plant then finds an easier route by growing other young shoots and the sap no longer moves very much in the old shoot. It becomes starved: its leaves become fewer and its flowers smaller until one day it is dead. It is important to remember this when pruning. The gardener should anticipate the natural life cycle of the rose by removing the parts it is about to discard.

Armed with these facts about the life cycle of the rose, the gardener can gain a special understanding of a plant's needs and learn how to make his roses thrive.

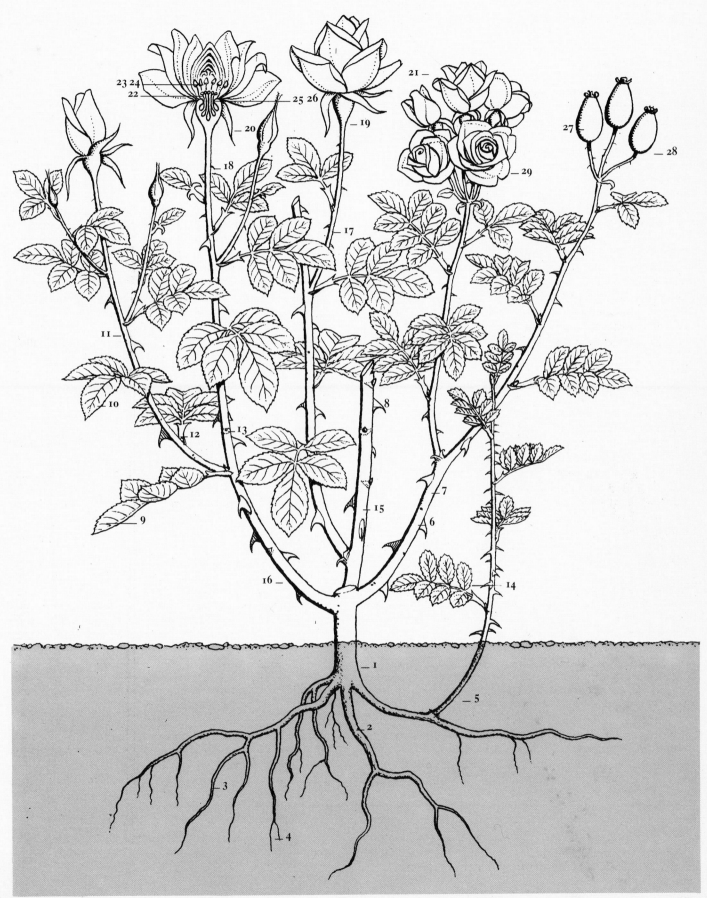

Planting and Cultivation

There is a rose for every climate. In general, the cooler the climate the deeper and more subtle are the colours. Intense sunlight bleaches yellow and pastel shades and limits the choice to red and pink varieties. Countries with hot, regular sunshine tend to favour floribunda roses which quickly repeat their flowers. Their hybrid teas are likely to be the 'cabbage' type with so many petals that they are slow to open. The latter type of rose does not do well in a cool, wet climate. In this type of climate hybrid teas are preferable which have around 30 petals to the bloom. The petals should reflex away from the centre of the bloom. If they lie close together like a cabbage they will spoil and go rotten before opening in a wet season.

Visiting nurseries

Look for a local specialist rose grower and visit his premises at least twice in the early summer and early in the autumn. Make a point of asking for garden varieties unless big exhibition varieties, requiring special attention, have taken your fancy. Ask the nurseryman for roses that suit your locality and the position you have in mind. Floribunda roses give a grand show but hybrid tea blooms are beautiful individuals which should be enjoyed at close range.

In addition to visiting your local nursery, it is a good idea to look at the roses on display in public gardens. Local rose societies and

Adaptability of the rose

Ground cover roses
These spread by means of long fronds which cover banks and tumble over low, retaining walls. Height can vary between 12–30cm (5–12in). The spread can be much greater.

Miniature roses
Grown in pots, troughs, rockeries and window boxes and are best spaced at around 30cm (12in). They grow from 12–30cm (5–12in) high.

Dwarf floribundas
Sometimes called cushion roses. These are used for edging paths and borders and for hiding the legginess of some of the taller roses. They can be planted as close as 30cm (12in) for a continuous or low hedge effect.

Floribundas
Grow from 45–90cm (18in–3ft) but can grow taller in certain conditions.

Hybrid teas
Grow around 75cm–1.07m ($2\frac{1}{2}$–$3\frac{1}{2}$ft) but a few exceptionally tall varieties will grow to 1.5m (5ft) high.

Shrub and species roses
For borders or informal hedges. Self-supporting up to a height of 1.5m (5ft).

Standard or tree roses
Usually budded at a height of 1m ($3\frac{1}{4}$ft), they grow upwards a further 45cm (18in) from this point.

Weeping standards
Used as centrepieces or special features. These weep down from the budding point which is usually at around 1.2m (4ft).

Ramblers
For an informal bramble effect, for use as pillar roses, or for climbing against a wall to a height of around 2.4m (8ft). The habit of growth is more lax than that of climbers.

Repeat-flowering climbers
For fences, pergolas and walls, these perform well up to a height of approximately 4m (12ft).

Climbing sports of hybrid teas and floribundas
These are the tallest-growing roses which can often reach to 9m (30ft) in height.

Climbing sports of hybrid teas and floribundas   Repeat-flowering climbers   Ramblers   Weeping standards   Standard or tree roses   Shrub and species roses

experienced amateur growers will often offer valuable advice on the rose varieties which do well in your area. Every rose has its day and looks its best during the first flush of flower. Any faults or proneness to disease do not show up until mid-season when mildew and black spot test the rose's defences. However, roses have been adapted to suit almost any situation.

Choosing the site

Ideally hybrid teas should be placed in the most sheltered, sunny spot in the rose garden. The free-flowering floribundas are better able to withstand windy sites. Very windy situations can benefit from the lovely colours of dwarf-growing roses which are almost immune to the buffeting which gales administer to the taller varieties.

Roses do not like to be overhung by trees and they should enjoy at least half of the day's sunlight. The rose is hardy and is not troubled by frost in temperate latitudes but in countries that regularly experience sub-zero temperatures care has to be taken to protect the bushes throughout winter with layers of straw or other insulating material held in place with stakes or twigs.

Tender, new spring growth in general, and standard roses in particular, are vulnerable to 'burning' and dehydration caused by moving sub-zero air. Even in windless conditions, frost – which is dense, heavy air – will actually 'flow' downhill and through gaps in hedges and walls. Sites that lie in the path of flowing frost, or which are situated in pockets or hollows that tend to encourage frosty conditions, should not be considered suitable for a rose bed.

Drainage

The best rose gardens have good soil drainage, either natural or contrived. Perpetually wet soil is sad and acid and does not favour the rose which, while having a reasonable tolerance for acid soil, much prefers a neutral (neither acid nor alkaline) condition. Plants that grow naturally in or around the site give a good pointer to the conditions. Rhododendrons, for example, probably indicate over-acid conditions. Thriving clematis will probably indicate alkaline conditions. Soil testing kits which require ordinary distilled water and which show the acidity or otherwise (the pH value) of your soil are available from most garden shops.

Soil types

Acid soils are relatively easy to treat with a dressing of lime, preferably hydrated lime. Alkaline soils in temperate climates are liable to produce conditions that lock up the magnesium in the soil and cause yellowing of leaves. Specialist knowledge is required to treat very alkaline soil thoroughly. Digging, and the addition of peat and other humus-forming matter, is beneficial but since alkaline soil locks up the soil magnesium, iron and other essential minerals, it is often easier to treat the plant with a specially manufactured product rather than the soil.

It is generally supposed that roses prefer to grow in clay but in fact, in common with most other garden plants, they prefer to grow in a medium loam of a neutral pH (about 7). The origin of the myth probably lies in the fact that roses will give a tolerably good showing on heavy soils that defeat other flowering plants.

Ordering roses

Try to place your order with the rose nursery as early as possible to ensure that yours is among the first to receive attention as soon as the nursery starts to send out roses. A nurseryman will sometimes take an order in good faith for a variety which, when harvested, fails to live up to his expectations. Unless you have made special arrangements with the nursery be sure to stipulate 'no substitutes'. It has become generally accepted nursery practice to make changes to an order when a variety becomes sold out.

Selecting roses

A specialist rose nursery relies upon the quality of its produce for the continued patronage of its customers and may be relied upon to serve you with sound, healthy rose bushes. Sometimes roses have to be bought from stores and garden shops which maintain an environment that is far from ideal to sustain a 'bare-rooted' plant. It is impossible to give the precise dimensions of a good rose bush as the habit of each variety dictates its individual proportions. A rose bush should be judged by its 'heft' rather than its size, so a sturdy cut-down plant is better than a long, thin one.

Container-grown roses

Nurseries and garden centres offer container-grown roses for year-round planting. Good plants will have several strong, new shoots growing from the base. Vigorous, healthy growth is more important than the quantity of flower buds the plants bear. Spindly growth and yellowing leaves demonstrate that the growing plants have been neglected and that their root formation will have suffered.

Where possible, choose containers which are designed to rot away naturally after being planted with the bush. Plastics pots, both rigid and pliable, must be removed as carefully as possible so as to prevent the soil from parting with the roots.

Choosing a healthy rose bush

A rose bush with three branches rather than two is better only if the combined girth of the former exceeds that of the latter. Branches should not be bruised, creased or broken, nor be completely devoid of thorns; all these conditions speak of heavy handling. A good root system will contribute even more than the top growth to the well-being of a newly planted rose bush. The root system should have many subsidiaries and not be just a carrot-like taproot that will have to produce a full set of capillary rootlets before it can support fresh growth. Rose bushes should look plump and fresh – the root system of a newly planted bush cannot cope with the task of reviving dehydrated top growth.

Hybrid teas   Floribundas   Dwarf floribundas   Miniature roses   Ground cover roses

How and When to Plant

Roses are best transplanted while they are dormant, that is when they have shed their leaves in preparation for the winter season. Ideally this should be done in late autumn but winter conditions vary so much throughout the world that it is difficult to lay down hard and fast rules. Compare, for example, the United Kingdom, which enjoys the longest season, from October through to March, with parts of Canada where planting cannot be considered until late April or May. Be guided as to the best planting time by the nurseryman to whom you have entrusted your order and plan according to his timetable. Container-grown roses can be planted at any time of year when the weather and soil conditions are suitable.

Preparing the rose bed

A rose bed should be prepared so that it will support bushes for more than ten years with no more than routine attention. If possible the ground should be dug to almost twice the depth of your spade, incorporating a liberal amount of manure, compost or other humus-forming material into the lower soil.

If natural conditions do not provide sufficient depth it will be necessary to add good quality topsoil in the form of a mound to provide at least 45cm (18in) of root space. Rose beds should be prepared about one month before the anticipated planting time to allow the soil to settle and form a stable planting medium.

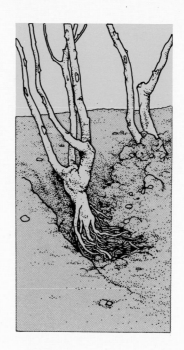

Heeling in

If conditions for planting are not exactly right, or if it is not convenient to plant the roses when they arrive, it is important that their good condition should be maintained until it is possible to do so.

Dig a short trench in friable soil about 30cm (12in) deep and as wide as your spade. Bank the soil from the trench against one edge of it. Lay the roots of the roses in the trench, leaning their branches against the bank. Fill in the trench, crumbling the soil so that it covers the roots and runs between the lower end of the branches. Firm gently with the heel to ensure that no air spaces remain to dry out the roots, and water the plants well.

The trench you have dug to cover the roots will now serve to house another row of bushes, and so on until your order is heeled in. The plants will now remain in good condition until permanent planting is carried out.

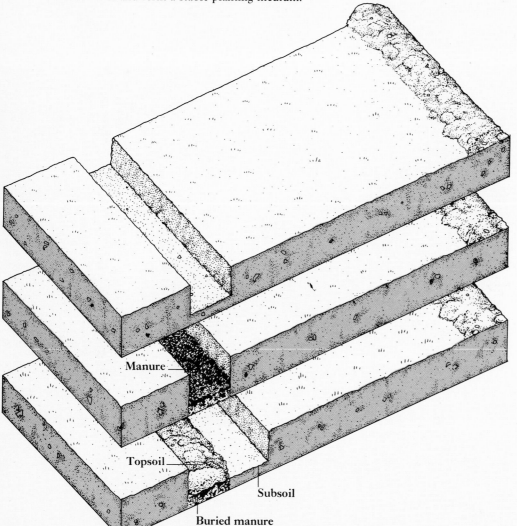

Manure

Topsoil

Subsoil

Buried manure

Double digging

1 Dig a trench as wide and as deep as the blade of your spade across the width of the rose bed and transport the soil to the other end of the bed.

2 Spread a liberal quantity of manure or humus-forming material along the bottom of the trench and fork this deep into the soil.

3 Turn the next spit of topsoil on to the buried manure and so form the next trench. Fork another application of manure into the subsoil.

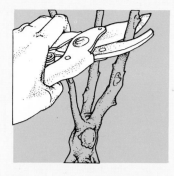

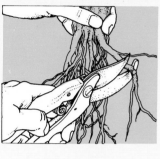

Preparing roses before planting

It is best to give roses their initial pruning just before you plant them. This will eliminate one back-bending operation and prevent you from trampling over the newly planted rose bed. This initial pruning will oblige the plant to produce new shoots that originate as close to the stock and scion union as possible. Cut too low and you endanger the life of the plant, too high and the bush will be inclined to grow top heavy.

The best point is about 10cm (4in) up the stem and just above an outward facing bud. Buds are small eyes that lie in the apex of the leaf stem and they are the points from which subsequent growth will originate. If an outward facing bud is not available move up the stem and make the cut just above the first available bud that points away from the centre of the bush.

Spacing

For the best results plant bush roses no more than 45cm (18in) apart. At this distance the bushes nurse each other; placed closer together they compete for nourishment, and if they are further apart weeds can grow and the rose bed will look sparse.

Climbers against a fence are ideally planted at around 2–3m (6–10ft) apart. Shrub roses for a hedge should be planted at 60cm (2ft) intervals alternately in two rows that are 45cm (18in) apart. Miniatures for borders are spaced at around 30cm (12in) apart. Always leave a distance of 30cm (12in) between the rose bushes and the border of the rose bed.'

Planting do's and don'ts

Do plant when weather conditions are suitable.

Do walk over the beds to squeeze out air pockets left by recent digging.

Don't put any fertilizer in the hole in such a manner that it comes into contact with the roots.

Don't plant into wet ground.

Don't plant in a drying wind.

Don't use newly creosoted stakes or poles for support.

Don't plant bushes too high or too low.

Do excavate a bigger hole for climbers or ramblers planted against a wall, and refill with good soil.

Do water regularly after planting if there is a prolonged dry period.

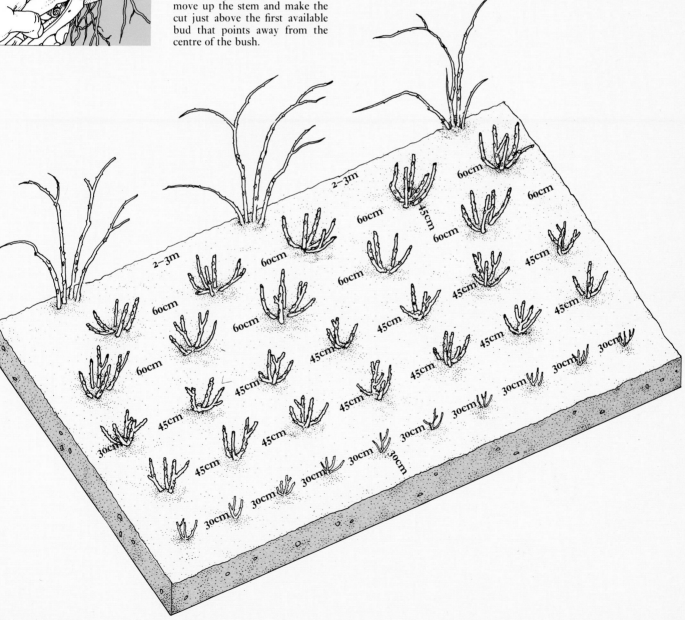

How and When to Plant

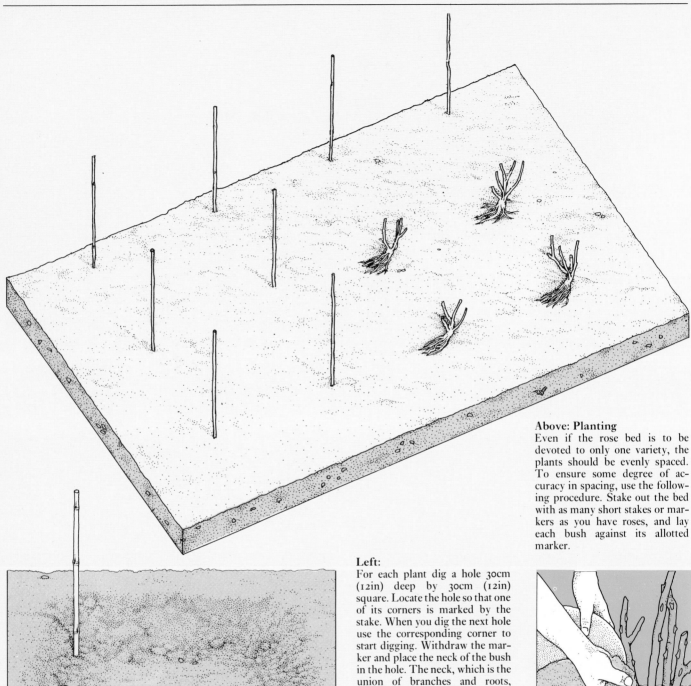

Above: Planting
Even if the rose bed is to be devoted to only one variety, the plants should be evenly spaced. To ensure some degree of accuracy in spacing, use the following procedure. Stake out the bed with as many short stakes or markers as you have roses, and lay each bush against its allotted marker.

Left:
For each plant dig a hole 30cm (12in) deep by 30cm (12in) square. Locate the hole so that one of its corners is marked by the stake. When you dig the next hole use the corresponding corner to start digging. Withdraw the marker and place the neck of the bush in the hole. The neck, which is the union of branches and roots, should be positioned so that when planting is finished the branches will be fractionally below or just at ground level. This position can often be established by noting where the previous soil mark on the stem is.

Left:
Spread the roots over as large an area as possible – make the hole bigger if necessary – and crumble a little soil back over the roots. Hold the rose in one hand to keep it steady. Press first with the hand to eliminate air pockets, then cover with more soil and tread lightly with the foot to firm the plant in position.

Above:
Now is the time to apply a long-lasting fertilizer (such as bone-meal) but wait until all the roses are planted, then dress the whole bed. Fork or rake over lightly to incorporate the fertilizer and to obliterate footmarks. Make sure the plants are well-watered to help settle the soil and ensure they have sufficient moisture.

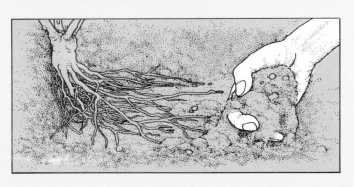

Planting container-grown roses

Planting roses in containers that break down naturally is simply a matter of digging a hole big enough for both bush and container. The compost surrounding the roots will give an excellent environment until the roots break out to forage for new food sources.

The removal of non-disintegrating containers almost inevitably causes root damage and the accommodating hole should be dug over-size to allow for a lining of moist peat to compensate the plant for the setback it would otherwise suffer.

Planting standards

Dig a hole 30cm (12in) square. Place the roots in the hole and excavate so as to ensure that only half of the knuckle of the tree will be covered by soil when planting is completed.

Now is the time to position the supporting stake which should measure approximately 1.4m (4ft 6in) by 3cm (1¼in) by 3cm (1¼in).

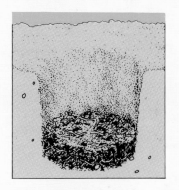

Planting roses in non-disintegrating containers

Dig a hole deeper and wider than the container, and line it with a bed of moist peat.

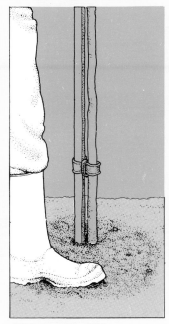

Place the container on the peat bed. Cut or pull away the container as gently as possible.

Remove the tree from the prepared hole to avoid damaging the roots while a stake is driven into the base of the hole as close as possible to the position previously occupied by the standard stem. Drive in the stake until its top is slightly below the level of the bottom-most graft on the standard stem. Keep offering up the standard to the stake to help with an accurate measurement.

Replace the standard, with the stem close to the stake and crumble the soil back around the roots. (A gentle shake helps the soil find its way through the roots.) Firm with the foot throughout. Use a specially made tree tie or garden string at the top and bottom to secure the standard to the stake.

Alternatively, a short piece of hose pipe 8cm (3in) in diameter, slit along its length, can be fitted around the stem to protect it from the chafing action of the string.

Fill in the hole with moist peat and firm with the fingers. Too much pressure will break up the root ball.

Water regularly until the plant is fully established.

Feeding, Mulching and Watering

Some gardeners regularly take advantage of the generosity of the rose. Its determination to give a reasonable display, even if left unattended, is more often acknowledged with a further period of neglect rather than rewarded with a good feed to redress the balance. For sturdy, healthy plants and an abundance of bloom regular feeding, like pruning, should become routine practice once or twice a year according to the methods you adopt.

First of all you must be satisfied with the physical condition of the soil in the rose bed. Soil of poor structure cannot properly impart essential minerals in solution to the roots. Thick clay will not allow the free passage of the mineral solution and light, sandy soil allows it to wash away too quickly.

Humus

Taking for granted that the rose bed is well drained, the first consideration should be the soil's humus content. Humus is thoroughly decomposed matter that was once involved in the life cycle of any living organism, animal or vegetable. It sustains the micro-organisms that abound in fertile soil to break it down into food that can be assimilated by a plant's roots. In heavy clay soils the humus acts to bind together quantities of very fine particles, and forms a granular structure that can be penetrated by both air and water. Humus has a stabilising effect on the relatively large grains found in sandy soils so that moisture and nutrients which would otherwise drain away are retained long enough for the roots to take full advantage of them.

Rose cultivation denies the soil its natural regenerating process, so the humus content must be artificially maintained. Sources of humus are well-rotted farmyard manure, peat and leaf mould, and composted vegetable matter. Both heavy and light soils need humus and a good quantity should be dug into the rose bed prior to planting. Thereafter a yearly mulching is necessary to maintain the humus content.

Organic fertilizers

Organic fertilizers are the concentrated by-products of animal or vegetable life. They are the most natural and satisfactory method of maintaining the soil's fertility – as well as feeding they provide the humus content. Well-rotted cow or horse dung is the best of all organic manures. Pig and poultry manure takes a long time to mature and should be used with considerable caution. Other organics include granulated peat, garden compost, spent hops, leaf mould, bone-meal, and hoof and horn. Sewage waste can be an excellent organic fertilizer but great care should be taken if its source is the product of an industrial community. Contamination by heavy metal salts can make the sewage deadly poisonous to all plant life. All of these may require a supplementary application of inorganic fertilizer to maintain the ideal chemical balance.

An organic fertilizer takes a long time to break down into its constituent plant nutrients and should be applied as a mulch early in the spring. All mulches should be lightly forked into the rose bed so that none of the goodness is lost to the atmosphere. Take care not to damage the roots of the bushes.

Applying bone– or fish–meal

Mulch

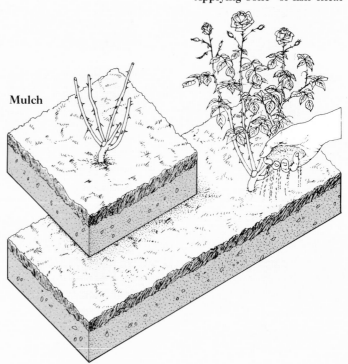

Sandy soil

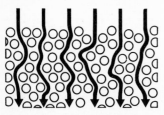

Sandy or granular soil allows nutrient solutions to pass too quickly through the top soil before they can be absorbed by the roots.

Clay soil

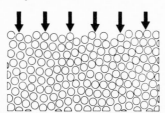

The fine grains of clay soil impede the passage of nutrients to the roots.

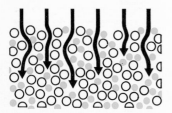

The addition of humus to sandy soil has a stabilising effect, inhibiting the passage of nutrient solutions long enough for the roots to take advantage of them.

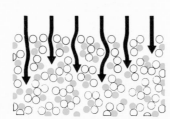

Humus binds together the fine particles of clay soil to form bigger granules, thus allowing nutrient solutions to penetrate to the roots.

How and when to apply organic fertilizers

Organics are slow acting but long lasting so they should be applied as early as possible in the growing season. The bulky organics such as farmyard manure, compost and peat are used as a mulch covering the rose bed to a depth of about 5cm (2in) and lightly forked into the top 10cm (4in) of soil.

The granulated organics such as bone or fish-meal should also be applied at the very beginning of each season, at the rate of 113gm to the square metre (4oz to the square yard) and then again later in the spring as the first flowers start to show. If costs permit, a mulch of granulated peat should be used in conjunction with the first application of bone or fish-meal to a depth of around 5cm (2in). The dressing should be scratched into the top 10cm (4in) of soil after application.

Inorganic fertilizers

Inorganic fertilizers are the refined constituents of soil chemistry: nitrogen, phosphate and potash, together with a number of trace elements. The proportion of each of these ingredients is balanced to suit the particular subject being grown. The correct amount of each chemical favoured by the rose is now so clearly defined, and the best manufactured brands are so well-formulated, that it is no longer necessary for the rose grower to purchase and mix his own chemicals.

Many excellent formulae have been developed over the years, each having its own special merits, but the recommendation of the Royal National Rose Society of Great Britain is as follows:

Ingredients	Parts by weight
Sulphate of ammonia	8
Superphosphate	16
Sulphate of potash	12
Kieserite	2
Sulphate of iron	$\frac{1}{2}$

Chalky soils induce a special deficiency which can be treated by doubling the last two ingredients.

Applying an inorganic fertilizer

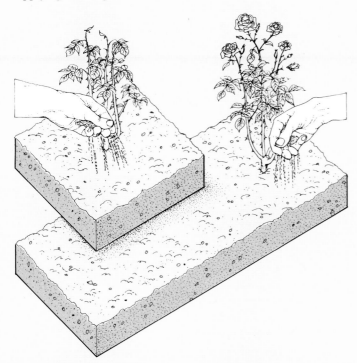

How and when to apply inorganic fertilizers

Inorganic fertilizers have an almost instant effect so they should not be applied until new spring growth appears on the bushes and the roots are taking up nourishment. While normal rainfall conveys the chemicals in solution down to the roots, it also washes them away so that a further application of fertilizer is necessary. The second application, in a season of normal, regular rainfall, should be made just after the first flush of bloom.

The Royal National Rose Society's formula should be used at the rate of 57gm to the square metre (2oz to the square yard) as the bushes come into leaf, and again as the first flowers fade. Rose fertilizers sold under brand names have their own rates of application which should be followed exactly.

Liquid fertilizers

A fertilizer in solution will penetrate to the roots much faster than if it were applied in granular form, giving an almost instant effect on the rose bush. Liquid feeding is usually employed by the keen rose exhibitor to supplement the generous application of fertilizer he has already applied at the start of the season. Very weak solutions are essential, otherwise the plants soon show signs of overfeeding. Liquid feeding should be carried out after rain, never on dry soil.

Watering

No matter how good the soil structure, or how rich the fertilizer, roses cannot thrive unless there is adequate moisture in the soil to convey the nutrients in solution to the roots. In regions that regularly experience arid conditions during the growing season it may be necessary to supplement the natural rainfall by irrigation.

The best method of artificial watering is known as trickle irrigation. The equipment for this consists of a stopped-off hose, punctured at regular intervals with very fine holes. This is laid on top of the soil among the roses. Water is fed into the system at low pressure to provide a constant drip from each aperture. Such a system embodies the essence of good watering practice in that it is constant, it penetrates deep into the soil without washing it away and it does not cause the soil to bake hard. This method also keeps water off the foliage where it can cause scorch marks and encourage disease.

If trickle irrigation is not possible, water each rose root area with a watering can, with or without a rose attachment. Give at least 5 litres (1 gallon) to each plant and apply it slowly so that it is absorbed deep into the soil and does not run off the surface. Light watering will only cause the roots to grow towards the surface of the soil and suffer even more from drought. Alternatively, water with a hose pipe to soak the soil thoroughly.

Methods for liquid feeding

Place a bucket of cow or horse manure, together with a house brick, into a coarse-meshed sack and suspend this in about 182 litres (40 gallons) of water for a week. Prod the sack occasionally to encourage circulation of the water through the manure.

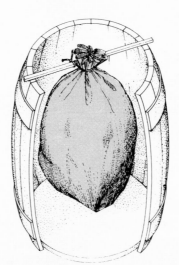

After a week, draw off a quantity of the liquid. Dilute it further until it is the colour of weak tea. Use the liquid fertilizer at the rate of 4.5 litres (1 gallon) to a bush at fortnightly intervals – on moist soil. Refill the container and leave it for another week before using more of the liquor, diluting as necessary. Recharge the sack after five weeks.

There are several good manufactured brands of liquid fertilizer that have an instant effect and are more convenient to use than the basic method just described. The rules, however, remain the same: a weak solution applied only to moist soil – and avoid contact with the foliage.

Pruning and Trimming

Happily, a rose bush will often thrive in spite of, rather than because of, the pruning treatment it receives each season. The bigger the bush the more flowers it will bear, hence a simple principle can be established: always prune rose plants with the aim of making them conform to the dimensions of your garden, rather than with the idea that lopping off branches will impart vitality to the plants. Vigorous plants will overcome a severe pruning but weak roses are best left alone or just trimmed. The art of pruning is reconciling this principle with the way in which a rose would grow if left to its own devices.

Roses differ from ordinary plants in that they replace their aerial shoots rather than extend them. Instead of forming a trunk and branches, they throw up a succession of basal shoots which are replaced as they atrophy. In their natural state roses are fierce competitors for light and space and, although modern varieties have been bred to manageable proportions, they still have to be tamed by an annual pruning to fit them for formal flower beds and borders. Gardeners interfere with this pattern by pruning the old shoots annually, so each rose compensates for its loss by producing new shoots which, being prime growth, will produce the best blooms. Various methods of pruning can be summed up as hard, long or trimming – it is best to adopt the style which will produce the size of bush required for your garden.

When to prune bush roses
Roses can be pruned at any time during their dormant season. The most conscientious way, however, is to remove some of the top growth in the autumn and follow this with proper pruning in the early spring. This procedure reduces the amount of branches on the bush so that it is not so vulnerable to winter winds, while the more precise pruning is reserved until early spring, when it can be seen how much unripe wood has been killed by frosts.

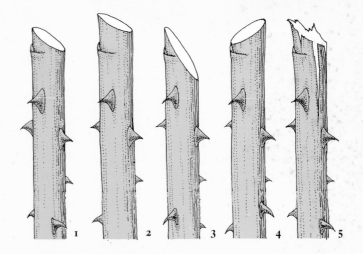

Pruning cuts From left to right:
1 Correct cut, just above the bud and sloping away from it, made with sharp secateurs.
2 Cut made too high.
3 Angle of cut too sharp.
4 Cut made too close to the bud and sloping in the wrong direction.
5 Jagged cut made with blunt secateurs.

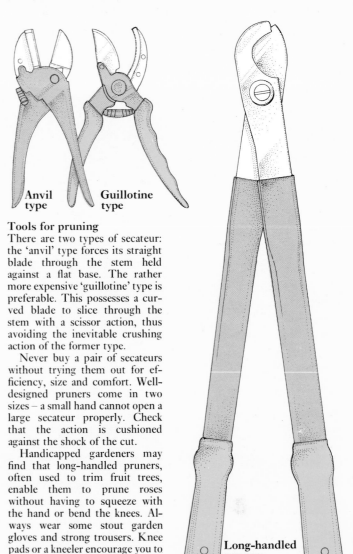

Anvil type   **Guillotine type**

Tools for pruning
There are two types of secateur: the 'anvil' type forces its straight blade through the stem held against a flat base. The rather more expensive 'guillotine' type is preferable. This possesses a curved blade to slice through the stem with a scissor action, thus avoiding the inevitable crushing action of the former type.

Never buy a pair of secateurs without trying them out for efficiency, size and comfort. Well-designed pruners come in two sizes – a small hand cannot open a large secateur properly. Check that the action is cushioned against the shock of the cut.

Handicapped gardeners may find that long-handled pruners, often used to trim fruit trees, enable them to prune roses without having to squeeze with the hand or bend the knees. Always wear some stout garden gloves and strong trousers. Knee pads or a kneeler encourage you to get close to the job.

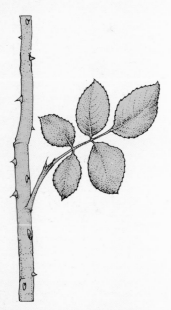

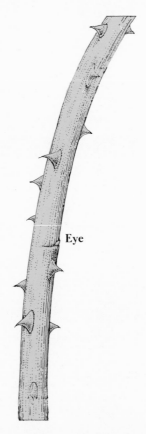

Eye

Shoots should always be cut above a bud or eye that faces away from the centre of the bush. These eyes occur in the apex of the leaf stem (which will usually have been shed by pruning time). Dormant buds can be found just above the small scar left by the departed leaf stem.

Long-handled pruners

Summer pruning

Pruning bush roses
1 Strong new growth from the base: cut back to around four eyes from the base. Choose an outward facing eye.

2 Cut away diseased and atrophied old growth.

3 Strong new growth from below last year's pruning point: prune about two buds up i.e. to the most convenient outward facing eye.

After the first flush of flower the lead shoot is trimmed back 15cm (6in) to the nearest bud. This accelerates the formation of new bud-bearing growth.

Pruning and Trimming

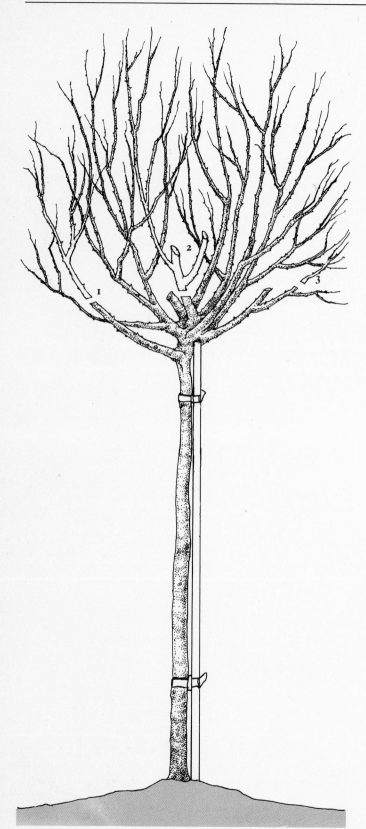

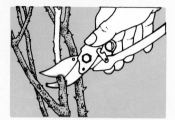

Pruning shrub roses
Shrub roses in borders or hedges should be pruned fairly hard for the first three years and thereafter just trimmed to maintain their shape. During the first year newly planted shrubs should be cut down to around 30cm (12in). Following the first and second years' growth they should be pruned back to around 45cm (18in). This treatment ensures that the shrubs produce plenty of basal shoots upon which the plants can rely for support. If the shrubs are allowed to grow unchecked they will become 'leggy' and top-heavy.

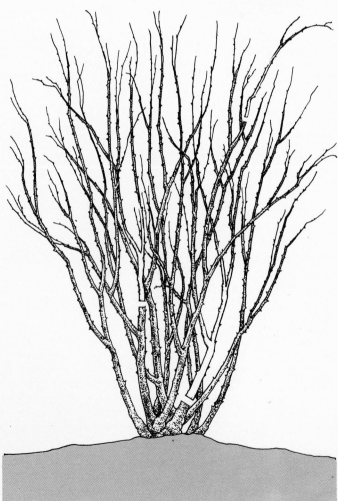

Pruning standard or tree roses
1 Strong new growth from the grafting point on the stem: cut back to the third or fourth eye from the grafting point. Choose an outward facing eye.
2 Old, diseased and atrophied growth: cut away to open up the centre.
3 Strong, new growth emanating from last year's pruning point: cut about two buds up i.e. to the most convenient outward facing eye.

Suckers

Suckers emanate from growth nodes on the rootstock onto which the cultivar (variety) has been budded. They will always grow from below the budding point. Therefore they can occur on the stem of a standard rose, but more often than not they grow from below the ground. Their appearance differs from the cultivar in that the sucker will probably have a seven – rather than the more normal five-leaf system, and thorns that differ in spacing and character.

It is important that suckers be removed at their union with the parent plant and not just pruned. This usually necessitates digging away some soil to expose the source of the trouble.

Pruning miniature roses

Miniature roses should be regarded as small flowering plants in their own right and not just as 'mini' roses. Healthy plants will keep on growing, so it is up to you to decide on the height that best suits their situation and prune accordingly.

The best maintenance technique is to trim the plants with scissors into compact little shrubs rather than prune them. When they have grown too big for their position cut them back fairly hard with secateurs. Most miniatures occasionally produce a particularly vigorous shoot that spoils the proportion of the plant. Cut this shoot away at any time of the year.

Sucker

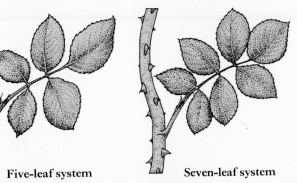

Five-leaf system **Seven-leaf system**

Removing suckers

Suckers are best torn away from the host root. This rather harsh treatment removes the growth node for all time. Otherwise they should be cut away, together with the nodule, using a knife rather than a pair of secateurs. Failure to excise all of the growth node will result in even more suckers growing from this point the following season.

Miniature roses are trimmed with scissors until they grow too tall.

Miniature roses which have grown too tall should be cut back hard.

Uncharacteristic long growth can be cut away at any time of the year.

Pergolas, Walls and Pillars

The difference between climbers and ramblers has become somewhat obscured by recent gardening practice. Rose gardens of yesteryear were in general much grander than the small plots we tend today. Originally climbers were intended to climb walls and pergolas, while ramblers were allowed to spread freely. Their long fronds were sometimes encouraged to strike new roots so that they spread in a similar way to strawberry plants. This treatment, which achieved the effect of a colourful bramble patch, can seldom be afforded today and ramblers have to be restricted to suit a more formal setting. Instead of being allowed to ramble outwards, they are trained upwards against a pergola or post in much the same way as true climbing roses.

Climbing roses and their habits

Ramblers
These are usually recognized by their clusters of small pompom-like blooms and seven-leaf systems. Like many of the species roses, they flower on the growth made the previous season. They flower for about one month in the early summer and thereafter produce only new growth for the following season. Unfortunately, soft growth during the summer is very vulnerable to fungus diseases and as a result the rambler is regarded as a harbinger of rust and powdery mildew. Examples: 'Excelsa', 'New Dawn', 'Dorothy Perkins'.

Hybrid tea and floribunda sport climbers
These are mutations of bush varieties in climbing form. Although they retain exactly the same flowers as the original, they adopt a habit of flowering only when they become established in their growing environment. This initial growth usually takes a couple of seasons but some of the more vigorous varieties will delay blooming for three or more years. Hybrid tea and floribunda sports are characterized by their ability to grow very tall, and by their two distinct flowering periods in early summer and early autumn. Varieties are always indicated by the word 'climbing'. Examples: 'Climbing Ena Harkness', 'Climbing Iceberg', 'Climbing Fragrant Cloud', 'Climbing Mrs Sam McGredy' and 'Climbing Masquerade'.

Recurrent-flowering climbers
These are the most modern of the climbing types, which have been bred to flower as they grow and throughout the whole season. Their height ceiling is around 4m (12ft). Examples: 'Compassion', 'Pink Perpêtue', 'Swan Lake'.

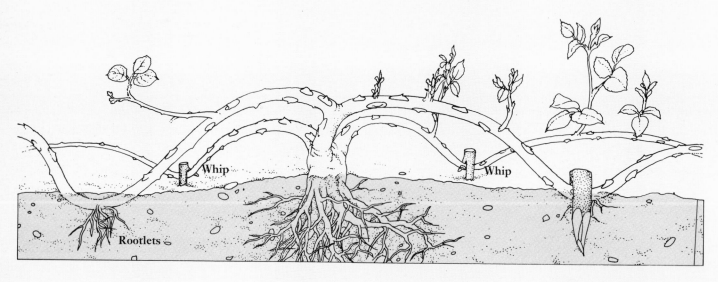

Whip

Whip

Rootlets

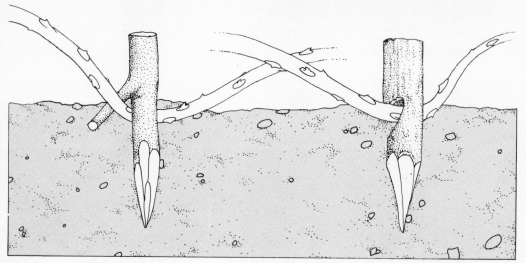

Pegging down ramblers for ground cover
The traditional technique of growing ramblers is to spread out the whips and peg them down at 1m (3ft) intervals. Some whips will grow new root systems, while others are trained low and horizontally to encourage bloom-producing lateral growth.

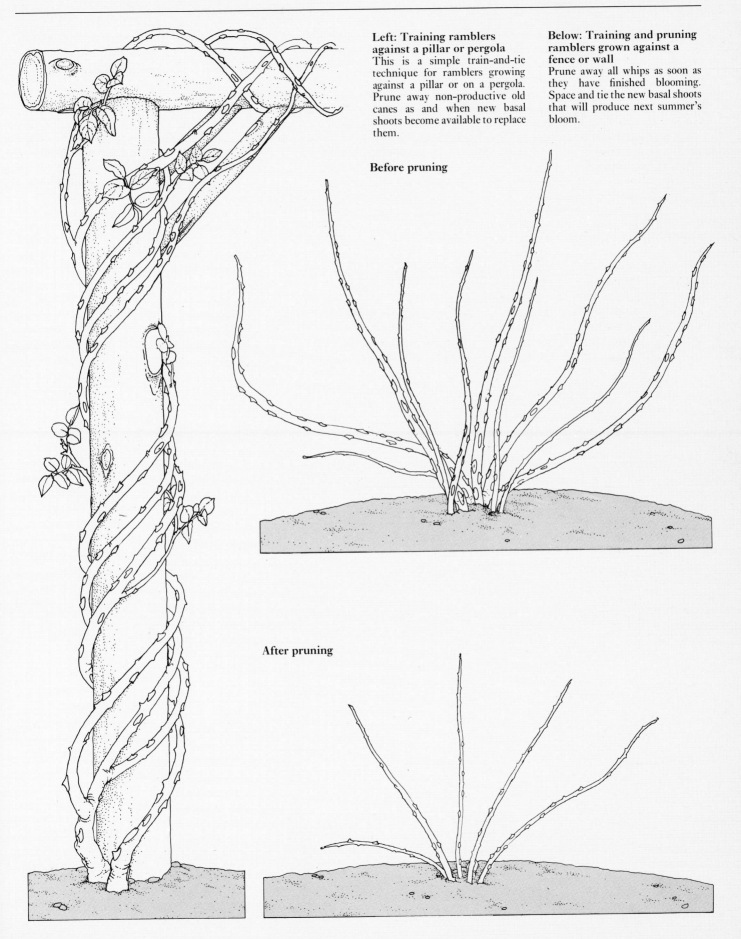

Left: Training ramblers against a pillar or pergola
This is a simple train-and-tie technique for ramblers growing against a pillar or on a pergola. Prune away non-productive old canes as and when new basal shoots become available to replace them.

Below: Training and pruning ramblers grown against a fence or wall
Prune away all whips as soon as they have finished blooming. Space and tie the new basal shoots that will produce next summer's bloom.

Before pruning

After pruning

Pergolas, Walls and Pillars

Training climbing hybrid tea and floribunda sports and recurrent-flowering climbers

Just as the fruit tree is trained in espalier fashion to promote fruiting spurs on the lateral growth, so should climbing roses be trained outwards rather than upwards. Letting the climber follow its natural inclination to grow upright results in a leggy unclothed base. Training induces the basal shoots to grow low and outwards, which encourages the lateral growths which give both height and cover, as well as flower.

Pruning

Pruning consists of removing non-productive old basal shoots and their associated laterals as and when there are vigorous new basal shoots to replace them. Whenever an obstruction prevents the basal shoots being trained horizontally, close to the ground, they should be led upwards and then outwards along a trellis or wires. The lateral growth which will result can be relied upon to give cover and flowers.

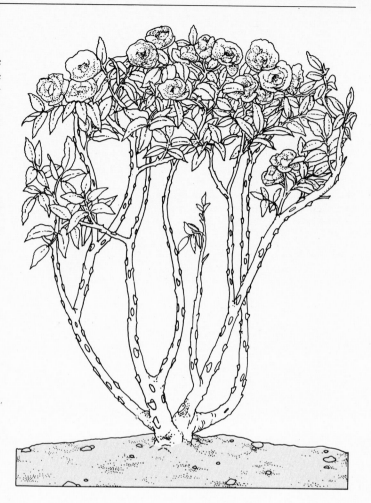

Below: Training basal shoots
Train basal shoots and their terminal growth low and outwards. This encourages flower-bearing laterals to grow, giving both height and cover.

Right: Encouraging flower-bearing laterals
Climbers which are allowed to grow upright become devoid of foliage and flowers at their base. Laterals grow at the top of the tree and become difficult to manage.

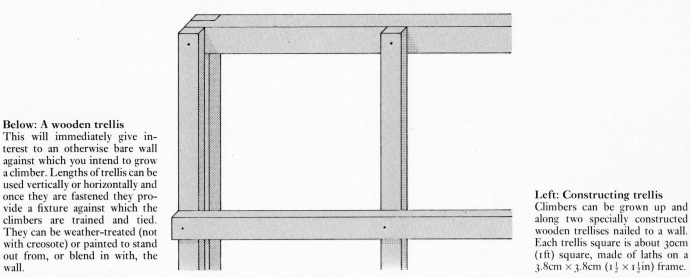

Below: A wooden trellis
This will immediately give interest to an otherwise bare wall against which you intend to grow a climber. Lengths of trellis can be used vertically or horizontally and once they are fastened they provide a fixture against which the climbers are trained and tied. They can be weather-treated (not with creosote) or painted to stand out from, or blend in with, the wall.

Left: Constructing trellis
Climbers can be grown up and along two specially constructed wooden trellises nailed to a wall. Each trellis square is about 30cm (1ft) square, made of laths on a 3.8cm × 3.8cm (1½ × 1½in) frame.

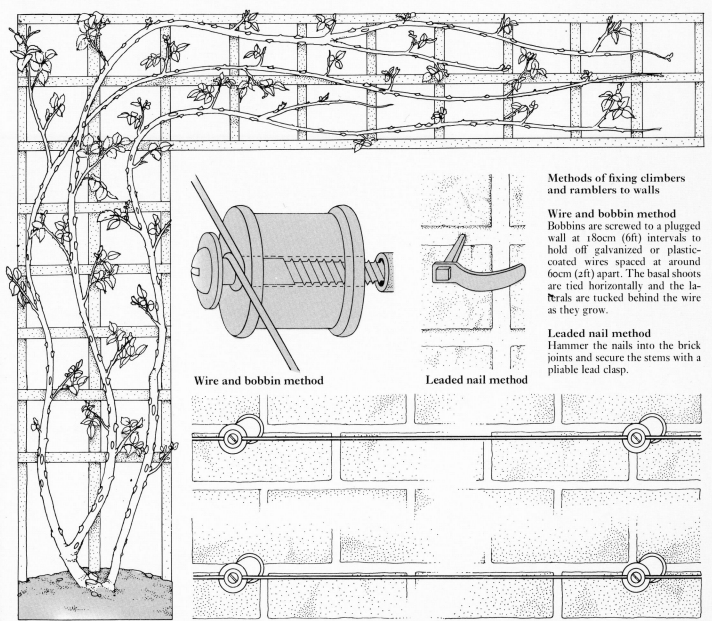

Wire and bobbin method

Leaded nail method

Methods of fixing climbers and ramblers to walls

Wire and bobbin method
Bobbins are screwed to a plugged wall at 180cm (6ft) intervals to hold off galvanized or plastic-coated wires spaced at around 60cm (2ft) apart. The basal shoots are tied horizontally and the laterals are tucked behind the wire as they grow.

Leaded nail method
Hammer the nails into the brick joints and secure the stems with a pliable lead clasp.

Roses for Hedges

Rose briars can be found growing naturally in most hedgerows, contributing dense, thorny growth that is impenetrable to many animals. It is not surprising therefore that various species of rose bushes have been selectively grown as hedges for many hundreds of years.

Sweet briar shrub roses were first planted to define boundaries and not for their remarkably fragrant foliage, pink flowers or bright orange hips. They were valued rather for their utilitarian qualities of abundant, impenetrable growth and inhospitable thorny branches. The charms of a rose hedge have only recently been incorporated into the garden landscape as a decorative rather than a functional feature. There are now many different shrub roses and floribundas available to give variety to informal or boundary hedges.

Planning

The style of the hedge will be determined by the characteristics of the variety of rose employed. A vigorous rambler rose forms a dense, tall, informal hedge and requires some support. A leggy floribunda/hybrid tea type grows slender and upright. The modern shrub roses have a great deal more spread with their height.

Planting distances vary according to the vigour of the variety. The bushes are usually planted in a double row at staggered intervals. The rows are best planted on both sides of any support that is to be incorporated into the hedge.

Rambler rose hedge

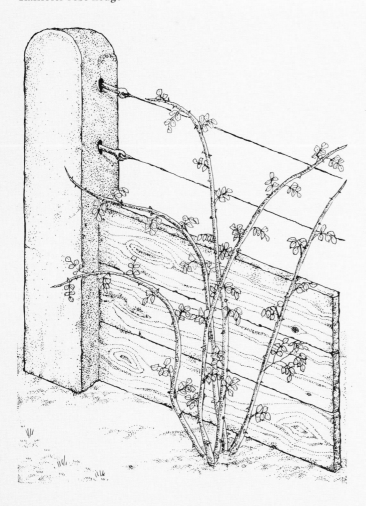

Preparation and planting

A rose hedge is a permanent feature, so great care should be taken in the preparation of the soil. The site should be manured and double-dug and finally dressed with a generous amount of bone-meal. The posts of any support should be set in position before digging commences to avoid unnecessary compaction of the soil – the wires and rails can be fixed afterwards. The posts should be treated against timber decay and sunk into the ground to a depth of 45cm (18in), preferably in concrete. Dig a wide hole to about a spade's depth, and plant the shrubs so that their roots spread out to provide a firm anchorage for the vigorous growth that will ensue.

Pruning rose hedges

Pruning methods for ramblers and climbers are described on pages 112–15. The principles of pruning and training remain the same when applied to a rose hedge. The only difficulty likely to arise is in matching the vigour and habit of mixed varieties. By pruning the bushes heavily or lightly, according to their performance during the previous season, a balanced display of each variety can be achieved.

Feeding

An annual dressing of bone-meal and a spring and summer application of rose fertilizer should be given to rose hedges which are expected to produce a lot of growth and bloom.

Shrub rose hedge

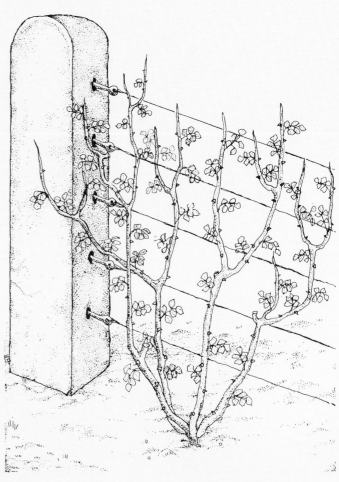

Suggested varieties for a rose hedge

Ramblers

Although they generally flower once only each season, most rambler varieties are suitable for a very tall rose hedge. They produce long, pliable whips which are easy to train, unlike some of the later developments that possess stiff and unyielding shoots.

Dorothy Perkins: Fragrant, rose-pink clusters. Dark, glossy foliage.

Excelsa: Big clusters of crimson double blooms. Dark green, glossy foliage.

New Dawn: Blush-pink double blooms in clusters. Fragrant with dark glossy foliage.

Modern recurrent-flowering climbers

Though not as tall and vigorous as ramblers, the modern climbers do have an extended flowering season which often lasts all summer long.

Danse du Feu: Sometimes called 'Spectacular'. Fragrant, scarlet double blooms in big clusters.

Golden Showers: Fragrant, bright yellow blooms. Dark, glossy foliage.

Pink Perpêtue: Fragrant clusters of bright, rose-pink double flowers. Blooms all season.

Swan Lake: Shapely white-tinged pink blooms, slightly fragrant, very free-flowering.

Modern shrub roses

These are perhaps the most satisfactory type of rose to grow as a hedge. The shrubs bloom throughout most of the summer and well into autumn. Growth is abundant, yet the plants are easy to train. Most varieties are disease resistant.

Ballerina: Soft pink, small, single blooms in clusters. The clusters are large and hydrangea-like, with a musk fragrance.

Chinatown: Clear, golden yellow blooms. Very sweetly scented with bright green foliage.

Dorothy Wheatcroft: Big clusters of bright red semi-double blooms.

Fountain: Rich velvet-red double blooms, fragrant and repeat-flowering.

Fred Loads: Clusters of fragrant vermilion-orange blooms. Vigorous and spectacular.

Joseph's Coat: Multicoloured blooms of gold, pink and red, borne in clusters. Vigorous and repeat-flowering.

Floribundas

Most of the modern floribundas are suitable for a border-type hedge up to a height of around 1m (3ft). Since they are not so vigorous as shrub roses, they are more suitable for internal rather than boundary hedges. Some varieties impart their particular characteristics to the hedge. For instance, 'Queen Elizabeth' is a rose that grows as tall as any of the shrubs but it has very little spread and a tendency to flower only at the top of the plant.

Informal shrub rose hedge

Support for a rose hedge

Boundary hedges should be provided with support: an open fence, a post and wire construction, or a rail of rustic poles fixed at a height of around 1m (3ft).

Support for a rambler rose hedge

Fencing panels 1m (3ft) high are supported by poles 2m (6ft) high. Wires are stretched between the poles to support the top growth. It is usual to plant a row of lower growing floribundas in front to hide the legginess of the ramblers.

Support for an external shrub rose hedge

A simple post and wire fence. The shrubs may be planted around 60cm (2ft) apart in two staggered rows, though planting distances vary according to the variety of rose.

Support for an informal hedge of shrub roses

The simple rustic pole and cross-bar construction prevents the shrubs from becoming loose and toppling in a storm.

Pruning hedge shrub roses and floribundas

Shrubs and floribundas should be pruned hard back for the first three years of their life as hedge plants. The principal aim is to encourage strong basal shoots close to the ground to support the massive top growth that is required for a hedge. The top growth will be spindly if it is allowed to grow too tall, too quickly. Just prior to, or immediately after planting, prune the plants down to around the fifth eye, leaving about 30cm (12in) of stem for shrubs and about 15cm (6in) for floribundas.

For the next couple of years prune the shrub roses down to about 45cm (18in) and the floribundas to about 30cm (12in). The growth will be quickly made up each season in spite of this treatment. The hedge which is eventually produced will be established upon a firm base and be self-supporting. Thereafter, the treatment of the hedge should be confined to trimming it into shape and to matching the habits of each variety in an assorted hedge. There is seldom any need to tie shrubs or floribundas to a support which merely serves as a feature while the hedge develops, or acts as a buffer against very strong winds.

Propagation: Budding and Grafting

Nature's most common method of propagation is by seed, but seed does not generally come true to the rose that bore it except in the case of wild roses. Nearly all garden roses are hybrids, not wild roses, and their seed is useless as a means of multiplying them. The rose grower is therefore obliged to resort to vegetative propagation, which cuts out the use of seed entirely, and uses instead a piece of the growing plant.

Nearly all roses grown for sale are propagated in nurseries by a method called budding, which is in fact a form of grafting. A piece of the desired rose is inserted upon the roots of another rose, which has its own top growth removed. This is a fast method of propagating roses because, as the roots are already there, the young plant can grow and flower with considerable vigour within twelve months. It is an economical method because the roots can be those of wild roses which may be raised cheaply from seed or cuttings. Also the inserted piece is very small, so that one plant can supply many of them. The operation can be performed in the open air, without expensive equipment or shelter. The method is acceptable horticulturally because the plants obtained are hardy and of reasonably even and similar growth.

The roses chosen to act as host, that is to supply the roots, may be grown from either seed or cuttings. They can be purchased if the grower does not wish to raise them himself. The kinds most generally used in Britain are 'Laxa', or *R. canina*, of which there are several selected forms, notably 'Inermis' and Pfander'. In warmer countries, 'Manettii' and 'Indica Major' are popular. In America *R. multiflora* is often used. There is a wide range of choice. A gardener who wishes to bud his own roses can take cuttings from the prunings of his rambler roses and use them as rootstocks. The Americans did this on a large scale using a red rose called 'Dr Huey'.

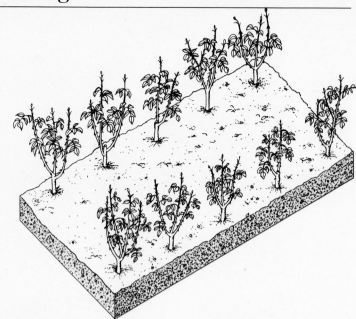

Planting rootstocks
When the host seedlings or cuttings have grown for their first season, they are lifted and transplanted. This is done partly to space them out for future work and partly to trim back the roots of seedlings, which if left in situ will form a long taproot instead of the fibrous root system which is needed. Cuttings are transplanted because they are inserted more deeply at the rooting stage than is desirable for the budding stage.

The cuttings or seedlings are planted about 20cm (8in) apart, in rows about 60–90cm (2–3ft) wide. They are ready to be budded when their sap is flowing in the summer, earlier than most people realize. It is a mistake to bud late in summer when the sap flow is reduced.

Selecting eyes
The piece of rose to be inserted is called the scion. The host plant is the stock, also known as rootstock or understock. The scion is very thin and only about 2.5cm (1in) long. Its essential part is an eye, which is a dormant growth bud, to be found just above the place where a leafstalk joins the stem. Its inessential part is the bark above and below the eye, sufficient to enable the propagator to hold the eye, and to anchor it.

Shortly before the operation is to be done, say the evening before, the eyes should be selected and gathered. They are best found on young shoots which are about to bear their first flower. These shoots should be showing a plump terminal bud or a young bloom. Most garden bush roses will have, on such a shoot, three to six eyes suitable for propagation. The top one, two or three eyes are usually insufficiently developed. The bottom one or two may be too flat or old. The eyes from the centre of the shoot are usually chosen, provided they have not already begun to grow into shoots themselves.

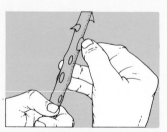

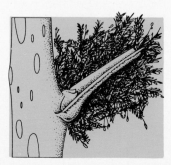

Cutting and trimming the shoot
The shoot is gathered by cutting immediately above one of the unsuitable eyes at the bottom. The flower (or flower bud) and the immature eyes at the top are removed. The remainder is the central part of the shoot, bearing the eyes chosen for use.

The leaves are cut off through their stipules, leaving a very short piece which will prove helpful for holding the eye. The thorns are rubbed off or carefully cut off without tearing the bark.

The shoot must then be kept fresh in clean water or damp moss until it is to be used. Such shoots, selected for budding, are known as budwood.

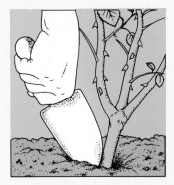

Making the T cut
The soil should be cleared away from the rootstock to expose its neck and, if necessary, the neck should be wiped clean.

With a sharp knife, the bark of the rootstock is laid open by a cut shaped like a T. The top of the T is cut first, covering about a third or a quarter of the rootstock's circumference.

The stem of the T is cut second. It should be a little longer than the eye one proposes to insert.

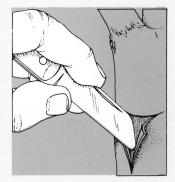

As the knife cuts upwards on the stem of the T and joins the top of the T, a slight twist will help the bark to spring open. If it does not open, either the operator is at fault in not cutting properly through the bark tissue or the rootstock is too dry for satisfactory budding; water it and try again the next day.

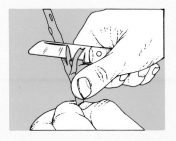

Preparing the eye
The budwood should be held firmly to cut out an eye to fit the T cut in the rootstock. Cut the eye from below, holding the budwood upside down, by cutting a thin sliver of wood about 2.5cm (1in) long, with the eye and the remains of the leafstalk in the centre.

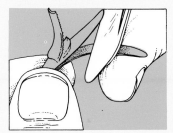

The part excised will consist of bark and a thin piece of wood. Flip out the wood with the point of the knife, so that only bark, eye and the leafstalk piece remain.

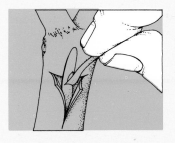

Inserting the eye
Slide this fragment (right way up!) into the stem of the T cut so that the flaps of rootstock bark enclose it. If the T cut proves too short to accommodate the scion, the scion may be trimmed so long as the eye itself is enclosed.

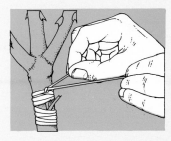

Securing the eye
Tie the eye in without delay so that the wound heals quickly. This may be done with raffia or some other material which ceases to be constrictive after a few weeks. The ties are made to over-lap, leaving the eye itself exposed, by holding a tail in the left hand and encircling the rootstock and the tail from bottom upwards.

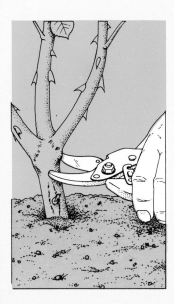

Removing the rootstock top growth
The eye should be knitted to the rootstock in three weeks, when constrictive ties may be removed. Any depression left around the rootstock should be gently filled with soil so that the eye is near soil level.

Next spring (see illustration), the rootstock is cut through to remove all its top growth close above the eye. This cut is through the neck; it should not be made through the shoots.

The eye will now grow. It is best to nip out the growing tip while the young plant is still very small, to force it to make more than one shoot. The young plant should flower the same summer if the variety is remontant.

Grafting
Grafting requires more complicated equipment than budding, such as heated frames and greenhouses. It is used as a means of increasing the supply of budwood rather than for raising plants for the garden. It may be carried out through the winter.

The simplest form of grafting is to cut through the rootstock straight away and discard all its top growth. Then cut through the bark, as one does for the stem of the T in budding, but continuing the cut up to the truncated top. The scion consists of one or two eyes on a piece of stem about 2.5–7.5cm (1–3in) long. Slice through the bottom third of this in a long diagonal, and insert it under the bark of the rootstock as in budding. Do not insert the whole of the diagonal cut in the rootstock; the top part should be clear above it. Bind with a grafting tie (thin twine is best), but not closely. The binding is used merely to hold the pieces together, not to bandage the wound in this case.

These grafts are united in two to three weeks when placed in a heated frame. They must then be transplanted into a greenhouse at a temperature suitable to keep them growing.

Propagation: Other Methods

Cuttings

Rooting plants from cuttings is a satisfying experience. Although budding gives quicker and more certain results, the patient gardener may have better long-term results with his cuttings, but only provided he is resolute in discarding the weaklings. Cuttings may be taken from roses from early summer to autumn. If taken in late summer or autumn, the cuttings can be rooted out of doors. Those taken earlier should be grown under good conditions for propagation in a greenhouse.

One cannot lay down hard and fast rules about which roses will root easily because some people will succeed with unlikely ones. In general the easiest roses to root are climbers, ramblers, shrubs, wild roses, miniatures and some floribundas, notably 'Queen Elizabeth' and 'Frensham'. The most difficult to root are hybrid teas, especially yellow ones, or any rose which has more than the average amount of pith, or which is slow to achieve the transformation of its cells into a woody state. If the choice exists, try to root the difficult ones under glass in the summer and leave the easier ones for outdoors in the winter. Miniatures are an exception, for their size makes them more vulnerable to damage in open ground, especially from being disturbed after frosts.

Choose young, firm wood of the current season's growth. For summer use under glass, it may be softer; for autumn use out of doors, it must be hard. Hard wood is most likely to be the lower 12–20cm (5–8in) of the shoot. The top of the shoot is not usually desirable. Cuttings of miniatures, naturally enough, are shorter.

Seed

Seed is only of use for raising wild roses or for breeding new varieties. Garden roses are almost all hybrids, and will not come true from seed. With rare exceptions, the seedlings of hybrids are inferior to the variety itself. Rose seed germinates over a long period and needs special treatment in most cases, otherwise only a few seeds germinate. The easiest roses to raise from seed are *R. multiflora* and *R. rugosa*, with some of their derivatives. There is little difference between raising rose seedlings and other seedling plants. Their main enemies are mildew, greenfly and birds; the latter enjoy pulling young seedlings out.

Rooting cuttings

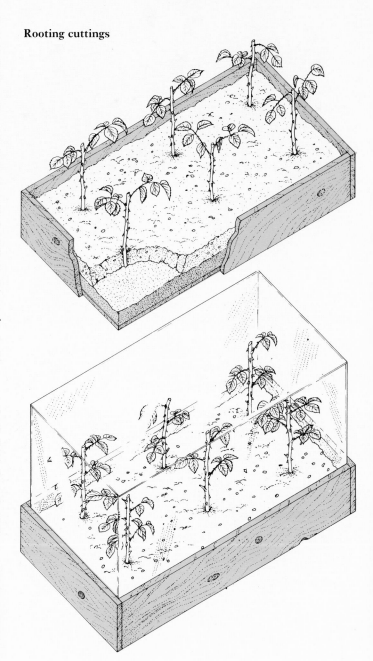

Autumn cuttings
There is very little to taking a rose cutting. First of all cut the shoot off the plant. It will probably have three to five leaves on it, unless it is one of those wild roses where the leaves are close together.

It is not necessary to cut the base of the cutting to an eye, any point will do. But cut the top so that it ends just above an eye, like a pruning cut.

Summer cuttings in heat
For summer cuttings under glass, remove only the bottom leaf or strip the bottom quarter if it is a close-leafed variety. Keep the rest of the leaves on. There is no need to remove any eyes unless the cutting is to be used as a rootstock. The eyes from below ground would prove to be suckers in that case. But if the cutting is to be an ornamental plant, the suckers will also be ornamental.

Rooting cuttings in heat
Dip the base of the cutting in a rooting hormone and plant it in good rooting soil or compost. The base of the cutting should be in close contact with friable and well-drained material. The favourite substance in the past was sand, which is now an ingredient of many modern composts.

Cuttings grown under glass in summer should be inserted so that the bottom quarter is under the soil. They need a humid atmosphere, ideally provided by a mist unit. Alternatively they can be enclosed in a case made by a frame of glass or polythene within the greenhouse. In the latter case the cuttings will need both spraying with water and ventilation. The grower will learn by experience how to balance these requirements correctly. The leaves of the cuttings fall off after a few days. They should be removed to prevent botrytis fungus.

Rooted cuttings in heat
After three weeks the cuttings should be rooted and will need less humidity and more air. Either turn off the mist and open the windows wider or else, if they are rooted in trays, carry them into a cold greenhouse.

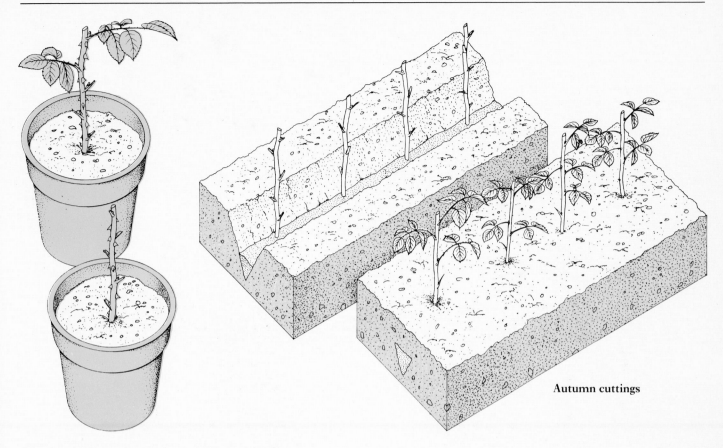

Autumn cuttings

Potting up rooted cuttings
The cuttings should be potted up about a week later and can be moved outside, provided that the change of temperature from one environment to another is minimal and gradual.

When the pots are full of root, the cuttings may be planted in their destined positions.

Rooting cuttings outdoors
For autumn cuttings outdoors, remove any leaves except for the top two. At this time of year the plants may be leafless.

The cuttings to be rooted outdoors in autumn need a sheltered position and fine soil. Their trench may be made by pushing a spade into the ground to make a V shape. Some sand or fine compost should go into the base of the trench. The cuttings should be inserted, close together, with at least half their length below ground. They will not root much, if at all, until the following spring. Meanwhile they are likely to be lifted after frost, in which case they should be firmed back again with the feet when the soil is dry.

In spring the cuttings grow leaves. Those which cannot root soon belie the promise of their leaves and die. The successful ones should be left all summer and may be dug up and transplanted the following autumn.

Storing seed
The seed is kept for a season in a mixture of slightly moist peat and sand. The mixture should be shaken up or turned over once a month. It is essential to keep out birds and mice which otherwise will eat the lot. The time to sow is in the subsequent spring and, if out of doors, preferably late enough to avoid early spring frost.

The storage period can be reduced for most roses by a process called vernalization. The seed is shelled out from the hips in autumn and stored in some slightly moist medium, such as vermiculite, for several weeks in a warm frame at about 18–20 C (65–70 F). It is then put outside for a similar period in a cold frame, where it experiences the alternate warmth and cold of winter. Breeders who use this method will normally sow the seed under glass before spring begins.

New Roses from seed

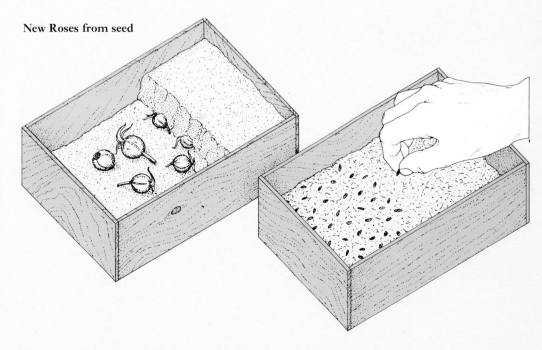

Controlling Pests and Diseases

Roses, in common with all living plants, are hosts to a number of parasitic organisms that feed upon and ultimately destroy their host unless the gardener intervenes with suitable counter-measures. Foremost in the war against pests and diseases is the rose grower's ability to provide an ideal situation for his roses, thus ensuring vigorous, healthy plants which are less likely to succumb to an attack of insect pests or fungal disease. Hence the first rule for controlling any parasite must be to feed the roses well and to maintain the good growing conditions of the rose bed.

Control of pests and diseases

All good garden shops stock the latest insecticides and fungicides specifically designed for use against rose pests. Formulations are frequently brought up to date or withdrawn, so that the recommendation of specific substances and advice on their application cannot be given. Great care should be taken by the gardener to carry out the manufacturer's instructions.

Hints for spraying pesticides

1 Identify the pest and obtain the appropriate insecticide or fungicide.
2 Use a sprayer with a lance jet and make sure the nozzle gives good atomization.
3 Spray on a calm day when rain is not expected.
4 Don't spray in bright sunshine or leaf scorch may result.
5 Read the instructions and follow them carefully.
6 Wear a mask and rubber gloves even if the product is safe.
7 Check the sprayer has not been used for weed control. If it has, wash it copiously or better still, obtain another sprayer.
8 Spray the underside of the leaves as well as the top.
9 Consider a repeat application about a week after the first to catch any pests or diseases that may have escaped or re-infested the plants.
10 Store safely any remaining concentrated insecticide or fungicide and wash your hands well after handling the container. Also wash the container and sprayer.

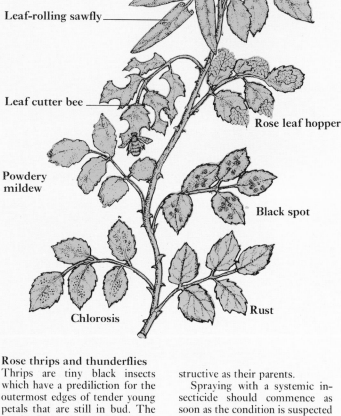

Cockchafer beetle
Rose thrip
Aphids
Rose slugworm sawfly
Caterpillar
Leaf-rolling sawfly
Leaf cutter bee
Rose leaf hopper
Powdery mildew
Black spot
Chlorosis
Rust

Insect Pests

Aphids (greenfly, blackfly)

There are several species of aphids. Their colour varies from black to near red although the most common type is green. Aphids occur in huge numbers on tender new rose growth from which they suck the sap and adversely affect the vitality of the plant. They are quick to breed and in favourable conditions will overwhelm a rose bed by smothering new buds and covering the foliage with sticky waste products. Fortunately they have many natural enemies such as sparrows and ladybirds. Aphids are relatively easy to control with systemic insecticides, but even so they can re-infect the roses within a very short time after treatment.

Since aphids are fed upon by birds and insects some people prefer to destroy them by using derris, or a mild spray of soapy water or detergent water (an egg-cupful of soft green soap or mild detergent to 9 litres or two gallons of water) rather than some of the more ruthless modern preparations. This does mean that the roses have to be sprayed at least once every week, perhaps more if rain washes away the effects of the spray.

Caterpillars

Moth and butterfly larvae feed on rose foliage and buds, leaving them holed and ragged. Although they are not responsible for extensive damage, caterpillars are the enemy of exhibitors who wish to produce flawless blooms and foliage. Because they seldom attack in large numbers the best way of dealing with them is to remove them by hand. Should they reach unmanageable proportions they are vulnerable to all the systemic insecticides.

Rose thrips and thunderflies

Thrips are tiny black insects which have a prediliction for the outermost edges of tender young petals that are still in bud. The result of their feeding is a distorted, misshapen bud with blackened edges to the petals, which will almost certainly be noticed before the insects themselves. The adult insect is winged. The nymphs are wingless but are almost as large and quite as destructive as their parents.

Spraying with a systemic insecticide should commence as soon as the condition is suspected and followed up one week later with another application. Delay in treatment may result in a ruined crop of bloom. Thrips can establish themselves in a rose bed very early in the season and remain undetected until the first blooms reveal the effects of their feeding.

Leaf-rolling sawflies

One of the most unusual rose pests is regrettably one of the most destructive. The eggs of the sawfly are laid in rows on the underside of the leaves early in the season, along with a toxin which causes the leaf to curl protectively round the eggs while they hatch. Leaves so affected are unable to serve the rose and result in a weakened plant.

Control in the past has been very difficult as the young larvae are protected from sprays by the curl of the leaf. Nowadays a systemic spray will easily check the sawfly larvae. The larvae descend into the soil and pupate, so following a bad attack the soil around the roses should be sprayed with a contact insecticide in the early spring.

Rose slugworm sawflies

The slugworm sawfly fosters its destructive young, usually one at a time, on the underside of rose leaves. The larvae have translucent, pale yellow skins through which it is possible to see the whole length of the food canal.

Rose leaf hoppers

In common with many other pests the leaf hopper exists for a great deal of its life on the underside of rose leaves. This pest is particularly damaging to climbing roses and causes pale mottled areas on the leaves. The effects of a severe infestation can result in premature leaf fall. Leaf hoppers are small, pale yellowish flying insects. They are often detected by the small leaps they make when the foliage is disturbed and the pale, empty skins left behind after their moult.

The eating habits of the larvae are to skeletonize the rose leaf by eating through the outer surface of the foliage, leaving only a network of ribs which soon wither and turn brown. Control is achieved with a systemic or contact insecticide.

Control is achieved with a systemic and contact compound spray. Particular attention should be paid to the underside of the leaves and the surrounding earth onto which the disturbed insects will fall.

Cockchafer beetles

There are several types of chafer beetles that are harmful to roses. They often invade the garden in great numbers, the adults having a liking for rose foliage, buds and blooms while the young larvae mercilessly devour the roots. The beetles fly at dusk to lay their eggs in light, sandy soil or to change their habitat. Prevention is better than cure, for chafer beetles can cause a great deal of damage in a short time. Dusting the bushes with a powder insecticide is particularly effective in warding off an impending attack.

Leaf cutter bees

Leaf cutter bees are similar to honey bees in appearance although the females, which cause damage to rose foliage, differ in that they make a nest in a wall or tree cavity in which to raise their young. They cut neat semicircular pieces out of rose leaves and carry them away to make cells in which to lay their eggs and store honey. Unless there are a great many of these creatures decimating the rose foliage, it will probably be more rewarding to observe their industrious habits than to set about destroying them. This can only be done by catching them with a net or using a fly-killer aerosol.

Fungus diseases

All the so-called diseases of the rose are fungus related. Fungi produce great quantities of spores which become embedded in the tissue of the plants they invade. Their parasitic existence usually culminates in the premature defoliation or even death of the host. Repeated attacks point to a regular source of infection which can be as close as decaying fallen leaf debris or as far away as an entrenched infection in a neighbouring garden. Control therefore is as much a matter of preventing fresh spores taking hold as of combating the symptoms of those already established in the plant. There are some varieties that are prone to attack from the most destructive fungus diseases: mildew, black spot and rust. If, in spite of treatment, the blight persists year after year and spoils enjoyment of the roses, the plants are better removed and replaced with more resistant types.

Diseases

Powdery mildew

Mildew is the most common disease of the rose. Young growth is vulnerable to attack but some varieties are more prone than others and will be smothered from top to bottom with what appears to be a powdery greyish-white covering. A spraying programme should be started as soon as tender shoots show signs of this powdery mould. These first symptoms only herald worse to come and a severe attack of unsightly mildew makes for very weak plants.

There are several methods of control that might be tried. The first should always be to consider the feeding of the roses to see if too much nitrogenous food is causing extravagant, defenceless growth. A little potash might be all that is necessary to redress the soil balance and harden up the growth.

Modern fungicides are now available in systemic form which enables them to attack spores hidden in the leaf tissue as well as the fully developed visible mildew. This treatment is to a certain extent waterproof and will have a much more lasting effect than a contact fungicide. However it is important to remember that the spray penetrates and persists only in the foliage on to which it is sprayed. Repeated applications will be necessary on new growth as it forms.

People who do not like using complex modern chemicals may feel more at home with one or other forms of the old-fashioned fungicides. A spray containing a weak solution of copper sulphate, for instance, appears to work off the powdery mould. Sprays based on the fungicidal properties of sulphur are still available and are very effective providing they are not applied too strongly or in hot, dry weather (this tends to burn the foliage) or expected to last after rainfall. Careful dusting of infected foliage with finely powdered sulphur can also be very effective.

Black spot

The second most common disease of the rose, but by far the most destructive, is black spot, so named because of the irregular, disfiguring black marks this fungus creates on the foliage. If allowed to run its course, premature defoliation seriously impairs the vigour of the plants and greatly reduces their span of life. The old methods of treatment were based upon limiting the spread of the disease by removing infected leaves from the bush and the soil and by sterilizing and spraying the mulch in early spring and autumn.

The modern way is to use a systemic fungicide specifically developed for use against black spot fungus. Systemic spray is absorbed into the foliage which in consequence is protected against invasion by new spores. A regular spraying programme that anticipates the onset of the disease, combined with the removal of infected debris, can now provide an effective control. Nothing, however, can actually remove the black spots which are areas of decayed leaf cells that once fed the disease.

Rust

The spores of rose rust first appear as rusty-orange coloured specks on the underside of leaves and stems. By mid-summer they turn black and are ready to survive the winter to re-infect the bush the following year. Rust can be an outright killer of newly planted roses, so infected plants should be destroyed to eliminate the source of the disease. Rust appears to be selective in the varieties it chooses to attack. Since there is no cure for the disease, particularly susceptible varieties should be excluded from the rose garden. Dig up and burn infected plants or, alternatively, cut off infected leaves and stems and spray regularly with a fungicide, remembering that the spores can become active after being dormant for years.

Chlorosis

Yellowing of the leaves is often mistaken for a disease but in fact it is usually indicative of a soil deficiency if widespread, or waterlogging if it is localized. The condition is common in lime soils which tend to 'lock up' the iron in the soil and deny the plant this essential trace element. Confirmation of a suspected deficiency is best sought from a rose-growing neighbour or the parks department of the local authority.

Treatment can be as simple as the application of a solution of ordinary Epsom salts, improving waterlogged soil conditions, or the use of sequestered iron.

Crown gall

This is a bacterial disease rarely seen on roses outside North America. The disease manifests itself in hard, irregular growths known as galls. If these appear on stems or roots the affected parts can be cut away and the wound sealed with Stockholm tar. If the crown (the point at which the plant was budded) is affected the whole plant may have to be destroyed by burning.

Roses in the Greenhouse

Roses grown in the open are subject to cold, wind and rain and cannot be expected to match the flawless perfection of blooms and foliage produced in a greenhouse. The glasshouse grower contrives to provide the ideal environment for roses, either to produce immaculate specimens for floral arrangements or to force the bushes into flowering a month or two earlier than those grown out of doors.

The greenhouse
Ideally, roses should have a light, airy location such as that provided by the lofty, high-walled glasshouses used by nurserymen. Most domestic-sized greenhouses are not capable of providing good air circulation while at the same time economically maintaining a relatively high temperature during the winter months. Most are also not big enough to allow for many plants. If the eaves are over 2.5m (8ft) high, roses may be planted directly into specially prepared beds and induced to give up to three or four crops of bloom a year for several seasons until they become exhausted. Roses respond well to light, airy surroundings but they are particularly vulnerable to draughty air currents. A localized attack of mildew is usually the result of a broken pane of glass or an ill-fitting door. Ventilation should come from high in the roof and not from vents in the walls of the greenhouse or from an open door.

The heating system should provide a constant temperature of between 13°C (55°F) and 16°C (60°F), depending on the degree of forcing required. Higher temperatures will only result in a loss of quality, so an efficient thermostat is essential. Shading from direct sunlight should be applied sufficiently early in the season to prevent leaf scorch but, since light is so important to the growing plant, it is a fine judgement as to when exactly the shading should be introduced. It is always better, however, to err on the side of caution as there is no cure for the unsightly scars of leaf scorch.

Planting
Rose planting areas in a greenhouse should be prepared in much the same way as outdoor beds. (See the chapter on 'How and When to Plant'.) Good, well-drained soil should be double dug to incorporate the initial application of manure. This should be done as much in advance of autumn planting as possible. While double digging, take the opportunity to run a hosepipe into the trench to flood the sub-soil which, if denied the benefit of regular watering or rainfall, can often become hard and dry. The bed will remain waterlogged for a while, so planting should be deferred until the excess water has drained away and the soil is firm and settled. Planting distances in the greenhouse bed can be as close as 30cm (12in) in any direction, but remember to allow for access to all blooms by keeping the beds not much wider than 1.2m (4ft).

Pot-grown rose bushes are suitable for the domestic-sized greenhouse where space can be allocated to only a few plants for a limited period of time. A 20cm (8in) pot is the best container in which to plant such a bush rose. Roses are best potted in a reasonably light, medium compost together with some long-lasting fertilizer. Place one or more pieces of broken crock in the bottom of the pot to aid drainage, then quarter-fill the pot with compost and compare the size of the roots with the pot. More often than not, the roots will be too large to fit without bending them double and it is generally considered better to cut off the extra-long roots rather than fold them over just to get them into the soil. Load handfuls of compost into the pot while holding the plant in position and use a dibbing stick from time to time to distribute the compost between the roots. Do not overfill the pot but leave a space of about 5cm (2in) between the top of the soil and the rim for watering and feeding.

Although the rose bushes should be potted as soon as they arrive in the autumn, they need not be moved into the greenhouse until the weather starts to get really cold. The ideal position for the 'once indoors' pots is on a well-drained layer of ashes or gravel which is packed around the base of the containers. The ashes or gravel can impart moisture to the pot when it is dry and accommodate the overflow during watering. The pots can be placed close to one another so that every bit of available greenhouse space can be exploited.

Forcing
Heating the greenhouse, in order to start the forcing process, should not be commenced before mid-winter. Daylight hours have an influence on the quality of blooms eventually produced, and heat alone will result in reducing the size of the blooms. To allow for the shorter days, a gentle heat of around 7°C (45°F) should be maintained for a fortnight and then increased a few degrees each week for two months until a temperature of around 16°C (60°F) is reached. This temperature should be maintained throughout the time the roses grow and bloom.

Feeding and watering
A light, medium compost with a built-in, slow-acting fertilizer supplies the potted roots with enough nourishment to give them a good start. Permanently planted roses will have the benefit of the manure that went into the preparation of their beds but, since both methods of growing are very intensive, there will be only a limited amount of soil to support each bush. The initial food supply, therefore, will have to be supplemented by quick-acting fertilizer while the roses are growing and flowering. Liquid feeding provides a constant supply of nutrients to the plants as well as taking care of routine watering.

There are several brands of liquid fertilizer that have a formulation and application rate suitable for roses. It is usual to dilute a quantity in a large plastic bin and distribute it by watering can directly onto the soil at the base of the roses, or into the pots. If warm weather causes the soil or pots to dry out before another feed is recommended, use plain water to moisten the soil. Feeding should be resumed only when the moisture content of the soil is back to normal, otherwise a harmful concentration of nutrient salts may result.

Summer treatment
Roses should be given time to recuperate after a period of forcing. Potted roses should be taken out of the greenhouse after they have flowered and plunged into soil for the rest of the summer and autumn. Dig a hole big enough to accommodate all the pot and bury it so that it will not require further attention until it is time to move it back into the greenhouse. At this time dig up the pot and remove the garden soil and also 3–5cm (an inch or so) of the pot soil. Replace the latter with a half handful of bone-meal and 2.5cm (1in) of fresh potting compost. Prune the bushes hard back in order to start the new forcing cycle.

Bushes planted directly into the greenhouse soil should be 'let down', or rested, for the whole of late summer and autumn. All ventilators and doors should be left open until the leaves have fallen. The bushes should be pruned hard back and lightly dressed with bone-meal before forcing commences once more. Always remove and burn prunings and dead leaves.

Problems

The most usual problem encountered when growing greenhouse roses is their vulnerability to mildew. Draught will aggravate this tendency and there are some varieties which are more susceptible than others. By far the best treatment for all fungus diseases is the electric sulphur evaporator that releases microscopic particles of sulphur into the greenhouse atmosphere to be deposited on leaves and stems and generally provides a hostile environment for mildew, black spot and rust spores.

Alternatively, there are regular sprays for rose diseases which must be applied as soon as trouble is identified and maintained throughout the active growing period of the roses. Systemic insecticides will control any pest attack but when they are used in the greenhouse special care should be taken not to inhale the spray mist. Always wear a mask and remember to retreat towards the door when spraying.

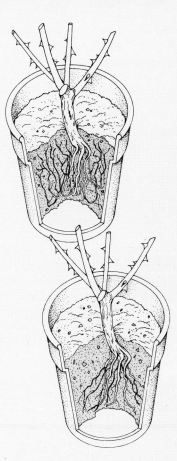

Above: Preparing the pot
A couple of pieces of broken crock placed in the bottom of the pot will aid drainage. Quarter-fill the pot with compost.

Above: Trimming to fit
It is much better to trim off roots that are too long for the container than attempt to fold them in. The crown of the bush should be just above the rim of the pot.

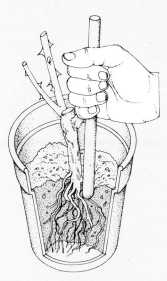

Above: Firming the compost
Use a blunt stick to force compost between the roots and firm it with your thumbs while filling the pot. Leave a space of about 5cm (2in) between the top of the soil and the rim of the pot.

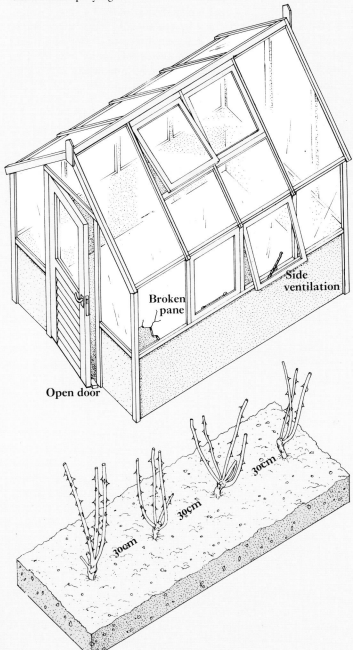

Open door

Broken pane

Side ventilation

Above left
Greenhouse roses abhor draughty air. Broken panes, side ventilation and permanently open doors will inevitably lead to a localized attack of mildew. Use air from ventilators on the ridge of the greenhouse.

Left
Roses can be planted as close as 30cm (12in) apart to exploit every bit of space in the greenhouse. Be careful to make the beds not much wider than 1.2m (4ft) or some blooms will be out of reach.

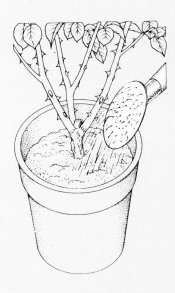

Above: Feeding and watering
When watering or feeding, do not wet the foliage or it will scorch and produce unsightly brown patches.

Growing Roses for Exhibition

How are you to judge the excellence of your roses unless you enter them in competition with those of other enthusiasts? If you feel you are growing specimen blooms or simply that you would just like to compare your roses with those produced by others, you can be certain that nearly every summer flower show will have a class for both novice and expert.

Timing

Experienced exhibitors plan to have their bushes in full bloom on the eve of the rose show. To this end they observe the usual time at which their bushes will be in full bloom and if necessary bring about a delay in flowering by pruning them back when they are well into spring growth.

Most local shows tend to occur after the normal first flush of bloom simply because it is easier to delay flower production rather than bring plants into flower prematurely. Long years of experience may be forgone by listening to rose show winners who will advise you of the best time to prune bushes for particular shows. When you have some idea of this date, extend your own pruning over a week either side, thus ensuring a constant production of blooms, whether the season be early or late.

Varieties

Rose judges work with the criterion that a large, perfect bloom will always beat a small, perfect one. The perfect hybrid tea bloom is full and double with a high, pointed centre and slightly reflexed petals forming a perfect symmetry. The ideal floribunda will sport a large flower truss with each bloom at its voluptuous best. A miniature rose should be petite, crisp and fresh. The catalogue of roses in this book lists some varieties which are especially suitable for exhibition but novelties to suit the specialist are always being introduced, so make a note of any newcomer that wins a prize.

Growing prize roses

Some dedicated exhibitors claim that it is possible to obtain specimen blooms only from maiden bushes and so they bud new roses every year. This may be an extreme viewpoint; however most exhibitors agree that a severe pruning, almost back to the ground (which allows only three or four main basal shoots to grow and produce bloom), is desirable. With either of these methods it is impossible to reconcile the routine of growing roses for a fine garden display with the ruthless dedication required to produce prize-winning roses.

Roses destined for exhibition should be treated to well-drained soil which has been manured and double dug. Top quality blooms are achieved by supplying the bush with as much nutrient as it can use. Unless the growing environment is ideal the roots will be unable to assimilate their regular weekly feed of potash-enriched liquid feed. A careful watch and a routine spraying programme against mildew, black spot or insect pests should be instituted. Once such pests and diseases have declared themselves visibly they may have already done irreparable damage.

The technique of disbudding ensures that all the vigour of one hybrid tea stem goes into the production of a single specimen. In floribundas the central bloom in the flower cluster usually develops first and is long past its prime before the rest of the flowers in the truss open. The central bloom should be removed as soon as possible with a sharp knife or pair of scissors so that the truss develops without the presence of a useless bloom. As the flower stems develop they need to be supported by a cane which

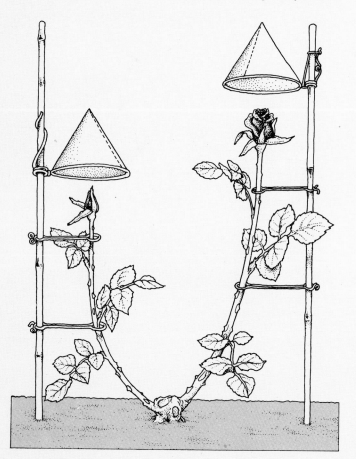

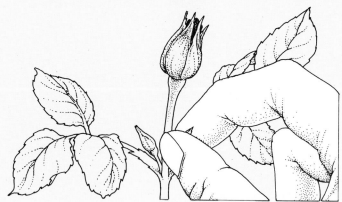

Left: Bloom protectors
Paper-covered wire twists or patent plant ties can be used to secure each stem to a cane for support, while at the same time preventing the developing blooms from chafing against the cane. Cone-shaped bloom protectors are made from a variety of materials including waterproof card and plastic. Methods of fixing vary. Clip them into position on the support as soon as the bud shows colour. As the stem grows, move the cones to maintain a space of around 5cm (2in) between the top of the bloom and the base of the cone.

Above: Disbudding hybrid teas
Disbudding produces the largest possible hybrid tea blooms by sacrificing the two smaller side buds. Before they have reached the size of a pea, rub or pinch out the buds on either side of the main bud. This directs all the stem's nourishment into the one bloom.

serves both to separate the developing blooms and carry a waterproof cone to protect them from rain and sun.

Cutting and preparing

Blooms which have unfolded their sepals and are showing colour usually have about three or four days to go before they reach perfection. Cones should be used to protect all blooms that look like opening in time for a rose show. Really large blooms which look as if they will mature a day or two ahead of judging time can be retarded by tying them up. The trick is to ease back the outermost petals with a camel hair brush and take a single turn of soft, thick knitting wool or worsted round the heart of the bloom. The tie should be secured with a couple of twists rather than a knot. From time to time brush the twists lightly to release the tension, taking account of the growth of the bloom. If the tie is not adjusted in this way the petals may become bruised. Remove the tie at the show just before judging commences. Cut your chosen blooms on the evening before the show and allow them to stand overnight in a cool place up to their necks in a bucket of water containing cut-flower nutrient. Blooms which are cut and staged without a good drink will quickly flag.

Transportation

Separate and secure the stems in the bucket with handfuls of crumpled wet newspaper. This will cushion the points of sharp thorns and prevent the water from slopping over on your way to the show. If you have to transport your roses in a box, a crumpled strip of newspaper packed under the necks of each row of blooms will save the outer petals from creasing. Damp newspaper packed round the cut ends of the stems will prevent them from drying out.

Left: Disbudding floribundas
The centre bud of a floribunda cluster usually develops well ahead of the others and is past its best before the rest of the buds open. The centre bud should be removed as deftly as possible so that no scar is visible to mar the spray when it is exhibited.

Transporting blooms
Above right
Flower stems can be protected against thorn or friction damage when being transported by cushioning them with handfuls of wet newspaper at the top and bottom of the container of water. The top layer prevents the water or cut-bloom nutrient from slopping in transit.

Right
Blooms travelling dry can be cushioned against damage by layers of crumpled newspaper under their necks and damp newspaper round the base of the stems. The stems are cut back a little and placed in water as soon as they reach the show.

Growing Roses for Exhibition

The techniques and tricks of exhibiting roses are learnt only after a long and dedicated apprenticeship, but there are a few basic points to ensure that novice exhibitors make a good start.

The schedule

Rose judges will not overlook one tiny breach of the show class rules. The most beautiful blooms in the world will not win a prize unless they are displayed according to the schedule. Immediately your interest is stimulated sufficiently to try showing your roses in competition, obtain a schedule from the flower show secretary and study the classes relating to roses. Local flower shows are perhaps less awesome for the beginner than shows specializing in roses, although the latter do more often have novice classes and provide the opportunity of displaying a wider range of material than the former.

Show rules are designed to eliminate all cause for argument so the terminology used is technical and precise. If, for instance, Class III is for a vase of six floribunda stems, it means six, not five or seven, and it means floribundas, not floribunda/hybrid tea types or shrub roses. Very probably it also means (read the rules carefully) they are to be staged in a vase provided by the show organizers.

Staging

The condition of blooms changes by the hour so it is always advisable to take at least twice as many as you intend to stage. Allow yourself plenty of time to find the show secretary to obtain and fill in the class card and receive your bowl or vase if it is to be supplied by the show. You should take your own packing for a vase. This can be either crumbled florist's block or the traditional reeds or non-floating drinking straws. The latter are gently squeezed into the vase and cut off level with the top so that they separate and secure the flower stems. The blooms are staged in them after they have been topped up with water.

At rose shows there are always classes for boxes of six or a dozen blooms. Although there are classes for the novice, the box sizes and furbishings can vary from area to area and it is perhaps best to start with vases and bowls and graduate to the boxes only when you have observed how others 'wire' the neck and dress the petals in this specialized method of staging blooms. Blooms should always be staged so that they are evenly spaced and do not touch one another. The length of stem should be in proportion to the container and the size of the bloom.

Staging roses in vases

The best way to show off hybrid teas in a vase is to arrange them in the shape of an inverted triangle, i.e. three blooms on the top, two blooms in the centre and one at the base of a six bloom arrangement. In a class for mixed varieties ensure that the various colours are separated and always place the smallest bloom at the bottom of the arrangement and the biggest at the top. Radiate the blooms in a bowl to form a well-spaced arc of flowers which do not touch but relate to each other, thus giving symmetry to the arrangement.

Floribundas should be presented with as many flowers to the truss as possible, although it is better to sacrifice a poor bloom than to allow it to remain and spoil the cluster. Space the stems evenly and avoid staging extra vigorous varieties that are out of proportion with their companions. Miniature roses should be staged to show off their dainty habit. The length of stalk should be in proportion to the size of the flowers.

Judging

The criteria for judging a rose are, first, that it should be at the peak of perfection at the moment it is judged and, second, that its foliage and presentation should be relevant to the class for which the rose is entered. Any blemish to the bloom will be noted and judged against its quality. Freshness of colour will count against a dull rival. The accolade of perfection will go to a bloom which is on the brink of opening rather than a flower that is overblown or shows signs of a split centre. Foliage should be clean and undamaged and the presentation should have balance and proportion.

Most competitions will require you to name the roses you have staged. Even if they do not, a crisp clean card bearing the names of the roses you have staged can provide a touch of showmanship that might tip the balance in the case of a tie. This card remains face up when your roses are judged but the stewards will see that your class card is face downwards.

Blooms can be held back from maturing for a few days and encouraged to produce a high centre by tying up the heart of the bud. Use worsted, thick knitting wool or raffia that has been soaked and softened. A double twist is preferable to a knot as it is desirable to slacken off the tension from time to time to prevent bruising. Release the tie when staging to test that the centre is holding, then retie the bloom until the last minute before judging takes place.

When staging blooms, try not to touch them but rather tease them into shape by blowing on them gently or using a camel hair brush. A bloom with a tight centre may be improved by softly brushing back the outer petals.

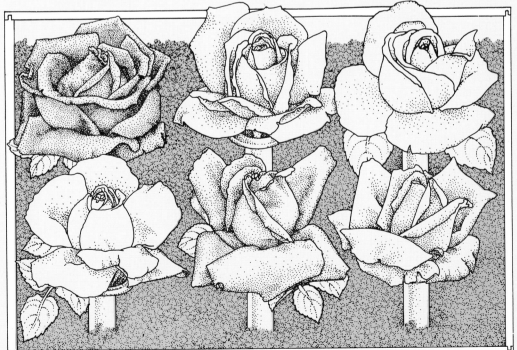

Above left
Three hybrid teas staged well apart in the shape of an inverted triangle in a typical show vase. This ensures that the judges can view each bloom fully.

Above
A bowl of mixed hybrid teas spaced so that each bloom relates to its neighbour but does not look overcrowded. Shorter-stemmed flowers should be placed at the front and the supporting mesh hidden by leaves.

Left
A special box with tubes and bloom holders is required for staging in box classes. Each rose is held in position by rings. To complete a good exhibit, cover the top surface of the box with moss, label clearly each variety and, if necessary, tilt the box forward slightly to show the blooms to their best advantage.

Planning a Rose Garden

Rose gardens have existed for many centuries but there is no set form for creating them. They can be formal or informal in style provided that consideration is given to basic horticultural factors and that the layout is soundly designed. A great deal of formality has been associated with rose gardens over the years. Early, traditional garden makers created geometrically-shaped beds laid out in regular patterns, often complemented by such features as sundials, summer houses, arches and statues. In contrast, the naturalistic or informal style of rose garden can be very successful and may possibly allow the rose gardener a greater range of choice and self-expression in its design.

Planning the design
Scale and balance are in the forefront of all good garden design. The actual shape of the beds in the formal rose garden is not so important as their scale, form and manageability. The wise designer also thinks about vistas and focal points. He tries to make full use of available space and never forgets the importance of free movement – both visual and physical – about the finished layout.

Balanced, well-proportioned beds are a great help when it comes to maintenance. Careful consideration should be given to their size so that they can accommodate the roses comfortably. If garden room is restricted, it is better to keep the design simple and plant shrewdly to avoid cramming. Formal, geometric shapes succeed together no matter how they are associated. Provided that balance, scale and form are sensibly evaluated, there are few problems. In developing a rose garden of natural style, however, all associated bed shapes should complement each other in a fluent way. This gives unity and flow to the design which is both pleasing to the eye and shows the roses to best advantage.

Colour and contrast
Blocks of the same colour are generally considered to be more effective than mixed colour arrangements. Formal rose garden design offers scope for colour blocking, making it particularly easy to arrange controlled blends or sharp contrasts, depending on individual tastes. Contrasting and grading colours is absorbing and worthwhile: reds may be contrasted with whites, pinks blended into reds, and the palest cream may be linked with bright yellow through a range of intermediate shades. There are many ways to arrange colour effects and a little careful thought is the only prerequisite. White blooms are always useful as coolers or buffers, preventing many a colour clash. They give liveliness to almost any combination of colours. Where there is no scope for blocks of the same colour and mixed roses have to be planted instead, whites can be used to link the different shades most effectively.

Foliage colours vary remarkably, and so do leaf sizes. It is worth giving this aspect of rose selection a thought, particularly when considering shrub roses. In all roses, however, there is a great range of colour and character in the leaves, spines and stems. Some of the sweet briars, for example, have beautifully scented foliage.

The informal rose garden lends itself more readily to less rigid colour treatment and gives the opportunity of including other shrubs (evergreen, flowering or otherwise) to serve as foils during blossoming and assist in offering permanent form to the planting design. Hip-bearing and late-blooming roses extend the display in the rose garden but selected shrubs of different kinds can be a useful addition. Rosemary (*Rosmarinus*) and lavender (*Lavandula*), with their silvery-green foliage, always blend well. *Viburnum tinus*, which flowers in winter and spring, offers a handsome dark-leaved background in the larger garden. Philadelphus, with its white flowers in the summer, looks well with red roses. Many rose gardens are improved by the winter-flowering *Viburnum farreri*. Clematis makes a good companion for climbing roses and conifers associate well with roses in all seasons.

Flowering times
Size and growth habit should be considered when selecting roses. Sizes should be carefully graded so that each rose has the chance to grow well and look its best. Flowering periods are also important, particularly when choosing climbing varieties. Some of these, such as the beautiful 'Albertine', carry only one flush of bloom while others, like 'Danse du Feu', will offer a secondary display later in the season. If space is restricted this may be a very important consideration indeed. Many other kinds of rose offer a fair continuity of blossom. This may be encouraged in hybrid teas by the shortening of flowered growth after the initial display. Cutting roses for indoor decoration also helps to prolong the flowering period.

It is worthwhile to try and find suitable varieties for given garden circumstances. Roses are remarkably tolerant but it will pay, for example, to plant strong growers in difficult situations. Shady walls are sometimes regarded as a problem but there is a number of climbing roses very willing to take on the challenge, including the pink 'Dr W. van Fleet' and the sweetly scented, pink 'Zéphirine Drouhin'. This lovely rose is subject to mildew in some years but preventive spraying very early in the growing season goes a long way towards curbing the problem.

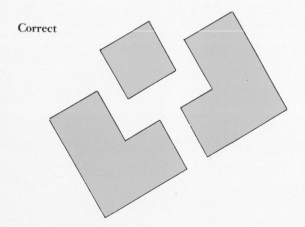

Correct

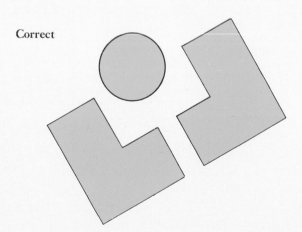

Correct

Formal   Conifers

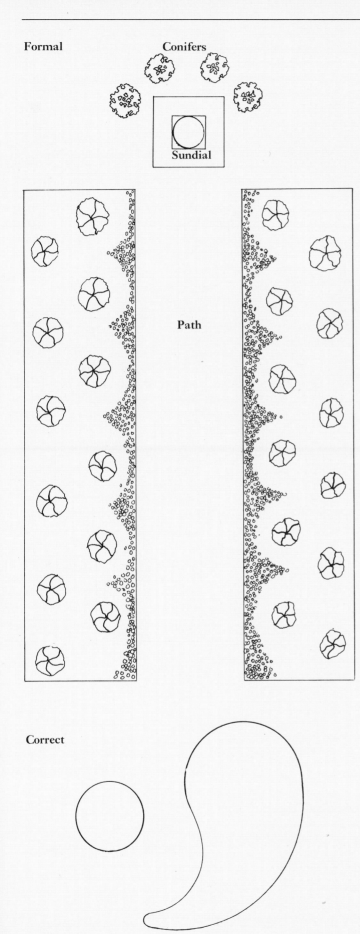

Sundial

Path

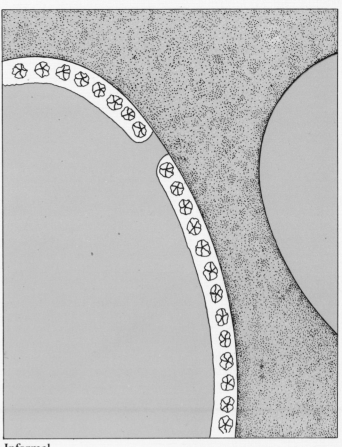

Informal

Left
A design for formal rose borders edged with small plants such as pinks (*Dianthus*), pansies (*Viola*), thrift (*Armeria*) and catmint (*Nepeta*). A vista is created with a sundial and grouped conifers.

Opposite page and below
Geometrically-shaped beds always combine well in formal rose gardens. With informally-styled gardens the bed shapes should complement each other to give unity to the design. The rectangular bed seen here is clearly alien to the tear-drop shape.

Above
Roses planted on one side only of an approach path give complete freedom of movement.

Correct   Incorrect

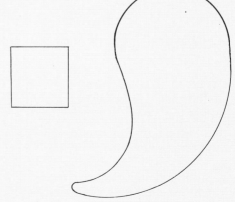

Town Gardens and Patios

Roses grow well in city gardens and look as much at home there as they do in country surroundings. The character of a city garden may be determined by its environment and this can influence the choice of landscaping style to some extent. It might be formal, in keeping with the style of the area and adjacent buildings; on the other hand the severity of the surrounding structures may be softened by a more informal approach.

The urban gardener may feel he is hampered by lack of sunlight. This should not preclude the rose as roses take to a degree of sunlessness and some will grow in permanent shade. Varieties which are prone to sun scorching may even produce better blooms in shady areas. Many industrial towns today do not present a handicap to the keen rose gardener. Where conditions are not ideal, however, it is always worth paying great attention to the basic matters of soil food, air and water. City dwellers without gardens can plant compact dwarf and miniature roses in window boxes or tubs placed on a balcony. Nowadays the town gardener is far from being limited in the variety of roses he can grow.

Roses for city gardens

There are several types of rose which can be exploited to the full in confined spaces. Climbers and ramblers can be used for covering walls and fences without taking up very much space. Properly installed support wires or soundly constructed trellis are essential for successful rose-growing on walls. If these are firmly attached at the outset they will hold roses secure as they are trained, pruned and tied over the years.

Every inch of a town garden has to be utilized, but it is often difficult to find low-growing subjects to plant close to a path and fill in the gap between the blooms of bush roses and the ground level without impeding movement along the path. Miniature roses

which grow to around 25cm (10in) in height and dwarf floribundas which do not exceed 45cm (18in) suit this sort of situation. Dwarf floribundas are sometimes called cushion roses because of their rounded, compact habit. If planted close together they form a low, continuous hedge. Miniatures can be planted as close as 15cm (6in) to a garden path and spaced at 30cm (12in) intervals. Dwarf floribundas require a little more room to be able to show off their abundance of bloom.

Miniature roses can be used effectively in rock gardens. Because they are small they can manage very well in a pocket of soil; in fact a restricted root space helps to maintain their desirable diminutive stature. The best effect is achieved by spacing them evenly throughout. Trim miniatures with scissors rather than prune them until they grow too large for their situation and then cut hard back with secateurs.

Patios and paved areas

The patio forms a link between house and garden and is often regarded as an extension of the home. It could be made larger rather than smaller if it is to be a feature and a real asset. The roses grown for the patio should be tailored to the area. Walls and overhead structures such as pergolas can be used for climbers and ramblers. Bush roses and miniatures can be grown in beds or gaps in the paving. Standard roses are suitable for restricted planting spaces and may be grown with bush roses to conceal their stems.

If patios or raised beds are constructed with retaining walls, spaces left in the wall faces can be used for ground cover roses and miniatures accompanied by other small plants such as pinks (*Dianthus*), thrift (*Armeria*) and aubrieta. Ground cover or prostrate roses may also be used to soften the appearance of paved areas and paths.

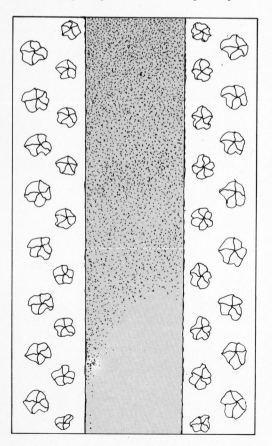

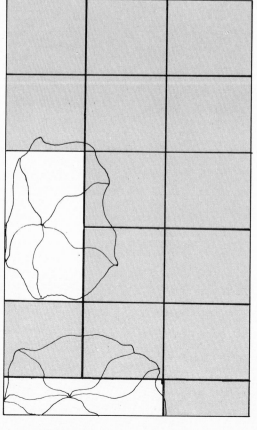

Far left
Miniatures can be planted as close as 15cm (6in) to pathways. Dwarf floribundas require a little more room; but both types of rose help to hide the bare lower branches of taller roses flanking a path.

Near left
Ground cover or prostrate roses such as 'Nozomi' can be used for softening the appearance of stone troughs or retaining walls. They can also lend charm and maturity to paved areas and paths. Each plant can be expected to grow about 1m (3ft) in any direction.

Rejuvenating Roses

Most roses can be considered past their prime after about 12 years of growing in a rose bed. At this time consideration is normally given to their replacement with new plants and perhaps more recent varieties. However, for sentimental or economic reasons, or after a long period of neglect, rose bushes sometimes have to be rescued and rejuvenated.

Pruning old hybrid teas and floribundas

There is often little difference in the appearance of an old, neglected rose bush and an old, cultivated one. Providing they are alive, they will both have produced a number of short, weak shoots sprouting from a hard, bark-encrusted stump that is more or less covered by the brittle stems of dead flower stalks. New growth is restricted by this decayed woody material which must be cropped back as close to the crown as possible with the aid of good secateurs, a pruning knife or even a small pruning saw. New growth that has managed to sprout through the encrusted stump will inevitably be slight and weak. These shoots are all that the rose has to survive on, so they should be pruned only lightly until they are replaced by strong new basal stems from the crown.

Suckers

The older the rose, the more likely it is that the bush was budded onto an understock prone to suckering. When a rose has difficulty in growing new shoots from an encrusted crown it will often engender sucker growth that saps the life of the old plant and eventually takes over. All suckers should be carefully removed by the method described in the chapter on pruning and thinning.

Replacement

A large bed of old roses will sometimes develop an unsightly gap that will need filling with new plants of the same variety. Very often such a bed has been inherited from a previous gardener and the name of the variety may not be known. If the name of the nurseryman who supplied the roses is known, write to him enclosing a mature bloom and a few leaves. State as much as you know about the habit of the plant and the approximate date it was supplied.

Rose societies often have a bloom identification service. Although some may not welcome enquiries through the post, they will have experts at their rose shows. Even when an old variety can be named, it may be that the only source is the original raiser. Rose societies and most growers can provide this information.

Climbers and ramblers

Climbers and ramblers that have been left to their own devices will have grown too upright. Most of the new growth will have occurred at the very top of the plants, leaving their lower branches bare of flowers and foliage. Reclamation of a climbing rose takes time. The big basal shoots should be teased over to a horizontal position as close to the ground as possible. This treatment encourages new lateral growth which provides both cover and blooms.

It may be necessary to tie the basal shoots with thin ropes which are attached to pegs hammered in the ground. In this way the shoots can be lowered gradually by tightening the ropes at regular intervals until they reach the required position. Old stems are thick and brittle so it may take a couple of seasons to bend them down without damaging them. Perseverance is usually rewarded by the appearance of vigorous new basal shoots breaking from the crown. These are easy to train and will eventually replace the oldest and most unmanageable branches.

Transplanting old rose bushes

Roses which have been established in a rose bed over a number of years have usually come to terms with their environment and are not making much new root growth. In sandy soil the roots are likely to be light and fibrous with one long taproot that has grown down in search of moisture. In wet clay soils the roots are coarse and look something like porous subterranean branches, totally devoid of fibre. Whatever the roots look like, they are fundamental to the existence of the plant.

An old rose bush that is to be transplanted should be dug up carefully in the dormant season. The spade should be inserted vertically into the soil at least 30cm (12in) away from the crown of the rose bush and forced back to lever both the roots and associated soil from the earth. This action should be repeated on all four sides of the bush until it is loose enough to be lifted, not pulled, from the ground, causing as little damage to the roots as possible.

Prune the bush hard in the manner previously described, cut away any excessively long taproots and prune clean any severed root. Replant the bush immediately to avoid root damage, incorporating some moist peat in the new hole. Follow this with a top dressing of bone-meal and keep the plant well-watered until new growth appears in the first flowering season. To encourage vigorous new root action do not use fertilizer until halfway through the first flowering season.

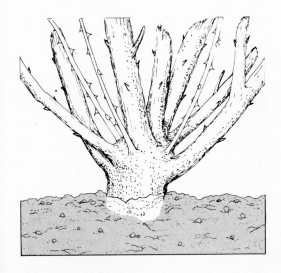
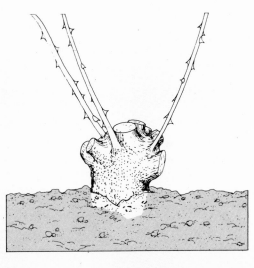

An old rose bush before and after remedial treatment
Far left: A typical old rose bush past its prime. The stump is covered with dead twigs and a few weak shoots.

Near left: The dead twigs should be cut hard back to the crown and the few weak flower shoots left lightly pruned.

Seasonal Survey of Care

Spring

Final pruning of established bush roses
Remove dead and thin growth from shrub roses
Finish planting new rose bushes
Water newly-planted roses
First application of rose fertilizer
Weed rose beds and apply pre-emergence weedkiller
Mulch with manure or peat
Watch for pests such as greenfly and caterpillars on new growth
Shade the greenhouse
Plant understocks

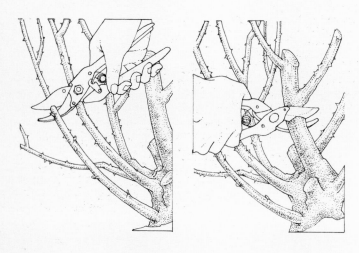

Summer

Order new roses for autumn planting
Second application of fertilizer
Water in the evening in dry weather
Disbud hybrid teas and remove central bud from floribunda
    flower clusters
Dead-head matured blooms
Spray for mildew and other diseases if necessary
Continue watching for pests
Prune ramblers after they have bloomed
Bud new roses on to understocks

Autumn

Preliminary pruning of bush roses – shorten main shoots
Prepare sites for new roses
Plant new roses (temperate climate)
Dead-head matured blooms
Continue to disbud hybrid teas
Open all vents in the greenhouse
Watch for pests and diseases in the greenhouse
Insulate roses against winter frosts (continental climate)
Re-stake standards if necessary
Remove shading from the greenhouse
Start pruning and training climbers and ramblers which
    produce only one flush of bloom in summer
Tie new stems of climbers into position
Remove suckers from established roses
Remove suckers from rootstocks
Dig up and discard non-productive old roses
Take cuttings of roses
Move pots into the greenhouse

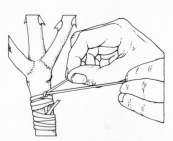

Winter

Fork in mulch
Cut out dead wood
Start pruning shrubs (except hip-bearing varieties) and climbers
Commence heating the greenhouse
Cut off budded understock tops
Continue planting new roses (temperate climate)
Plant new roses raised at home from cuttings or budding
Continue to cut back stems of established bush roses
Plant rootstocks for budding later
Continue watching for pests and diseases in the greenhouse
Order new roses for spring planting

The Fellowship of the Rose

Roses foster friendly feelings. This is soon discovered by anyone with good roses in his garden upon the enquiries and comments he receives from passers-by. (It was once a common custom for British railwaymen to wear a rose in their buttonhole and many a retired ticket collector will swear to the good humour his flower induced.) The natural outcome of their common interest was for rose growers to band together by forming societies to multiply the love and knowledge of the rose. Nearly all rose societies owed their inception to exhibitors who wished to stage well-organized shows in pursuit of their hobby. It naturally followed that every conceivable aspect of the rose received study as members began to ask one another questions about their favoured flower.

The Royal National Rose Society

The first rose society on a national scale was founded in London on 7 December 1876, by a band of enthusiasts led by Canon Hole. Several other clergymen were among the founders. They shared the conviction that cultivation of the rose must give benevolent relief to many people from the tedium of their daily labour. In those days of grimy industrial toil alcohol provided much of that relief, to the horror of the clergy. It happened that Canon Hole visited a rose show run by some Nottingham coal-miners and the probability is that they inspired him to found the National Rose Society. As both clergyman and rose grower himself, he had found an excellent means of combining business with pleasure.

The Society now has the prefix 'Royal', by command of Her Majesty Queen Elizabeth II. Its membership is about 40,000, and its headquarters are at St Albans in Hertfordshire. Shortly after its inception it began to issue publications to its members; its *Rose Annuals* are a feast of information for any lover of roses. It also maintains at St Albans an important rose garden in which hundreds of different varieties, some of them rare, may be seen.

In 1928 the National Rose Society followed an example set by the French over 20 years earlier: to grow new varieties of roses in order to make recommendations of their worth from a less biased point of view than that of the rose breeder. Some of the originators' claims about their roses were wildly exaggerated, with a blithe silence as to failings, much to the disappointment of people who tried to grow them unsuccessfully. This situation has now altered, thanks to scrupulous judging and administration by the Society. The varieties which emerge with certificates or medals from their trials are clearly known to have performed admirably during their three years of testing. Although infallibility is not claimed, a high standard of reliability is certainly maintained.

The American Rose Society

The American Rose Society was founded in 1899 and in time began to publish its valuable *American Rose Annual*. The great distances and varied climates in the United States made it impossible for one trial ground to supply reliable information for the whole country. The Society therefore began to inform its members by collating experiences with rose varieties over the whole country. On the information thus provided over the first five years of a new rose's life in commerce, they can make a national average assessment as a guide to their members. They call it the 'proof of the pudding'.

It probably arose from this operation that a bold project was tackled by Dr J. Horace McFarland, a master printer and a president of the Society. He decided to collect and print information about every rose available in the world. The resulting work was *Modern Roses*, published in 1930. It is now in its seventh edition, with details of about 12,000 different roses. The American Rose Society, now located at Shreveport, Louisiana, continues *Modern Roses* in association with other organizations. The Society is the international authority for the registration of rose names.

Australasia and Europe

In 1900 the National Rose Society of Victoria was founded in Melbourne, Australia. Over the next 60 years all the mainland states and Tasmania, except for the somewhat infertile Northern Territory, formed their own societies. In 1972, the six state societies decided to form the National Rose Society of Australia while at the same time maintaining their own existence. Their *Australian Rose Annual* is a valuable contribution to the world's knowledge of the rose. New Zealand has an active society which produces a fine Annual.

Similar developments can be reported from many other countries. France, for example, has a most distinguished record by both professional and amateur societies. La Société Française des Roses is situated in Lyon. The Verein Deutscher Rosenfreunde, at Baden-Baden, outdid *Modern Roses* in 1936 by the publication of August Jäger's *Rosenlexikon*, which gives information on nearly 18,000 different roses. Probably the world's most complete rosarium is at Sangerhausen in East Germany.

National rose societies exist also in Argentina, Belgium, Bermuda, Canada, Czechoslovakia, India, Israel, Italy, Japan, Poland, South Africa, Sri Lanka and Switzerland. Trials of new varieties are a function performed by the majority of national societies.

The World Federation of Rose Societies

Many national societies belong to a worldwide rose organization, the World Federation of Rose Societies, of which a Belgian lady, the Baronne Gaston de Gerlache de Gomery, was the first president in 1968. One of the purposes of the World Federation is to meet every two years in a member country, in the hope that leading rosarians from all over the world will attend. Thus the host country may benefit from the knowledge of the experts; the experts may have their experience widened by their hosts; and the interest and pleasure in growing roses may be enlivened internationally.

National and international societies are by no means the only ones. There must be thousands of local rose societies throughout the world which enable rose growers to meet and learn from one another about their favourite flower.

Plant Patents

It is generally accepted that inventors and artists should be paid for the pleasure they give to humanity. When buying a book, for example, the purchaser knows the author will receive his royalty from the money paid. But with plants, until recently, it was different. According to general opinion plants grew for free – and their production was not easily controlled. Yet it could be argued that of all the originators in the world, the plant breeder has a unique importance. His work might well be the factor to save a nation from starvation. In spite of this, he was left to fend for himself while writers, music-makers, mechanics and chemists had rights of property conferred upon their inventions. Very slowly this injustice is being put right.

The first plant patents

In 1930, a climbing rose called 'New Dawn' made history by acquiring United States Plant Patent No. 1. The holder of the patent was given rights in his rose for a period of 17 years. The famous French breeder, Francis Meilland, worked hard to convince European legislators of the need for similar laws. They were slowly introduced in France, Germany, Denmark, Switzerland and other places but many countries still have no plant patent laws. The British passed their Plant Varieties and Seeds Act in 1964 and again a rose was the first plant to receive a grant of rights. It was 'Aventure', an orange-red hybrid tea bred by a Frenchman, Paul Croix. The British rights are granted for 15 years but unfortunately 'Aventure' did not last the full period.

The general principles under which rights are granted are that the plant must not already be in commerce; it must be different from any other; and it must maintain its stability of character. If those factors are in order the breeder then receives his rights, which are to license others to grow his variety for sale. It is left to him to decide what conditions and charges he will make. Obviously they must be acceptable to his prospective customers or else he will do no business; and they must be fair, or else some law or other will call him to heel. Under British law, there is nothing to stop anyone propagating plants for pleasure. It is only if sale is the object or the consequence of propagation that the rights apply.

Royalties

In most countries, the holders of rights decided that the best way of controlling their rights was to charge a royalty on every plant sold and to require the seller to put a special label on the plant. Provided that every plant is labelled, the labels themselves render a true account. If an unlabelled plant is found to be sold, it is evidence of a theft of the royalty.

British nurserymen, used to growing a wide range of varieties, were not pleased with the prospect of hanging assorted labels on their plants. Nor could they feel at ease when labels, hitherto a cheap commodity and treated accordingly, were in fact a kind of money, lying at risk of loss around their packing sheds. So they devised a cheap and simple method. Instead of paying for each plant sold, they elected to pay a correspondingly lesser sum for each plant propagated. Then it was only necessary to know that one had budded a thousand 'Grandpa Dickson', for example, to pay for them and dispose of them without further trouble or expense. This scheme is operated by the British Association of Rose Breeders on behalf of nearly all the world's breeders who hold a grant of rights in Britain.

The justification of any law which confers rights upon an originator is in the acceleration of progress in the field concerned. Money can be an incentive, enabling writers, inventors and plant breeders to continue their work without taking on other jobs to finance it. Money is also necessary for funding research.

Rose breeding is a type of research in which the most profound results are likely to be achieved by putting into garden roses some feature which has hitherto been virtually confined to wild roses. Many examples of such features could be given, but three simple ones will suffice: the scent of sweet briar leaves; the beautiful hips of *R. moyesii*; the vitamin C content of the 'Dog Rose'. If a rose breeder took on one of these projects, the likelihood is that he would raise and discard hundreds of thousands of seedlings over a period of 20 years or more with no certainty of any success at the end of it. Over the period he would have budded, grown and carefully observed some thousands of plants whose destination must eventually be the bonfire. It takes money to pay for research and the best possible justification of plant breeders' rights is that this type of research is proceeding apace in breeding establishments in many countries.

The rose world is closely united internationally. The breeders who are the originators of the plants rely on the nurserymen to propagate and distribute their roses. The people who buy and grow the bushes are represented by their rose societies. In turn, the rose societies give the utmost help and support to the breeders and nurserymen by critical trial of the new varieties and by a continuous analysis of the merit of varieties. Thus, when the rose societies of countries such as Japan, Germany, Britain or Italy announce the results of their trials, it will be found that among the winners are varieties from all around the world; and the pick of the world's roses may be found in the catalogues of all but the most parochial nurserymen.

Certainly there is rivalry between the world's rosarians: the kind of rivalry in which each person does his best but cannot resist the impulse to admire his rivals' achievements. Breeders, nurserymen and exhibitors freely exchange knowledge to help one another. This happens at all levels, whether internationally, nationally or privately.

Naming roses

One consequence of the rose's international currency is the difficulty of names. What trips off a German tongue nearly chokes a Frenchman. 'Irish Mist', a sweet, romantic name to the Ulsterman who bred it, was less so to the German who wished to sell it because it becomes in German 'Irish Dung'. Nurserymen in every country need a suitable name for each variety but if a rose has different names throughout the world much confusion can be caused.

The international community of breeders has therefore suggested that the variety name should be a code associated with the breeder, which should always be printed in catalogues along with the more popular name. Thus, when a rose is listed as 'Meinatac' syn. 'Susan Hampshire', for example, it is clear it came from Meilland and is a tribute in Britain to an admired actress. It probably has another name in France, and another in America, and maybe still others in Japan or Spain or Switzerland; but by 'Meinatac' it is clear in each case which rose it is.

Glossary

Aerial shoot (or growth) Growth of the character of the parts of the plant above ground, as opposed to roots.

Anther The top part of the stamen; it bears the pollen.

Banksianae A section of the sub-genus Eurosa.

Bare-rooted A plant with no soil round the roots.

Bark The outer covering of a stem.

Basal shoot A shoot arising from the base of the plant.

Bedding A method of growing roses to fill completely a small area which is usually isolated, or else separated from other plots.

Bicolour A rose of two colours. Normally one of the colours is on the inner surface of the petals and the other on the outer surface.

Blind (shoot) A growth which ought to produce a flower bud but which stops growing beforehand.

Blow A term describing the act of a flower in opening its petals too quickly to please an exhibitor; from the common phrase 'fully blown'.

Bracteatae A section of the sub-genus Eurosa.

Bud 1 An unopened flower. 2 A synonym of 'eye'.

Budding A type of grafting commonly used to propagate roses.

Budwood Stems designated to be used for budding.

Bush A shrub. The word is often used by rosarians to imply a small, compact shrub.

Calyx The leafy protective covering of the flower bud, opening into five sepals.

Caninae A section of the sub-genus Eurosa.

Carolinae A section of the sub-genus Eurosa.

Chromosome A microscopic thread of tissue which bears the plant's genes.

Cinnamomeae A section of the sub-genus Eurosa.

Climber A rose whose inherited nature is to grow through and lean on other plants in order to flower in the sun. Its stems are fairly stiff but do not stand securely without support.

Cluster A group of flowers together on one shoot.

Compost 1 A mixture of soil and other ingredients, prepared to a specific formula. 2 Manure broken down by bacterial activity from vegetable refuse, with or without animal matter. The term 'garden compost' is sometimes used to indicate this meaning.

Cone A bloom protector of conical shape used by exhibitors to shade and shelter a flower still growing on the plant.

Crown See Union.

Cultivar An abbreviation of 'cultivated variety'. It is used to distinguish deliberately cultivated varieties from botanical varieties which arise naturally.

Cutting A piece of rose stem prepared so that it will root for the purpose of propagation.

Dead-heading Removing old flowers from the plant soon after they have bloomed.

Disbudding The removal of flower buds while they are very young. The object is to divert their 'strength' into another bud in order to obtain an extra-large bloom.

Dormant Asleep, in the sense that the growth processes are not being stimulated. This happens in winter mainly owing to low temperature and lack of sunlight.

Double A flower with many petals. A bloom with over 15 petals may be called double unless it opens unusually quickly or contains some petals much smaller than others. A rose with over 15 full-sized petals will have these arranged in at least three circles.

Double digging Digging the soil two or more spits deep and ensuring that each spit is returned to the same layer it came from. Another term for this operation is 'bastard trenching'.

Eurosa One of the four rose sub-genera. It is by far the largest and contains all but four of the species. It is divided into ten sections. The meaning of the word is 'true roses'.

Exhibition class A specification of what is required in a competition for roses at a show. Commonly it is just called a 'class'.

Exhibition variety A variety which is successful at producing flowers for cutting and showing but less successful at growing suitably in the garden. Some varieties suit both purposes and these are likely to be included in lists of exhibition varieties.

Eye An axillary growth point, before it has started to grow. The word 'axillary' describes the eye's position, which is at the upper angle made by the junction of the leafstalk and the stem. Also known as a 'bud'; hence the dictum: 'in the axil of every leaf there is a bud'. The eye is the central piece taken for the operation of budding.

Fertile hybrids A hybrid that bears seed capable of growing, as opposed to sterile hybrids which bear no viable seed.

Fertilization The successful conception of a seed by means of the fusion of the male pollen cell with the female egg cell. The correct name for these cells is gametes.

Fertilizer Any plant food added to the soil. See manure.

Fibrous root system A root which includes many fine growths. A fibrous root system indicates that the soil is well-cultivated and that the plant is in good condition.

Foliar feed An organic or inorganic manure (fertilizer) which is applied directly to the leaves.

Forcing Causing roses to flower sooner than they naturally would by the application of heat in a glasshouse. If carried to its extreme, using minimum ventilation, the grim expression used is 'sweating them out'.

Free flowering A term implying that a

Glossary

variety may be compared favourably with similar sorts in the number of blooms it produces. It would be more useful if one was always sure what similar sort the writer had in mind.

Frond See Terminal growth.

Fungicide A chemical to prevent or cure plant diseases.

Gallicanae A section of the sub-genus Eurosa.

Garnette type Roses after the style of the variety 'Garnette' which is a red floribunda grown under glass for the flower markets. It is remarkable for its durability as a cut flower but is not generally considered to be an attractive garden rose.

Genes The microscopic particles which are borne upon the chromosomes and contain the influences which cause hereditary factors to be manifested in a living organism.

Genus A group of plants, such as roses, which can be separated from all other plants by the factors they bear in common. The word implies generation, or being born.

Grafting A method of propagation by implanting a piece of the plant one wishes to increase upon a host plant.

Ground cover A variety of rose used to cover the ground closely; it is usually of a trailing nature.

Hesperrhodos One of the four sub-genera. It consists of two species from the United States, hence the name, which means 'western roses'.

Hip The fruit of the rose. May also be spelt 'hep'. Note that this word is exclusive to roses.

Humus The substance which is the result of decomposition of organic matter in the soil. It is dark in colour, spongy in texture and of the utmost value in the soil.

Hybrid A plant whose parents are not both of the same true species. Nearly all roses found in gardens are hybrids.

Indicae A section of the sub-genus Eurosa.

Inflorescence 1 The flowers borne together on one stem. 2 The flowers of a rose or of a group of roses flowering at one time; hence first inflorescence, etc.

Inorganic manures (or fertilizers) Manures which do not operate through the living organisms of the soil, but which are ready-made imitations of the plant foods these living organisms eventually produce.

Insecticide A chemical to prevent or kill insect pests.

Knuckle A thick or protruding joint. The term is used in this book to describe the base of a standard stem where other basal shoots have been removed in the course of growing the stem.

Laevigatae A section of the sub-genus Eurosa.

Lateral shoot (or growth) A shoot that has grown from an eye on the side of a stem, as opposed to basal shoots. A lateral shoot which becomes large and originates fairly low on the plant may be called a main shoot. If it is small and near the top of the plant it may be known as top growth. This leaves laterals with the sense of being useful, flower producing wood.

Leaf The leaf of a rose consists of a stalk bearing from three to 19 leaflets and the two rudimentary green growths at the foot of the stalk. The leaflets are arranged in opposite pairs with one at the terminus (and are therefore always of an odd number). Such an arrangement is called 'pinnate'.

Leaf joint The place where a leaf joins the stem. The proper name for it is 'node'. The area of the stem between two nodes is the 'internode'.

Leaflet One of the components of a leaf. Most garden roses have five or seven leaflets to a leaf but the number is apt to vary, even on the same shoot.

Leafstalk The stalk of the leaf joining it to the shoot. Its proper name is 'petiole'.

Maiden A rose plant during its first growing season after being budded. At the end of that season it is normally sold.

Manure Matter (originally dung) spread on or dug into the soil to feed plants. Many other manufactured substances are now used, not only on the soil but also on the leaves. It seems better to call them all manures rather than to use terms such as fertilizers or feeds, which separate them into different categories instead of comparing them under one. See Inorganic and Organic manures

Modern shrub roses A term used in this book to group together various roses of strong, shrubby growth, raised in the twentieth century.

Mulch A kind of manuring in which the purpose of feeding is allied with, or subservient to, the purpose of smothering weeds and conserving moisture in the soil.

Mutation A variation from the normal, generally in growth or colour, owing to a change of behaviour by one or more genes. See also Sport

Natural hybrid A hybrid that arose without human intervention. Wild roses fertilize one another quite frequently and it is likely that many thought to be true species are in truth natural hybrids which perhaps originated long ago.

Nodule A little swelling, especially upon the roots where nodules frequently prove to be a point of origin for suckers.

Old garden roses A term loosely applied either to most roses of the 19th century or earlier, or to the oldest of those groups grown in Europe, namely Gallicas, Damasks, Albas and Centifolias.

Organic manures Manures or fertilizers which originate from animal or plant remains and which break down in the soil to form plant foods.

Pedicel A flower stalk; usually the short piece between the bloom and the nearest leaf below.

Pergola A structure to support climbers or ramblers, giving the effect of a pathway covered by roses. It requires piers at each side, each joined at the top to its lateral and opposite neighbours by beams of adequate strength, and well above head height.

Petal The part of the flower comprising the petals is called the corolla, which means a 'little crown'. A petal is therefore a component of the corolla. In the past, botanists called petals 'leaves', thus *centifolia* literally means 'a hundred leaves' but was used to describe roses with many petals. The reason for this is the botanical dictum that the parts of the flower are in reality modified leaves.

pH A scale by which a chemical reaction of the soil is measured to determine its degree of acidity. The lower the figure, the more acid; the higher, the more alkaline. The point of neutrality is 7. Roses usually grow best in the range 4.5 to 7.5 but there are exceptions, and other factors must be taken into account.

Pimpinellifoliae A section of the sub-genus Eurosa.

Pinnate See Leaf

Pistils The female organs in the flower. Each consists of a stigma joined, by a stem known as the style, to an ovule in the seed pod below. The pollen adheres to the stigma and penetrates the style to reach the ovule.

Pith The cellular tissue at the centre of the stem. Its proper name is the 'medulla'.

Platyrhodon One of the four sub-genera. It contains one species from China which has the unusual quality of having bark which flakes off.

Pollen The floury dust, usually yellow, which is borne on the anthers. It contains the male fertilizing agent (gamete).

Pollination The act of applying pollen to the stigmas, whether by human intervention or by another agency such as wind or insects.

Propagation The increase of plants by any means.

Prickles The usual word for thorns in botanical descriptions.

Pruning The removal of parts of a plant in order to direct its growth in a desired manner.

Quartered Term applied to a flower in which the petals are folded in three or four groups, instead of in a single cone. It therefore opens as if the centre were quartered. Many old garden roses display this form owing to their petals being short.

Rambler A rose whose inherited nature is to grow along the ground or through other plants on which it rests its weight, eventually to flower in the sun. Its stems are tenuous and can therefore be artistically used to provide a falling effect. A less confusing name is 'trailer'.

Recurrent See Remontant

Reflexed Describes a petal which bends outwards or backwards without losing its firmness.

Remontant Flowering a second time, or more often, in a season. Botanically, it is more concise, precise and admirable than the commonly used alternatives such as recurrent flowering, repeat blooming, etc.

Repeat flowering See Remontant

Root The subterranean part of the rose, having no appearance of the aerial parts.

Root hairs (or rootlets) Small, delicate extensions of the roots. Another term for these is 'feeding roots'.

Rooting hormone A substance which encourages roots to grow; it is applied to cuttings in order to prompt them to make roots. The rooting hormones sold may be a compound of such substances and are based upon research into the materials made by the plant itself. Various enzymes or hormones are made according to the next immediate development required by the plant, e.g. root, colour, scent.

Rootstock The name for the host plant on to which a rose is budded or grafted, except in the case of standard roses when it is more usually referred to as the 'stem'. The correct name in each case is 'stock'.

Sap The juice of a plant. It is water, with minerals dissolved in it, subject to as many complex chemical changes as the plant requires. Some of it circulates and some is enclosed in the cells.

Scion The correct name for the part of the rose implanted on to a stock in the course of propagation.

Seed The product of fertilization, eventually to be detached from the hip in order to become a new plant. Rose seeds are of a type known as 'achenes', which have a woody shell, within which is a kernel surrounded by a skin, or testa.

Seedling A plant grown from seed. Although it means a young plant in common speech, rosarians (especially breeders) extend it to cover mature plants.

Seed pod The hip. The correct term for an immature seed pod is ovary, and for a mature one, hip. In practice, the term seed pod is sometimes used in both cases.

Semi-double A flower having approximately eight to 15 petals. See also Double

Sepal A component of the calyx.

Serrated Toothed or fimbriated at the edge. The word is derived from the Latin for a saw.

Sexual propagation Propagation by seed.

Shoot A young growth. When a shoot becomes mature it is often still called a shoot, although 'stem' is more correct.

Shrub A woody, perennial plant which has several stems coming from its base (instead of only one, in which case it is a tree). All roses are therefore shrubs although a distinction is made to separate the climbing types. The word 'bush' means exactly the same as shrub, although it is sometimes used to suggest a smaller, denser shrub.

Shrub rose The foregoing entry illustrates the vacuity of this expression. It is used to suggest roses which are grown as large shrubs rather than as bedding plants.

Side shoot See Lateral shoot

Simplicifoliae One of the four sub-genera. It consists of one species from Iran. Because it does not have pinnate leaves it is officially a separate genus: *Hulthemia*. However, it is certainly a close relation to the rose.

Single A flower with five petals. The term is sometimes used to describe roses with up to eight petals.

Species A distinct kind of rose which reproduces itself exactly by seed borne and fertilized by itself. In practice, many rose species produce a varied population of seedlings, thus suggesting they are in fact hybrids themselves.

Glossary

Sport The common word for a mutation, or naturally arising variation.

Stamens The male organs in the flower, each consisting of a stem (the filament), topped by the anther.

Standard A rose budded on the stem of its host plant at a desired distance clear above the ground. The American name is 'tree rose'.

Stem 1 A mature shoot. 2 The stem which is cut off with a bloom. 3 The stock for a standard rose.

Sterile Unable to set seed.

Stigma The top part of the pistil. Its purpose is to provide an adhesive landing ground for pollen.

Stipule The small, green growths on each side of the lower part of the leafstalk.

Stock See Rootstock

Style The columnar stem of the pistil.

Sub-genus A group of plants within a genus, distinguishable by characteristics different from the rest of the genus.

Sub-lateral A side shoot which has grown from another side shoot.

Sub-soil The soil below the top 30cm (12in).

Sucker An aerial shoot originating from the roots. It enables a plant to survive even if the parts above ground are destroyed. If the plant was budded, the sucker will be growth from the rootstock, not the rose that grows on it, and should be removed.

Synstylae One of the sections of the sub-genus Eurosa.

Systemic A substance, usually used to kill insects or fungi, which is absorbed into the sap of the plant and therefore is effective for longer than a substance which remains only on the exterior of the plant.

Taproot The long root of a seedling which is put down for immediate anchorage. Because taproots are unfavourable for transplanting, seedlings are dug up after their first season and their taproots are shortened.

T cut The cut made in the stock when budding it; so named because of its shape.

Terminal growth The top part of a shoot. The term is not in common use except for climbers and ramblers.

Thorn A prickle, usually found on the bark. Sometimes it is found in modified form on the back of leaves and, in three sub-genera, also on hips.

Trailer An alternative, and perhaps better, word for rambler.

Transplanting Taking a plant from one place and planting it in another.

Truss See Cluster

Understock See Rootstock

Union The place where scion and stock were joined.

Variety Correctly refers to a plant different from its own species and which arose naturally, i.e. a botanical variety. Those which arise in cultivation are, strictly speaking, cultivated varieties (see Cultivar).

Vegetative propagation Propagation by asexual means, namely by causing a part of the plant other than seed to grow into a new plant. The methods used for roses are budding, cuttings and grafting.

Vermiculite A derivative of mica, which retains moisture. It is used by rose breeders to store seed, and by other horticulturists for rooting cuttings.

Vernalization The treatment of stored seed to induce it to germinate by imitating the ideal conditions of spring. With rose seeds it is achieved mainly by changes of temperature.

Weeping standard A trailing (or rambler) rose budded on a tall standard stem and, if necessary, trained to be pendulous.

Whip A long, young pliable shoot, usually of a rambler or climber.

Wood 1 Mature tissue in the stems. 2 A collective description of mature stems.

Classification of the rose

It has never been easy to split the rose into clearly defined sections, whether botanically, historically or horticulturally. The reason for this is that one section is liable to merge into another. Nevertheless, in 1971 the Royal National Rose Society of Great Britain proposed a simple classification as a guide to show gardeners what they might expect of the various sections; a further purpose was to classify the show schedules issued by many societies for rose shows. Nobody pretends it answers all problems. It leaves out nearly all considerations of botany, history and origin; only time will show how useful it is to gardeners and exhibitors.

The RNRS divided roses into 3 groups: Modern garden roses, Old garden roses and Wild roses. The Old and the Wild were more or less left according to tradition. Modern garden roses were divided into 4 sections, according to whether they were climbers or not, and whether they flowered only once or repeated their bloom. Taking into account the various modern types, the following 12 classes account for all Modern garden roses:

1. Summer-flowering shrub
2. Repeat-flowering shrub
3. Repeat-flowering bush, large flowered (hybrid tea)
4. Repeat-flowering bush, cluster flowered (floribunda)
5. Repeat-flowering bush, polyantha pompon
6. Repeat-flowering miniature
7. Summer-flowering rambler
8. Summer-flowering climber
9. Summer-flowering climbing miniature
10. Repeat-flowering rambler
11. Repeat-flowering climber
12. Repeat-flowering climbing miniature

The intention was to abandon the terms hybrid tea and floribunda when 'large flowered' and 'cluster flowered' became popularly accepted; and in 1979 it was announced that for exhibition schedules this step was being taken.

Index

A

Abrams, F. Von, 79
Ackermann, 32
'Adolphe Horstmann', 76
Adonis, 12
'Aglacia', 88
'Aimée Vibert', *53*
'Albéric Barbier', 91, 93
'Albertine', 93, 130
Albrecht V, 32
'Alec's Red', 68, 76
Alexander, 74, 75, 76
Alice in Wonderland, 56
All-America Rose Selections Award, 76, 77, 78, 92
'Allgold', 66, 68, 76, 82, 83, 85
'Alpha', 66
'Alpine Glow', 79
'Altissimo', 93
'Ama', 83
American Rose Annual, 135
American Rose Society, 135
'Amberlight', 68
'Amethyste', 93
Amour Triomphant, L', *23*
Andrews, H. C., 29, 32
'Angela Rippon', 94
'Ann Aberconway', 82
'Anne Cocker', 68
'Ann Elizabeth', 76, 85
'Anne Poulsen', 81
'Anne Watkins', 83
'Antoine Ducher', 54
Aphrodite, 12
Apollo, 13
Apothecary, 19, 38
Armada jewel, *21*
Armstrong and Swim, 93
Armstrong Nurseries, 76
'Arthur Bell', 68, 77, 82, 93
Art Nouveau, 27
Arts and Crafts movement, 25, 27
Aubriet Claude, 32
Aurora, 12
Austin, D., 89
Australian Rose Annual, 135
'Austrian Copper', 74
'Austrian Yellow', 46, 48, 54, 74
'Autumn Damask', 51, 52
'Aventure', 136
Avicenna, 38
Avout, Pieter van, 13

B

'Baby Carnival', 94
'Baby Crimson', 95
'Baby Faurax', 82
'Baby Gold Star', 94
'Baby Masquerade', 94, *94*
'Baby Rambler', 88
'Baccara', 68
Bacchus, 12
Baden-Baden Gold Medal, 76, 82
Bagatelle Gold Medal, 93
'Ballerina', *87*, 89, 117
'Ballet', 68
'Bangor', 84
'Banksian Yellow', 46

'Bantry Bay', 92
Barry, Madame du, 22
Basseporte, Madelaine de, 28
'Beauté', 76
Bees Ltd, 77
'Belle Blonde', 93
'Belle de Crécy', 50
'Belle Isis', 89
Bennet, Henry, 54, 64, 65
Bentall, J. A., 89
Berlin wool roses, 37
Berlin woolwork, 25, 37
Besler, Basil, 28, 32
Bess of Hardwick, 36
'Bettina', 68
'Big Chief', 76
Birth of Venus, *12*, 20
Bizot, 93
'Blanc Double de Coubert', 88
'Blanche Moreau', 51
'Blessings', 68, 76
'Blush Noisette', 52
'Bobby Charlton', 76
'Bobby James', 93
Boerern, Jackson and Perkins, 84
'Bonfire', 82
'Bonfire Night', *80*, 82
Books of Hours, *30*
Bosschaert, Ambrosius, the Elder, 22, 23
Botanical illustration, 20, *21*
Botticelli, 12, 20
'Boule de Neige', 53
Bowles, Carrington, 32
'Brasilia', 76
Breughel, Jan the Younger, 13
Breughel, Jan the Elder, 22
'Bridal Pink', 68
British Association of Rose Breeders, 62, 136
Brookshaw, George, 32
Brunfels, 32
Brutelle, L'Heritier de, 32
Bry, Johann Theodor de, 32
'Buccaneer', 93
Buisman, G. A. H., 89
'Bullata', 51
Burne-Jones, Edward, 25, 37

C

'Camaieux', 50
'Canary Bird', 61
Cants of Colchester, 77
Capability Brown, 56
'Capt. Thomas', 92
'Cardinal de Richelieu', 50, *51*
'Catherine Mermet', 53
'Celsiana', 51
'Celestial', *50*, 51
Cellini, Beuvenuto, 34
C Gregory and Son, 76, 79, 93
Chambard, C., 93
'Champion', 76
Champney, John, 52
'Champney's Pink Cluster', 52
'Chapeau de Napoleon', 51
Charlemagne, Emperor, 13
Charles I, 22
'Charles de Mills', 50
'Charles Mallerin', 78
'Charles P. Kilkam', 78

'Charlotte Armstrong', 79, 85, 92
'Château de Clos Vougeot', 93
Chaucer, 19
Chelsea Flower Show, 68
'Cherokee Rose', 46
'Cheshire Life', 68
'Chestnut Rose', 46
'Chicago Peace', 77
'China Rose', 46
'Chinatown', 82, 117
'Chivalry', 76
'Chrysler Imperial', 78
'Circus', 82, 93
'City of Belfast', 68, 82
City of Belfast Gold Medal, 79, 82, 84, 93
'City of Leeds', 82, 85
'Cläre Grammerstorf', 82
Clef des Champs, 32
Cleopatra, 15
'Climbing Goldilocks', 93
'Cochet-Cochet', 88
Cocker, Alec, 66, 76
'Coeur d'Amour', 79
'Colibre', 95
Collection of Roses from Nature, A, 28, *31*
'Colour Wonder', 76, 78, 79
'Columbine', 82, 83, 84, 92
'Commander Jules Gravereaux', 93
'Common Moss', 51
'Compassion', 91, 92, 112
Concert, The, *21*
Confucius, 16
'Constance Spry', 89
'Copenhagen', 92
'Coral Dawn', 92, 93
'Cornelia' *87*, 88
'Coryana', 83, 84
Costa, Lorenzo, *21*
Council Chamber, 25
Crane, Walter, 27
Crataeras, 38
'Crimson Glory', 77, 83
'Crimson Perpetual', 53
'Crimson Shower', 93
'Criterion', 68
Croix, Paul, 136
Crouchback, Edmund, 19
Cupid, 12
Cybele, 12

D

'Dacapo', 95
'Dainty Maid', 89
'Dame de Coeur', 76
'Dame of Sark', 82
'Danse du Feu', 84, *91*, 92, 93, 117, 130
'Dany Robin', 95
'Darling Flame', 95
Dean of Roses, The, 24, 25
'Dearest', 68, 82, 85
'Dekorat', 76
Delaney, Mrs, 27
'Delbard-Chabert', 93
Devoniensis', 53
'Dicbar', 84
'Dick Koster', 83
'Dickson', 93
Dickson, Pat, 66, 76, 79

Dicksons Roses, 76, 77, 79, 82, 83, 84, 85
Diana, 13
'Diorama', 68, 76
'Doctor Verhage', 68
'Dr Huey', 118
'Dr A. J. Verhage', 76, 77
'Dr W. van Fleet', 92, 130
Dodoens, 32
'Doris Tysterman', 68
'Dorothy Perkins', 91, 93, 112, 117
'Dorothy Wheatcroft', 89, 117
Dot, P., 89, 94, 95
'Double Delight', 76
'Dreaming Spires', 93
Dreer, H. A., 92
'Dresden Doll', 94
'Duchess of Portland', 52, 53
Duel of the Roses, 17, *17*
'Duftwolke', 77
'Duke of Mildew', 77
'Duke of Windsor', 76

E

Ecluse, de l', 32
'Eden Rose', 79
Edmund, Earl of Lancaster, 19
Eduardo Toda, 94, 95
Edward I, 19
Edward IV, 19
E. G. Hill & Co., 78
Ehret, Georg Dionysius, 28, 31, 32
'Electron', 78
Elements of Flower and Fruit Painting, 32
'Elizabeth Harkness', 77
'Elizabeth of Glamis', 68, 81, 82, 84
Elizabeth I, Queen, 20, 40
'Ellen Poulsen', 95
'Ellinor le Grice', 66, 82
'Else', 81
'Emily Gray', 93
'Ena Harkness', 83, 92, 93, 112
'Ernest H. Morse', 76
'Escapade', 82
'Estrellita de Oro', 94
'Ethel Sanday', 77
'Etoile de Hollande', 93
'Evelyn Fison', 66, 68, 78, 82, 83, 84
'Evening Star', 77
'Excelsa', 112
Eyck, van, 32
'Eye Paint', 82, 117

F

Fabergé, Carl, 34
egg, *34*
Fabriano, da, 32
'Fairy, The', 89
'Fairy Moss', 94
'Fashion', 95
'Felicia', 88
'Felicité Parmentier', 51
'Five King', 95
'Fire Signal', 85
'F. J. Grootendorst', 88
'Flaming Peace', 77
Fleurs Animées, Les, 29

'Fleur Cowles', 68, *71*
'Flora', *13*
'Flora Delanica', 27
'Floradora', 85, 95
Flora in the Garden, 13
Floral Telegraph, The, *24*
Flores des Serres et des Jardins de l'Europe, 55
Florilegium Novum, 32
Florist, The, 32
'Flower Girl', 85
Flower Painters,
    Dutch, 30, 32, 36, 37
    French, 28, 32
    Italian, 32
    royal, 32
Flowers, Language of, 29
'For You', 95
'Fountain', *87*, 89, 117
Fragonard, 23
'Fragrant Cloud', 68, 76, 77, 85, 112
France, La', 53
'François Juranville', 93
'Franklin Engelmann', 79
'Frau Dagmar Hartopp', 88
'Frau Karl Druschki', 53
'Fred Loads', 89, 117
'Frensham', 81, 83, 86, 120
'Fresia', 83
'Freude', 76
'Fritz Nobis', 89
'Frosty', 95
'Frühlingsgold', 89
'Frühlingsmorgen', 66, *66*, 84
Fryers Nurseries Ltd., 76, 85
F. Turbot and Co, 85
Fuchs, 32

G

Garden of Pleasant Flowers, 22
'Garden Party', 76
'Garland, The', 93
'Gartenstolz', 89
Gaujard, J., 79
'Gavotte', 77
'G. de Ruiter', 76
'Général Jacqueminot', 53
'Général Schablikine', 53
'Georg Arends', 79
'George Dickson', 78
Gerard, John, 32
'Gertrude Westphal', 84
'Gioia', 78
'Giralda, La', 89
'Gloire de Dijon', 52
'Gloire de France', 51
'Gloire des Rosomanes', 53
'Gloria, Dei', 78
Goes, van der, 32
Goey, De, 88
'Golden Delight', 68
'Golden Giant', 78
'Golden Glow', 92
'Golden Masterpiece', 77
'Golden Rose of Bâle', *19*
'Golden Rose of the Hague', 95
'Golden Showers', 92, 117
'Golden Times', 68
'Golden Wings', *87*, 89
'Goldilocks', 66, 82, 83, 84, 85, 95
Gold Medal and Award for
    Fragrance, Belfast, 76

Gold Medal Japan, 79
Goodyer, John, 38
'Gooseberry Rose', 46
'Gottfried Keller', 54
'Governador Braga da Cruz', 77
'Grand Gala', 77
'Grandpa Dickson', 68, 76, 77, 85, 136
'Grandville', 29
'Grenada', 76
Grete Herball, 30
'Grey Dawn', 68
'Grootendorst', 88
'Gruss an Teplitz', 85
Guirlande de Julie, 32

H

Hague Gold Medal, The, 78, 79, 83
'Hamburger Phoenix', 84, 92
'Handel', *91*, 92
'Hanne', 77
Harkness, Alexander, 76
Harkness, Jack, *66*, 89
Heem, Davidsz de, 22
'Heidelberg', 92
'Helen Traubel', 68
Henderson, 32
Henrietta Marie, Queen, 22
Henry Edland Memorial Medal for
    Fragrance, 76, 77, 82, 85, 92
Henry IV, 19
Henry VII, 20
Henry VIII, 19
Herbal, 38
Herball, 32
Herbals, 28, 32
Hershey Rose Gardens,
    Pennsylvania, 63
'Herzog von Windsor', 76
'Highlight', 79
Hilliard, Nicholas, 20
Hilling, T., 89
'Hispida', 89
Historia Plantarum Rariorum, 28
Hoefnagel, Georg, 32
'Holiday', 84
Holmes, R. A., 89
Hortus Eystettensis, 28, 32
Hortus Floridus, 28, 29
'Hugh Dickson', 53
'Hume's Blush Tea-scented China', 53
'Hume's Tea-scented China', 48
Huysum, Jan van, 22, 24, 32
Huysum, Jacob van, 28

I

'Iceberg', 68, *80*, 81, 83, 84, 93, 112
'Iced Ginger', 83
'Illona', 68
'Independence', 79
'Indica Major', 118
'Inermis', 118
International Rose Test Garden, *63*
'Irish Beauty', 82
'Irish Gold', 77
'Irish Mist', 83, 85, 136
'Irish Wonder', 82
Isis, 15, 83

J

'Jack Frost', 68
Jackson and Perkins Co., 77, 92
Jacob, Theodor, 21
James Cocker and Sons, 76, 79
Jardin du Roy tres Chrestien Henry IV, Le, 32, 36
J. Mattock Ltd., 82, 83, 93
'Joanna Hill', 78, 89
'Jocelyn', 68
John Sanday (Roses) Ltd., 77
'John Waterer', 77
'Josephine Bruce', 77
'Josephine Wheatcroft', 95
'Joseph's Coat', 68, 93, 117
'Julie Rose', 68
Juno, 79
'Just Joey', 68, *74*, 77

K

Kändler, J. J., 34
'Kara', 94
'Karen', 81
'Karl Herbst', 79
'Kathleen Ferrier', 89
'Kathleen Harrop', 93
'Kerrymann', 83
'King of Hearts', 77, 78
'King's Ransom', 77
'Kirsten', 81
'Kiskadee', 83
Knossos, Palace of, *14*, 15
'Königin der Rosen', 76, 77, 78
'Königin von Danemarck', 51
'Korbell', 84
Kordes, W., 74, 81, 89, 90
'Kordes Perfecta', 77, 85
'Korlita', 78
'Korona', 82, 85, 92
'Korp', 68, 77
'Korresia', *80*, 83
Koster, D. A., 83
'Kronenbourg', 77, 78

L

'Lady Godvia', 89
'Lady Hillingdon', 53
'Lady Mary Fitzwilliam', 53
'Lady Seton', 68, 78
'Lady Sylvia', 77, 78
Laffay, 64
Lambert, 89
Lambert, P., 88
Lammerts, Dr W. L., 85, 92
'Lavender Lassie', 89
Lawrence, Mary, 28, 32
LeGrice, E. B., 66, *66*, 82, 84
Lens, Louis, 78
'Leverkusen', 92
Ligozzi, Giacomo, 32
'Lilac Charm', 68, 84
'Lilli Marlene', 83, 84
'Lilli Marleen', 68, 83
Lindley, John, 32
Litakor, 78
'Little Darling', 83, 84, 85
'Little Flirt', 95

'Little Sunset', 95
'Lolita', 78
Louis XV, 22
Ludwig, Emperor, 13
'Lydia', 77, 93
Lyons silk weavers, 36

M

'Macpow', 76
'Macrat', 84
'Mactru', 85
'Madge Whipp', 77
Madrid Gold Medal, 79
'Magnifica', 89
'Maiden's Blush', 51
'Maid Marion', 89
'Major Roulet', 95
'Mallerin', 92
'Maman Cochet', 53
'Manettii', 118
'Ma Perkins', 78, 84
'Maréchal Niel', 52, 54
'Margaret McGredy', 78
'Margot Fonteyn', 84
'Margot Koster', 83
'Majorie Fair', 89
'Marlena', 66, 68, 84, 95
Mars, 12
Martyn, John, 28
Mary Queen of Scots, 36
'Mary Sumner', 81, 84
'Masquerade', 81, 82, 84, 93, 94, 112
'Matangi', *80*, 84
'Max Graf', 89
'Maxi', 84
McGredy, Sam, 66, *67*, 90, 91
'McGredy's Yellow', 79
Medici, Marie de, 36
Meilland, Alain, 66, *67*, 78, 95
Meilland, Francis, 136
'Memento', 84
Memling, 32
'Mermaid', 89, *91*, 93
'Mimima', 94
'Minvetto', 95
'Mischief', 68, 78, 79, 83
'Mister Lincoln', 78
'Mme Abel Chatenay', 53
'Mme Alfred Carrière', 52
'Mme A. Meilland', 78
'Mme Butterfly', 78
'Mme Caroline Testout', 53
'Mme Hardy', 51, *51*
'Mme Isaac Pereire', 53
'Mme Legras de St Germain', 51
'Mme Léon Cuny', 83, 84
'Mme Louis Laperrière', 68
'Mme Pierre Oger', 53
Modern Roses, 135
'Modesty', 12
'Molly McGredy', 84
Monnoyer, Jean-Baptiste, 28, 29
'Mon Trésor', 95
'Moon Maiden', 68
Moore, Ralph, 94, 95
Morey, D., 77, 93
Morris, William, 37
'Mothers' Union', 84
'Moulin Rouge', 82, 95
'Moyne de Morgues', Jacques Le, 32
'Mozart', 89
'Mrs John Laing', 53, *53*

'Mrs Sam McGredy', 93, 112
'Mullard Jubilee', 78
Müller, Dr Franz, 54

N

Napoleon, 24
National Rose Show, 25
National Rose Society, 25
National Trust, 68, 74, 78
'Nelkeurose', 88
Nero, 15
'Nevada', 87, *87*, 89
'New Penny', 95
'New Dawn', 79, 92, 93, 112, 117, 136
'News', 68, 84
New Treatise on Flower Painting or Every Lady her own Drawing Master, A, 32
Nightingale and the Rose, *16*
'Niphetos', 53
Noisette, Philippe, 52
Norman, A., 83
'Nuage Parfumé', 77

O

Obel, de l', 30, 32
'Old Blush', 48, *49*, 52
'Old Master', 84
'Opa Potschke', 79
'Opera', 79
'Ophelia', 78, 88
'Orangeade', 83, 84
'Orange Belinda', 68
'Orange Sensation', 89
'Orange Sweetheart', 66, 84
Order of the Golden Rose, 19
Orleans, Gaston d, 32
'Ormiston Roy', 89
Os, van, 22
'Our Princess', 83

P

'Paddy McGredy', 68, 78, 83, 84
'Paestana', 52
'Paint Brush', 94
'Papa Meilland', 78
'Para Ti', 95
'Parfum de l'Haÿ', 88
'Parkdivektor Riggers', 66, 79, 92
Parkinson, 22
'Park's Yellow Tea-scented China', 48, 52, 53
Parsons, Alfred, 32, 33, 55
'Pascali', 68, *74*, 78
Passe, Crispin de, 28, 29
'Paul's Scarlet Climber', 92
Paul, William, 57, 58, 64, 93
'Peace', 68, 74, *74*, 75, 76, 77, 78, 79, 81, 85
'Pearl of Canada', 95
Pedigree Hybrids of the Tea Rose, 64
'Peer Gynt', 76, 78
Pemberton, Rev J. H., 88, 89
'Penelope', 68, 88
'Peon', 94, 95
'Perfecta', 76

'Perichon', 52
'Perla de Alcanada', 95
'Perla de Montserrat', 95
'Perle des Rouges', 95
Pernet-Ducher, Joseph, 54
'Pernille Poulsen', 84
'Persian Yellow', 48, 54, *55*
'Petite de Hollande', 51
'Pfänder', 118
'Phyllis Bide', 89
'Picasso', 66, 81, 83, 84
'Piccadilly', 66, 77, 79, 82
Pietra-dura, 34
Pindar, 15
'Pineapple Poll', 68
'Pink Favourite', 79
'Pink Grootendorst', 88
'Pink Parfait', 68, 82, 85
'Pink Perpêtue', *91*, 93, 112, 117
'Pisanello', 32
Plant patents, 136
Poitiers, Diane de, 34
Pompadour, Madame de, 22, *23*, 35
'Pompon de Paris', 95
Pope Leo IX, 19
Portland Gold Medal, 79, 92
'Portland Trailblazer', 76
Portrait of a Young Man, 20, 21
Pot-Pourri, 40, *40*, 41
Poulsen, D. T., 79, 81, 82, 83, 84, 92
'Pour Toi', *94*, 95
'Precious Platinum', 66, 79
'Première Ballerine', 79
'Président de Sèze', 51
Prevost, Jean-Louis, 28
'Prima Ballerina', 68, 77, 78, 79, 92
'Princess Hélène', 53
'Priscilla Burton', 66, *67*, 84
'Prominent', 77
Provins, 19, 38

Q

'Quatre Saisons', 51
'Queen Elizabeth', 59, 68, 76, 78, 80, 84, 85, 89, 117, 120
Queen Elizabeth II, H.M., 79
Queen Mother, 82
'Queen of Roses', 76
Queen's Silver Jubilee Appeal in Great Britain, 95

R

Ramsden, Omar, 27
Recevil des Plantes, 28
'Red Dandy', 77
'Red Devil', 66, 79
'Red Favourite', 82
'Red Gold', 85
'Red Imp', 95
Redouté, Pierre-Joseph, 24, 29, 32, 33
'Red Planet', 66, 76, 79
R. Harkness and Co, 76, 77, 82, 85, 89, 92
Rhodanthe, 13
'Rimosa', 95
'Ripples', 68
Robbias, della, 32
Robert, Nicholas, 28, 32
'Robin Hood', 83

'Rob Roy', 68
Roessig, 32
Rohde, Elanour Sinclair, 40
Roman de la Rose, 18, *18*, 19
Rome Gold Medal, 76, 79, 85
Rosarum Monographia, 32
Rosa,
    acicularis, 47
    arvensis, 46, 90
    banksiae lutea, 46, *49*
    beggeriana, 47
    canina, 39, 47, 50, 118
    centifolia, 40
    centifolia foliacea, *33*
    chinensis, *33*, 46, 48, 90, 94
    corymbifera, 50
    ecae, 47
    eglanteria, 47
    fedtschenkoana, 47
    filipes, 46, 93
    foetida, 46, 48, 54
    foetida persiana, 54
    foliosa, 47
    gallica, 19, 48, *48*, 50
    gigantea, 46, 48
    helenae, 46
    hemisphaerica, 48, 54, *54*
    hugonis, 47, 61
    kordesii, 66, *91*
    longiscuspis, 46, 93
    lutea, *33*, 38
    macrophylla, 47
    moschata, 46, 50, 52, 90
    moyesii, 47, 136
    multibracteata, 47
    multiflora, 46, 59, 81, 90, *91*, 118, 120
    mundi, 48
    nitida, 47
    odorata, 90
    palustris, 47
    pendulina, 47
    persica, 44, 46
    phoenicia, 50
    roulettii, *94*, 95
    rox burghii, 46
    rubrifolia, 47
    rugosa, 47, 66, 86, 88, 120
    sempervirens, 46
    sericea pteracantha, 47
    setigera, 46
    sinowilsonii, 46
    spinossissima, 47, 81
    stellata, 46
    virginiana, 47
    webbiana, 47
    wichuraiana, 46, 61, 66, 85, 90, 91
    willmottiae, 47
    xanthina, 47, 60
Rosary of passion, 13
Rose Amateur's Guide, 64
Rose bush of Hildesheim, *13*
Rose care,
    beds, 102
    breeding, 64, 65, 66
    budding, 118
    cutting, 68
    feeding, 106, 107
    fertilization, 64, 65, *65*
    grafting, 118
    mulching, 106, 107
    pests, 122, 123
    planting, 100, 101, 102, 103, 104, 105

pollination, 65, *65*
propagation, 65, 118, 119, 120, 121
pruning, 108, 109, 110, 111
rejuvenating, 133
rose sickness, 58, 59
trimming, 108, 109, 110, 111
watering, 106, 107
'Rose de Canelle', *30*
'Rose de Provence, The', *30*
Rose design,
    Assyrian reliefs, 26
    Baccarat paperweight, *35*
    Byzantine metalwork, 26
    ceramics, 17, 22
    Christian ivories, 26
    coinage, 19
    Damascus ware, 17
    diamond, rose-cut, 34
    dress fabrics, 36
    Egyptian tomb painting, 15
    embroidery, 20, 22, 36, 37
    enamelling, 34
    engravings, 28, 29
    Flemish miniaturists, 30
    Florentine mosaics, 34
    furniture, 22, 26
    glass, 35
    Hellenistic marble columns, 26
    heraldry, 19
    Isnik wares, 17, *17*
    Italien keyboard instruments, 26
    Jacobite glass, *35*
    jewellery, 20, 34
    Limoges enamels, 36
    manuscripts, 30
    Mesopotamia friezes, 26
    mosaick, 27, *27*
    Mycaeneán gold jewellery, 26
    paperweights, 35
    perfume label, *38*
    Phoenician stelae, 26
    plaster, 20
    porcelain, 34, 35
    postage stamps, 29
    printing, 32
    Rhodian wares, 17
    Shiraz ware, 17
    stone, 20
    stylized rose, 26
    table top, *27*
    textiles, 36, 37
    valentines, 25
    venice lace, *36*
    wallpaper, *27*
    window, 26, *26*
'Rosa Gaujard', 79
'Rose landia', 68
Rose, life cycle, 98
'Rosemary Rose', 68, 85
'Rosenberger', *104*
Rosen, Die, 32
'Rose of Provins', 19
Rose, parts of, 98
'Roseraie de l'Haÿ', 88
Rose Society of Northern Ireland, 62
Roses of Heliogabalus, 15
Rosette, patera, 27
Rose Garden, The, 57, 64
Rose gardens, 56, *57*, 58, 59, 60, *61*, 62

    Municipal Rose Gardens, Madrid, 63

Index

Queen Mary's Rose Garden, Regent's Park, 62
Renaissance, 20
Royal National Rose Society, *62*
Skansen, *62*
Westbroek Park, 62
Rose illustrations, 28, 29, 30, 32
  botanical drawing, 32
  Dutch, 32
  flower books, 29
  French, 32
  printing, 28, 29, 32
Rosenlexikon, 135
Rose-en-soleil, 19
Rose, Minden, 22
Rose noble, 19, *19*
Roseraie de l'Hay-les-Roses, la, 63
Roses, 29, 32
Roses, Les, 24, 29, 32
Roses Cultivées à l'Hay, 57
Roses et Rosiers, 57
Rose Sunday, 19
Rosette, 26, 27, 34
Rose use,
  arrangement, 20, 70, *70, 71*
  cosmetics, 38
  for exhibition, 126, 127
  hip syrup, 39
  medicines, 38
  oil, 38
  perfumes, 38
  petal bath, 39
  petal preserve, 39
  petal wine, 39
  rosewater, 20, *25*, 38
  soaps, 38
Rose varieties,
  alba, 48, 51, 56, 60, 88
  arctic, 47
  briar, 116
  bush, 86
  cabbage, 37, 50
  centifolia, 56, 60, 61
  China, 48
  climber, 54, 56, 61, *61*, 66, 90, 112, 120, 133
  climbing sports, 100
  container-grown, 105
  Damask, 19, 40, 48, 50, 51, 56, 60, 79
  Dog, 19, 25, 38, 39, 92, 136
  du Roi, 53
  dwarf floribunda, 100
  evergreen, 46
  floribunda, 54, 59, 61, 62, 66, 100, 112, 114, 117, 120, 133
  floribunda bush, 81
  gallica, 48, 50, 56, 60
  Garnette, 68
  ground cover, 100
  hedges, 116
  hips, 38
  hybrid, 48, 54, 64, 66
  hybrid musks, 86
  hybrid perpetual, 53, 54, 56, 74
  hybrid tea, 54, 62, 66, 68, 100, 101, 112, 114, 126
  hybrid tea bush, 74, 75, 81
  miniature, 54, 56, *58*, 59, 94, 100, 111, 120, 128
  modern shrubs, 86, 117
  moss, 50, 51, 61
  musk, 46, 52
  noisettes, 52

old bushes, 133
old hybrid teas, 133
Pemberton Hybrid Musks, 86
pink, 58
pink cabbage, 25, 36
Portland, 52
Prarie, 46
rambler, 56, 61, 90, 100, 112, 117, 120, 133
recurrent flowering climber, 117
repeat-flowering climber, 100
repoussé, 34
rubra, 88
scabrosa, 88
Scotch, 47
shrub, 60, *61*, 100, 120
shrubbery, *57*
slipped, 19
Species, 100
sport climbers, 112
standards, 56, 100, 105
suckers, 111, 133
sulphur, 48
tea, 48, 53, 74
tree, 56, 100
Tudor, 19, 20, 26, 36
weeping standards, 100
western hybrids, 48
wild, 54, 120
'Rosina', 95
'Rosmarin', 95
'Rosy Jervel', 94
Roulet, Major, 94
'Royal Dane', 79
'Royal Gold', 93
Royal Horticultural Society, 62, 68
Royal National Rose Society of
  Great Britain, 62, 86, 107, 135
  Certificate of Merit, 76, 77, 78, 79, 82, 83, 84, 85, 88, 89, 92, 93, 95
  Gold Medal, 76, 77, 78, 79, 82, 83, 84, 85, 88, 89, 93
  Presidents International Trophy, 76, 77, 78, 79, 82, 84, 85, 89
  Trial Ground Certificate, 76, 77, 78, 79, 82, 83, 84, 85, 89, 92, 93
'Royal Salute', *94*, 95
'Royal Virgin', *31*
'Rudolf Timm', 83
Rudolf II, Emperor, 32
Ruiter, G. de, 85, 94
Ruysch, Rachel, 22

S

Sackville-West, Victoria, 61
'Saframo', 53
'Sam McGredy', 81, 84
'Saratoga', 77
'Satchmo', 85
Sayer, Robert, 32
'Scarlet Gem', 95
'Scarlet Pimpernel', 95
'Scarlet Queen Elizabeth', 85
'Scented Air', 85
'Schneewittchen', 83
'Schneezwerg', 88
'Schoolgirl', 83, 91, *91*, 93
'Scotch Rose', 54, 64
'Sea Pearl', 85
Seasons or Flower Garden . . ., 32
Seghers, Daniel, 22

'Semi-plena', 51
'Semperflorens' 94
'Shepherdess', 83, 85
Shepherd, R., 89
'Shepherd's Delight', 89
'Shot Silk' 89
Siege of the Castle of Love, The, 19
'Signora', 79
'Silver charm', 68
'Silver Jubilee', 66, 79
'Silver Lining', 79
'Sir Lancelot, 68
Sisley, Jean, 64
'Sissi', 76
Sissinghurst, *60*
'Slater's Crimson China', 48
S. McGredy International, 76, 77, 78, 79, 82, 83, 84, 85, 92, 93, 95
Socrates, 40
'Soeur Thérèse', 89
'Soleil d'Or', 54
'Sombreuil', 88
'Sonia', 68
'Sonia Meilland', 66
'Son, The', 85
'Southampton', 85
'Southport', 83
'Souvenir de Claudius Denoyel', 93
'Souvenir de Claudius Pernet', 78
'Souvenir de la Malmaison', 53
Spaendonck, Gerard van, 22, 24, 28, 32
'Spartan', 77, 78, 81, 82, 85
'Spectacular', 92, 117
'Spong', 51
'Stanley Gibbons', 68
'Starina', 95
'Sterling Silver', 76
'Sunsilk', 68, 85
'Super Star', 68, 74, 76, 79
'Susan Hampshire', 136
'Sutter's Gold', 68, 79
'Swan Lake', 112, 117
'Sweet Briar', 47
'Sweet Fairy', 95
'Sweet Promise', 66
Swim and Weeks, 78, 79
Swim, Herbert C, 67

T

'Tabler's Choice', 82
Tantau, Mathias, *67*, 76, 77, 79, 85, 89, 94
'Tantau's Triumph', 83, 84
Temple of Flora, 29
'Tenor', 93
Thornton, Dr Robert John, 29
Tiffany, Louis Comfort, 34
'Tiki', 82
'Tiptop', 85
'Titania', 95
'Tom Brown', 68
'Tom Thumb', 94, 95
'Tony Jacklin', 85
'Topsi', 85
'Tour de Malakoff', 51
Tradescant, John, 22
Tres Riches Heures du Duc de Barry, 30
'Trier', 88

'Troika', *74*, 79
'Tropicana', 79
'Trumpeter', *80*, 85
'Tuscany Superb', 51, 84

U V

'Ulrich Brunner', 53

Vallet, Pierre, 32, 36
'Variety Club', 82
Venus, 12, 15
'Vera Dalton', 83
'Versicolor', *48*
'Victor Verdier', 53
'Ville de Chine', 82
Vink, J. de, 95
'Virgo', 83
'Visa', 66
Vitamin C, 38

W

Walscapelle, Jacob, 22
'Wedding Day', 93
'Wee Man', 95
'Wendy', 95
'Wendy Cussons', 79
'Wheatcroft's Baby Crimson', 95
'Whisky Mac', 68, 76
'White Butterfly', 78
'White Cockade', 92
'White Masterpiece', 77
'White Spray', 68
'William Allen Richardson', 52
'William Lobb', 51, *51*
Willmott, Ellen, 32, 33
Wisley, 62, *62*
W. Kordes Sohne, 76, 77, 78, 83, 84, 89, 92, 95
Woburn Abbey, 68
World Federation of Rose Societies, 135

X Y

Xerxes, 12

'Yellow Cushion', 85
'Yellow Sweetheart', 95
'Yesterday', *87*, 89
'Young Quinn', 68
'Yvonne Rabier', 85

Z

'Zambra', 95
'Zéphirine Drouhin', 53, *53*, 91, 93, 130
Zephyr, 13
'Zorina', 77, 94